education
be smarter.

New PSAT 10/11/NMSQT
Strategy/Practice Guide

Developed in conjunction with Test Prep Genius

New PSAT 10/11/NMSQT Strategy/Practice Guide

C2 Education is a registered trademark of C2 Educational Center, Inc.

2015 Edition

This product was developed by Test Prep Genius, a premiere education support services company that delivers a comprehensive package for education institutions and services.

C2 Education: http://www.c2educate.com/
Test Prep Genius: http://www.tpgenius.com/

Development support was provided by C2 Education and Edward Kim, the Director of Curriculum. Please report any errors or feedback to the nearest C2 center and support@tpgenius.com.

Table of Contents

Section 1
The New PSAT

Introduction: The Redesign
Our Mission – YOU
Test Structure Changes
Subject-specific Changes
How to Use This Book
About the National Merit Scholarship®

Introduction: The Redesign
College Board's Announcement

The Announcement
On March 5, 2014, in Austin, Texas, College Board President David Coleman presented a renewed mission by the organization to provide a redesigned SAT and PSAT. Still in the midst of implementing vast changes to their AP Courses, College Board announced that in spring of 2016, high school students would begin taking a radically changed, redesigned standardized test.

President Coleman and a number of College Board's team members had been integral in guiding and executing the mission to develop the Common Core State Standards (CCSS). To align with the CCSS, College Board and President Coleman continued their work with the SAT and PSAT by re-assessing test questions and the structure of the existing exam.

In order to provide high school students with a stronger predictive assessment for college success, College Board redesigned the PSAT in drastic ways. The new PSAT is very different in both test structure and test questions; the new exam will strive to answer one very important question: Is the average high school student prepared for first-year college work?

The PSAT 10/11 will be designed for sophomores and juniors to take during the school year in October; the PSAT 8/9, which is covered in another book, will be designed for 8th graders and freshmen to take during the school year in October.

Our Mission – YOU

Test Prep Genius has one mission: to provide you with curriculum and support that maximizes your progress without wasting time. Instructional content should be short and effective; practice material should be plentiful.

Test Prep Genius is excited to offer you the C2 Education PSAT 10/11/NMSQT Strategy Guide. This guide will show you short, effective strategies for every major concept the new PSAT incorporates.

We wish you the best of luck in your work, progress, and results on the new PSAT!

Test Structure Changes
Overall Changes to the New PSAT

There are major structural changes to the new PSAT 10/11 that you should keep in mind. These changes were made to better meet the needs of the average high school student and to provide you with an optimized exam.

Timing and Question Counts

Reading:	60 minutes for 47 Questions
Writing and Language:	35 minutes for 44 Questions
Math:	70 minutes for 48 Questions

Total Time = 2 hours and 45 minutes

Raw Scores

Raw Scores are calculated based on the total number of questions you answered correctly. You will not be penalized an extra -0.25 points for answering questions incorrectly since the College Board wants to encourage educated guessing without penalty on the new exam.

Score Reporting

Your final new PSAT 10/11 score is composed of two pieces – 1 Math Score, 1 Reading and Writing Score.

Both Math and Reading and Writing Scores are scaled from 160 to 760 for a total PSAT 10/11 score ranging from 320 to 1520. Why the weird scale? The College Board wants to be able to take your PSAT scores and New SAT scores to compare them to each other on one composite scale. The PSAT 8/9, PSAT 10/11, and New SAT score will be compared to gauge the progress each student has made on the tests.

Although the old PSAT only provided a general report with the overall section scores and a student error report by question, the new PSAT 10/11 offers a detailed breakdown of scores. Parents, students, college admission officers, and counselors will gain greater insight into your abilities by using these scores.

1 Total Score
The Total Score is your composite score ranging from 320 to 1420.

2 Section Scores
The 2 Section Scores are your respective scores in Math and in Reading and Writing ranging from 160 to 760.

3 Test Scores
The 3 Test Scores are your individual scores for Math, Reading, and Writing. The Math, Reading, and Writing Scores are scaled from 8-38.

2 Cross-Test Scores

The Cross-Test Scores are two scores that look at specific topics that are covered on the new PSAT: History/Social Studies and Science. These scores are scaled from 8 to 38 and provide insight into your mastery over the aforementioned topics across all sections, not just one.

7 Subscores

There are also 7 Subscores for Math, Reading, and Writing that provide insight into each major content dimension within the subjects. Content Dimensions are general categories of concepts and question types that make up each section on the exam. Two of the subscores are common in both Reading and Writing. All subscores are scaled from 1 to 15.

Math Subscores
Heart of Algebra
Problem Solving & Data Analysis
Passport to Advanced Math

Reading Subscores
* Words in Context
* Command of Evidence

Writing Subscores
Expression of Ideas
Standard English Conventions
* Words in Context
* Command of Evidence

Indicates common subscores across different sections

Subject-specific Changes
Changes to each subject: Evidence-based Reading & Writing, Math, Essay

There are detailed changes to each subject on the new PSAT:

Evidence-based Reading

The new Reading section is no longer broken into three sections; it is one long 60-minute section with 47 questions.

There will be 4 single passages and 1 paired passage, and all passages will stay within a 500-750 word count; the paired passage will have 1000-1500 words. There are also specific topics for the passages to be used – 1 U.S. and World Literature passage, 2 History/Social Studies passages, and 2 Science passages.

1 of the History/Social passages and 1 of the Science passages will also contain graphics, which will be incorporated in some way, shape, or form on a number of questions. The graphics will be somewhat challenging, utilizing high data density, several variables, and complex interactions. Your goal will be to understand the core information the graphic intends to show and how it ties into the passage as a whole or in part.

Reading passages will range in text complexity from grades 9 – 11. However, they will focus on topics and content relevant to today's students instead of focusing on outdated literature and facts like the old PSAT's passages.

Each passage will definitely contain 1 Words in Context question and 1 Command of Evidence question.

> The Words in Context questions are similar to passage vocabulary questions in the old PSAT Reading – the old PSAT presented questions like "In Line 87, the word ____ most nearly means". The new PSAT provides similarly phrased questions but focuses on vocabulary that has different connotations depending on the context of the passage; the vocabulary is also noticeably easier so students do not need to rote memorize words. Students should focus on utilizing vocabulary in different ways. For example, the word "synthesis", as presented by the College Board, has different meanings in science and business.

> The Command of Evidence question is a new question type. For certain questions, you will rely on definitive proof within the passage to answer them. Sometimes, a Command of Evidence question will follow directly after, to ask you to select the specific lines used for reference when answer the previous question.

Despite the changes to the Reading section of the new PSAT, keep in mind that Reading Comprehension is still just Reading Comprehension. You must read each passage carefully, take notes, and answer questions that test your understanding of what you read.

Evidence-based Writing

The new Writing section is no longer broken into two sections; it is one short 35-minute section with 44 questions.

There will be 4 single passages with 400-450 words each. Like Reading passages, Writing passages will have set topics, but also specific styles of writing. There will be 1 passage each based on Careers, History/Social Studies, Humanities, and Science; each passage will have exactly 11 questions. Passages will incorporate various writing styles: 1 Nonfiction Narrative, 1-2 Argumentative, and 1-2 Informative/Explanatory. While the writing styles may not impact your understanding of each passage, the topics may if you favor certain topics over others.

Like Reading passages, Writing passages will also incorporate 1 or more graphics in 1 of the passages. These graphics will serve a similar purpose for the passage – to present data that correlates to the bulk of the passage but your focus will be incorporating grammar, graphic information, and language to answer questions.

Writing passage will range in text complexity from grades 9 – 11. The passage topics mentioned before will be relevant to today's student.

Each passage also contains 1 Words in Context question and 1 Command of Evidence question. The focus of the majority of questions will be on the key grammar rules and English conventions we use in the proper English language.

Math

The new PSAT Math has been changed from a 3-section component to a 2-section component. One section will allow you to use a calculator, but the other section will not! This is a major change College Board has focused on because it is important the students can solve math problems with and without tools like calculators.

The Calculator section will have 31 questions for you to complete in 45 minutes. 27 of these questions will be multiple-choice questions and 4 questions will be grid-in.

The No-Calculator section will have 17 questions for you to complete in 25 minutes. 13 of these questions will be multiple-choice questions and 4 questions will be grid-in.

To contribute to the Cross-Test scores for Science and History/Social Studies, 16 questions (8 questions for each Cross-Test score) will be focused on topics in Science and History/Social Studies.

Math will be broken down into a number of major content dimensions:

Heart of Algebra will focus on your mastery of Pre-Algebra and Algebra I. You will solve equations, manipulate expressions and inequalities, and interpret formulas.

Problem Solving & Data Analysis will focus on your ability to analyze relationships using ratios, proportions, percentages, and units, and summarize qualitative and quantitative data. This dimension essentially assesses your ability to apply concepts from the Heart of Algebra and other mathematical concepts to word problems and complex situations.

Passport to Advanced Math will contain higher-level math concepts such as re-writing expressions using structure or analyzing and solving quadratic equations and higher-order equations. Polynomials will also appear.

Additional Topics in Math covers miscellaneous topics found in Geometry and basic Trigonometry. You will utilize area and volume formulas, investigate various shapes and their properties, and work with trigonometric functions. This dimension will contribute to the total Math Test Score but will not be displayed as a subscore on your score report.

The Calculator section will contain problems from all four content dimensions listed above but the No-Calculator section will not have Problem Solving & Data Analysis questions. This means that the Calculator section will contain all the problems for Problem Solving & Data Analysis!

How to Use This Book
Maximizing your experience with this book

The C2 Education PSAT 10/11/NMSQT Strategy Guides are designed to provide you with strategies, concept lessons, and deeper understanding into solving the problems you will see on the new PSAT. While you will need to spend sufficient time studying the materials in this book, we have simplified the best approach to every concept on the new PSAT.

Whether or not you have also obtained the TPGenius 2016 Redesigned Strategy & Practice Guide, there are dozens of practice workbooks available from many other education services with hundreds of practice problems. Regardless of the practice workbooks you have at your disposal, you should take the lessons and strategies you learn from this guide and apply them to the practice questions you tackle.

This guide splits "lessons" by specific concept or question type. Take lessons one or a few at a time – the most important thing is for you to carefully absorb all the knowledge you need to master and conquer the new PSAT.

There are two workbooks in this series for the PSAT 10/11/NMSQT:

The **New PSAT 10/11/NSMQT Strategy/Practice Guide** has a huge volume of practice problems for you to tackle and one full-length practice test at the end of the book for you to try. This edition is designed to provide a more comprehensive look at the test for students who need more practice problems covering a wider variety of approaches and methods.

The **New PSAT 10/11/NMSQT Strategy Guide Intensive Prep** is designed to be more compact and condensed – while there are about the half the number of practice problems compared to the Practice Edition, there are two new, full-length practice tests for you to try. This edition is geared towards students who prefer a direct, get-in-get-out method for tackling the PSAT and for students who have little time to prepare.

We wish you the best of luck in your work, progress, and results on the new PSAT!

About the National Merit Scholarship

The National Merit® Scholarship Program recognizes students with excellent academic performance. High school students enter the National Merit® Program by taking the PSAT® during October of their school year. Many high schools offer the PSAT on a set day each year for students free of charge.

Entry Requirements

Students must adhere to the following requirements in order to enter the National Merit® Program via the PSAT:

1. Students must take the PSAT/NMSQT® no later than their third year in grades 9 through 12, regardless of grade classification or educational pattern.
2. Students must be enrolled as a high school student, progressing normally toward graduation/completion of high school, and planning to enroll full-time in college no later than the fall following completion of high school.
3. Students must be citizens of the United States or be a U.S. lawful permanent resident or have applied for permanent residence in the U.S.

All students may take the PSAT/NMSQT®, but must adhere to the above requirements in order to be entered into the National Merit® Program.

National Merit® Program Recognition

Based on PSAT/NMSQT® score performance, students are recognized and notified by their high school administrators of said recognition. There are multiple levels of recognition:

- **Commended Students**: In September, approximately two-thirds of approximately 50,000 top test scorers receive Letters of Commendation in recognition of their academic potential. Commended Students achieve high scores but score just below the level required for participants to be recognized as Semifinalists. Commended Students do not continue in the competition for National Merit® Scholarships, but may become candidates for Special Scholarships, which are sponsored by corporations and businesses.
- **Semifinalist**: In September, approximately one-third of approximately 50,000 top test scorers receive notifications that they have qualified as Semifinalists. Semifinalists are the highest scorers in each state; these Semifinalists will receive scholarship application materials from their respective high schools. Semifinalists may advance to Finalist standing by meeting high academic standards and all other requirements explained in the information provided to Semifinalists.
- **Finalists**: In February, approximately 15,000 Semifinalists are notified by mail at their home addresses that they have become Finalists in the program. High school principals are also notified and sent certificates to present to each Finalist.
- **Winners**: Winners of the National Merit Scholarship® are chosen from the Finalists based on abilities, skills, and accomplishments without regard to gender, race, ethnic origin, or religious preference. NMS committees select winners based on Finalists' academic records, information about school curricula and grading systems, two sets of test scores, the high school official's written recommendation, student activities and leadership roles, and the Finalist's personal essay.

Types of National Merit Scholarship® Awards

From March to mid-June, approximately 7,600 Finalists are awarded a Merit Scholarship® award. There are three types of awards:

1. **National Merit® $2500 Scholarships**: All Finalists compete for these scholarships, which are awarded based on state representation. Winners are given these single payment scholarships for college tuition or other use.
2. **Corporate-sponsored Merit Scholarships**: Corporate sponsors can designate these scholarships to children of their employees, associated communities, or Finalists with career plans the sponsor wants to encourage. These scholarships can be renewable for four years of undergraduate study or as single payment one-time awards.
3. **College-sponsored Merit Scholarships**: A number of sponsor colleges select winners based on which Finalists have been accepted for admission to respective schools. These awards are renewable up to four years of undergraduate study.

Special Scholarships

Every year, approximately 1,300 National Merit® Program participants, who are outstanding but not Finalists, are awarded Special Sponsorships by corporations and business organizations. Students must meet each sponsor's criteria and submit an entry form to the sponsor organization. These scholarships are renewable up to four years of undergraduate study or as one-time awards.

For more information, check out the National Merit® website:
http://www.nationalmerit.org/

Section 2
Evidence-based Reading

Explicit and Implicit Information
Understanding Relationships
Author's Intent
Structure
Analyzing Arguments
Citing Textual Evidence
Words in Context
Word Choice
Analogical Reasoning
Analyzing Multiple Texts
Quantitative Information

Explicit and Implicit Information
Concept & Strategy Lesson

Many of the questions on the PSAT 10/11 will require you to identify information that is stated *explicitly* and *implicitly*. *Explicit* information is clearly stated in the passage. *Implicit* information is not clearly stated and is instead implied.

EXPLICIT INFORMATION QUESTIONS

Explicit information questions are the most straightforward questions on the PSAT 10/11. They are essentially reading comprehension questions that ask you to recall information that is clearly stated in the passage. They can often be recognized by the use of phrases like *according to the passage* or *based on information in the passage*.

HOW TO ANSWER EXPLICIT INFORMATION QUESTIONS

Explicit information questions are looking for information that is stated in the passage. Wrong answer choices will usually fall into one of the following categories:

- NO EVIDENCE: Choices that are not clearly stated in the text, that require a leap of logic, or that require outside information.

- TOO SPECIFIC: Choices that provide details that are not mentioned in the text or that focus on a tiny detail of the part of the passage referenced in the question.

- TOO GENERAL: Choices that discuss a large group when the passage discusses specific members of a group or choices that contain extreme words like *all, every, always,* or *none*. The correct answer will very rarely contain extreme words.

- DIFFERENT AREA: Choices that reference a different part of the passage than the one referenced in the question.

- INCORRECT BASED ON INFORMATION GIVEN: Choices that negate information in the passage or that are proven wrong by information in the passage.

TO ANSWER EXPLICIT INFORMATION QUESTIONS:

Step 1: Locate the part of the passage being referenced by the question.

Step 2: Examine the answer choices. Eliminate any choices that fall into one of the "wrong answer choice" categories.

Step 3: Of the remaining choices, choose the one that is most clearly supported by the passage.

IMPLICIT INFORMATION QUESTIONS

Implicit information questions are less straightforward. They require that we use logic to make inferences based on information in the passage. They can often be recognized by the use of phrases like *suggest*, *implies*, *infer*, or *conclude*.

HOW TO ANSWER IMPLICIT INFORMATION QUESTIONS

The best strategy for these questions is to use active reading when reading the passages.

Active reading requires taking notes and using marks like underlining to highlight main ideas, arguments, evidence, and other important details of the passage. By noting main ideas, arguments, and evidence, you can gain a better understanding of the author's intent in writing, his attitude toward his subject, and his overall tone. This information provides valuable clues to help answer implicit information questions.

As with explicit information categories, incorrect answer choices for implicit information questions also tend to fall into one of several categories:

- <u>INCORRECT BASED ON INFORMATION IN THE PASSAGE</u>: Choices that are disproven by something stated in the passage.

- <u>DO NOT MATCH THE AUTHOR'S TONE OR ATTITUDE</u>: Choices that take a different stance than the author or that do not reflect the author's tone.

- <u>NOT COMPLETELY ANSWERING THE QUESTION</u>: Choices that might be supported by the passage, but that fail to completely answer the question being asked.

- <u>ONLY LOOSELY RELATED TO THE PASSAGE</u>: Choices that are not closely related to the information that is stated in the passage.

TO ANSWER IMPLICIT INFORMATION QUESTIONS:

Step 1: Locate the part of the passage being referenced by the question.

Step 2: Examine the answer choices. Using your notations on the passage, eliminate any answer choices that fall into one of the "wrong answer" categories.

Step 3: Of the remaining choices, choose the one that is most clearly supported by the passage.

Understanding Relationships
Concept & Strategy Lesson

The reading passages on the PSAT 10/11 have many working parts. As a result, readers will have to know exactly how to relate ideas in the text to each other.

UNDERSTANDING RELATIONSHIPS QUESTIONS

Several questions will ask how one part of the passage relates to another. This could be an idea that the author states (and how it relates to the evidence the author gives), relationships between events mentioned in the passage, or relationships between individuals mentioned or quoted in the text. If the reading is a paired passage, these questions may ask about the relationship between ideas or topics mentioned in both. These questions usually use words or phrases such as "what is the relationship...", "connects with," "related to", or "caused by."

TYPES OF RELATIONSHIPS

1) <u>Cause-and-Effect/Sequence</u>
   What happens first? What happened next? These relationships are generally chronological in nature – perhaps a new technology has built on the innovations of previous technology, or a lawsuit cited in the passage came about as a result of a certain crime committed.

2) <u>Comparison-Contrast</u>
   While trying to argue a point, an author may bring in another idea to either provide contrast or show similarity. Are these two things alike in any way? Or are they completely different? Do they support or refute the other?

3) <u>Adding Support</u>
   Especially after the author makes some sort of claim, the passage will often offer evidence to support the claim. This may include citing a study or quoting an expert whose opinions agree with the author.

4) <u>Personal Relationships</u>
   These relationships are between people mentioned in the passage. Are these two people related, or are they coworkers? Do they have similar views, or is the author showing us the difference between their viewpoints?

TO ANSWER UNDERSTANDING RELATIONSHIPS QUESTIONS:

Step 1: Find the two parts of the passage mentioned in the question.

Step 2: Determine the relationship between the two situations or ideas (cause/effect, part/whole, comparison/contrast, claim/support) or people (parent/child, rival/rival, colleague/coworker).

Step 3: Eliminate any answer choices that do not fit the relationship you have determined, or that simply do not make sense in the context of the passage.

Step 4: Choose your answer from the remaining answer choices – whichever choice has more support from the passage.

Author's Intent
Concept & Strategy Lesson

Everything you read on the PSAT 10/11 was written for a reason. The author may have a point he or she is trying to argue, or perhaps he or she is sharing information or just trying to tell a story. Many questions on the PSAT 10/11 will ask you to determine and describe what the author's intent was when writing the passage. These include questions that focus on central ideas and themes, the author's purpose, and the author's point of view.

CENTRAL IDEAS AND THEMES

When reading a passage, it's important to keep an eye on the big picture. This can often be difficult since the passages are often long and contain many different ideas. Consider how you would summarize the primary ideas of the passage. If you were asked what the question is about, how would you respond?

One way to determine this is to make small notes to the side of the passage that summarize each paragraph while you read. By the time you've finished reading, you should be able to look at your notes to get an abbreviated version of the passage itself, put in simpler terms.

These notes can be immensely helpful in determining the central idea or theme. Questions that ask about central ideas and themes usually use the phrases "main idea", "primary point", or "central theme".

ANALYZING PURPOSE

Knowing what the passage is *about* is just one aspect of these questions. You'll also need to know *why* the author wrote this passage. Say you've just read a passage on cloning. Good – you know the main idea. Now why was the author writing this? Has the author taken a stance for or against cloning? Or has the author simply given you the information with no bias? If the passage is a selection from literature, the author's intent is likely simply to relate an incident, or describe a character's personality.

In addition, you want to determine the author's intended audience – is it a friend? A specific scientific community? The world? Is the language very simple and clear, or is it highly technical? Speakers or writers will write differently and phrase their ideas differently depending on the audience to whom they're speaking.

Questions that ask about analyzing purpose will usually use the phrases "what is the author's purpose?" or "why did the author write this?"

POINT OF VIEW

Not every passage is written by an EPA official or American President. Often a big part of determining the author's intent is to figure out where he or she is coming from. Is the writer writing from a position of authority? How formal or informal is the language used? What is the writer's tone? Does the writer himself/herself have a vested interest in what he or she is writing about? You would get very different viewpoints on genetic experimentation from a multinational science corporation and a protestor against said genetic experimentation, for example.

TO ANSWER AUTHORIAL INTENT QUESTIONS:

Step 1: While reading the passage, make notes alongside the paragraphs as you read. This should give you a general idea of the main ideas or themes of the passage.

Step 2: If the question is asking for the main idea or theme of the passage, use the information you gathered in step 1 to determine the main idea and/or theme. Then eliminate any answers that do not match your summary, and pick the answer that best fits the passage.

Step 3: If the question is a purpose or point of view question, identify the speaker and audience of the passage. Then eliminate any answers that do not match the passage or contradict it; from the choices remaining, choose the answer that is best supported by the passage.

Structure
Concept & Strategy Lesson

When you read a passage, the ideas aren't simply arranged in the order the author thought of them. Each speech, excerpt, or report has been carefully thought out in order to best communicate its ideas. Ideas progress through the text. Answering questions about the passage's structure will be difficult, as this skill requires a thorough understanding of everything the passage is trying to say.

These questions will ask about the whole passage's organization, and also will ask about the role of specific paragraphs within the passage.

OVERALL TEXT STRUCTURE QUESTIONS

The best method to approach text structure questions is – before you look at the questions – analyze the structure of the passage as you read. There are several ways a passage could be arranged:

1. chronologically and/or cause-effect
2. thesis statement followed by support (evidence or quotes from experts)
3. from general statements to specific statements
4. contrasting ideas – pro/cons of a situation, problems and solutions, examples and counter-examples

As you read, write notes in the margins of the test that you can refer back to when answering questions. Note shifts of subject or tone between paragraphs. Watch out for instances in which the author gives more evidence to support the claim, refutes an opponent's claim, provides explanation, changes topics, or describes multiple aspects of a situation or problem.

With this "road map" of the passage, answering overall text structure questions should become much simpler. Questions about the passage's overall structure will use phrases such as "what is the structure of the passage as a whole?" or "In the passage overall, how does the author arrange his arguments?"

PART-TO-WHOLE STRUCTURE QUESTIONS

These questions ask what role certain paragraphs, sentences, and phrases play in the structure of the passage as a whole. Is that third paragraph providing additional evidence, or is it refuting a previously stated point? Look for phrases such as "the author included the information in lines 42-53 in order to…" or "what purpose does the third paragraph (lines 22-29) play in the passage as a whole?"

TO ANSWER STRUCTURE QUESTIONS:

Step 1: While reading, note any shifts in tone, subject, or purpose that you spot in the passage. Note how individual paragraphs or arguments play a role in the development of the passage's ideas.

Step 2: Identify whether the question asks about the passages overall structure or the role that part of a passage plays.

Step 3: If the question is a part-to-whole question, look at the part of the passage being referenced and determine how this part of the passage relates to the author's main ideas.

Step 4: Eliminate any answer choices that do not suit the structure based on your notes.

Step 5: Choose the answer that best represents how the passage is structured or how the cited portion of the passage contributes to the author's main ideas.

Analyzing Arguments
Concept & Strategy Lesson

When you try to make an argument, you can't simply state your opinion and be done with it. You've got to back yourself up with proof. The same goes for the writers of the passages you read on the PSAT 10/11. Many of the passages you read will be making a central claim and you must not only identify the main idea but determine how the author argues it – and how convincing that claim actually is.

ANALYZING ARGUMENTS QUESTIONS

There are three main types of analyzing arguments questions:

1) Claims and Counterclaims
2) Analyzing Reasoning
3) Analyzing Evidence

CLAIMS AND COUNTERCLAIMS

Claims and counterclaims questions ask you to identify the claims or counterclaims that the author makes in the passage. Remember that a claim is an argument made by the author, and a counterclaim is an opposing argument used to support the author's main argument. The best way of answering these questions is through process of elimination.

> **TO ANSWER CLAIMS AND COUNTERCLAIMS QUESTIONS:**
>
> **Step 1:** If the question asks about a specific claim made in the passage, find that argument and reexamine the paragraph in which the claim appears.
>
> **Step 2:** Eliminate answer choices that disagree with the information found in the relevant part of the passage.
>
> **Step 3:** Eliminate answer choices that use extreme language, such as *always* or *never.*
>
> **Step 4:** Of the remaining choices, choose the one that best reflects the information in the passage.

ANALYZING REASONING

Analyzing reasoning questions are a bit trickier because they can come in several forms. Some analyzing reasoning questions ask what assumptions the author or his sources make. Another asks you to identify the author's reason for including a word or phrase in the context of making an argument. These questions require you to understand the reasoning behind the author's argument and whether his reasoning is valid. Examples of faulty reasoning include:

Faulty causation: When the author identifies a causal relationship that isn't true.

Circular reasoning: When an author restates an argument in order to support that argument. An argument cannot support itself.

Over-generalization: When claims are too bold or all-encompassing.

Over-simplification: When the author's reasoning fails to acknowledge the complexity of the issue.

TO ANSWER ANALYZING REASONING QUESTIONS:

Step 1: If the question asks about an assumption made by the author, determine whether the author's argument would be weakened if that assumption were invalid. Eliminate any answer choices that don't agree with this assessment.

Step 2: If the question asks you to evaluate whether the author's reasoning is strong, look for evidence of faulty reasoning. Eliminate any answer choices that don't suit your findings.

Step 3: Of the remaining choices, choose the one that best reflects your assessment of the author's rationale.

ANALYZING EVIDENCE

Analyzing evidence requires you to determine whether the evidence the author uses is relevant or pertinent to the argument the author is making. If the author is citing an expert, is that expert a good source? (A climate scientist could tell you more about global warming than, for example, a wildlife scientist.) Are the statistics the author cites clearly supporting the author's argument, or are they misleading?

Evidence can generally be divided into four basic categories:

Examples: Provide context to support a claim made by the author.

Analogies: Illustrate the author's claim.

Statistics: Numbers used to support a claim. Statistics can often be misleading, so pay very close attention to what they actually prove.

Testimony: Information from an expert. Both the source and the information are important.

TO ANSWER ANALYZING EVIDENCE QUESTIONS:

Step 1: Determine what king of evidence is used. Eliminate answer choices that do not seem to fit this type of evidence.

Step 2: Determine whether the evidence is authoritative and relevant to the author's claim. Eliminate any answer choices that don't seem to fit your assessment of the evidence.

Step 3: Pick the answer that best defines the evidence and its relevance.

Citing Textual Evidence
Concept & Strategy Lesson

Citing textual evidence questions will appear on every reading passage on the PSAT 10/11. These questions ask you to identify which part of the passage supports your answer to an earlier question.

APPEARING IN PAIRS

Citing textual evidence questions will always appear within a pair of questions. The first question of the pair focuses on analysis, asking you to draw a conclusion or make an inference about something in the passage. The second question in the pair is the citing textual evidence question, which provides four sets of lines from the passage and asks which one provides the best evidence in support of the answer to the analysis question.

ANSWERING CITING TEXTUAL EVIDENCE QUESTIONS

Because citing textual evidence questions always appear in pairs, they can help you to figure out the answer to the analysis question. After all, the answer to the analysis question must always be supported by one of the sets of lines in the citing textual evidence question, which can narrow down the possibilities and identify the part of the passage in which the answer to the analysis question can be found.

It is easier to answer citing textual evidence questions when you are already able to answer the analysis question:

> **TO ANSWER CITING TEXTUAL EVIDENCE QUESTIONS**
> **WHEN YOU *DO* KNOW THE ANSWER TO THE ANALYSIS QUESTION:**
> **Step 1:** Using the answer to the analysis question, look for important words, phrases, or ideas in each of the sets of lines identified in the citing textual evidence question. Eliminate any answer choices that don't contain these important ideas.
>
> **Step 2:** Of the remaining answer choices, choose the one that most clearly supports the answer to the previous question.

Other times, the citing textual evidence question and the analysis question can work as a pair to help you answer both questions:

**TO ANSWER CITING TEXTUAL EVIDENCE QUESTIONS
WHEN YOU *DON'T* KNOW THE ANSWER TO THE ANALYSIS QUESTION:**

Step 1: If you cannot answer the analysis question, start by eliminating any answer choices in the analysis question that are wrong.

Step 2: Look at the line sets provided in the answer choices for the citing textual evidence question. Eliminate any answer choices in the analysis question that cannot be supported by one of the citing textual evidence line sets.

Step 3: Eliminate any answer choices in the citing textual evidence question that do not support one of the answer choices provided in the analysis question.

Step 4: Of the remaining options, choose the pair of answers that have the clearest relationship to one another and that are most strongly supported by the passage.

Words in Context
Concept & Strategy Lesson

Every reading passage on the PSAT 10/11 will test your knowledge of vocabulary through words in context questions. Unlike the sentence completion questions of prior iterations of the PSAT 10/11, these words in context questions won't test "PSAT 10/11 words" that you almost never see in academic contexts. Instead, these questions test words that are likely to be used in normal conversations or in academic texts, but that can have multiple meanings depending on their context.

ADDRESSING WORDS IN CONTEXT QUESTIONS

Words in context questions are easy to spot because they always appear in the same format:

As it is used in line _##_, "_word_" most nearly means...

The answer choices will always be either a single word or, much more rarely, two- or three-word phrases. You will need to use the context of the sentence or paragraph to determine which answer choice best matches the meaning of the word in question.

TO ANSWER WORDS IN CONTEXT QUESTIONS:

Step 1: Cover up the answer choices for the words in context question.

Step 2: Reread the sentence that the original word appears in, replacing the original word with one of your own choosing. The word you plug in should suit the context of the sentence to retain the sentence's original meaning.

Step 3: Uncover the answer choices and eliminate any choices that don't suit the sentence based on the word you chose in step 2.

Step 4: Of the remaining choices, choose the one that best suits the sentence's intended meaning.

Word Choice
Concept & Strategy Lesson

The PSAT 10/11 will test your ability to analyze an author's choice of words within a given passage. Remember that an author almost always chooses his words carefully, so an author's choice of words is typically done with some purpose in mind.

ADDRESSING WORD CHOICE QUESTIONS

Word choice questions will usually either ask why an author has chosen a particular way of phrasing something or how the author's choice affects the passage. Answering word choice questions will often require that you understand the author's intent in writing the passage; after all, the author's choice of words will generally be determined by the author's purpose in writing.

TO ANSWER WORD CHOICE QUESTIONS:

Step 1: Underline the words or phrases indicated in the question.

Step 2: Carefully reread the paragraph containing the words/phrases indicated in the question. In the margins, jot down the purpose of the paragraph within the passage.

Step 3: Using your knowledge of the author's intent in writing the passage and the purpose of the paragraph containing the words/phrases, begin eliminating answer choices that do not reflect your findings.

Step 4: Of the remaining choices, choose the one that best suits the author's intent and the purpose of the paragraph.

Analogical Reasoning
Concept & Strategy Lesson

The PSAT 10/11 will ask you to identify similar situations through analogical reasoning questions. These questions ask you to analyze something in the passage and to apply the characteristics of that something to another, unrelated situation.

ADDRESSING ANALOGICAL REASONING QUESTIONS

Analogical reasoning questions will usually ask which of a given set of situations most closely mirrors a situation given in the passage. These questions typically require that you go beyond the superficial details of the passage to analyze the deeper meanings. For example, the situation in the passage might involve a politician hoping to address the achievement gap in education by attacking the root issue of poverty. The superficial details here are the actor (the politician) and the problem (the achievement gap). The underlying detail is the means by which the politician hopes to address the problem -- by solving the root of the problem.

TO ANSWER ANALOGICAL REASONING QUESTIONS:

Step 1: Reread the portion of the passage referenced by the question. Analyze the situation to find its deeper meaning.

Step 2: Carefully read each of the answer choices provided. Determine which details are just superficial and ignore these details.

Step 3: Compare the situation in the passage to each answer choice. Eliminate answer choices that only share superficial details.

Step 4: Of the remaining choices, choose the one that best mirrors the deeper meaning of the situation in the passage.

Analyzing Multiple Texts
Concept & Strategy Lesson

The PSAT 10/11 reading section will often present paired passages that require that you analyze multiple texts. These questions will require that you be able to identify the points of view of two different authors in order to compare or contrast the passages.

ADDRESSING ANALYZING MULTIPLE TEXTS QUESTIONS

Some multiple text questions will ask how the author of one passage would respond to information or claims made in the other passage. Other questions may ask about the differences or similarities between the points of view of the two authors. Regardless of the form the question takes, all multiple choice questions are made easier through active reading. To answer these questions, it is important to be able to identify the main ideas/claims, author's intent, and style/tone of each passage.

TO ANSWER ANALYZING MULTIPLE TEXTS QUESTIONS:

Step 1: Carefully take notes regarding the author's main arguments/ideas, intent, and style/tone while reading each passage.

Step 2: Eliminate any answer choices that fail to accurately identify the main ideas and point of view of both passages.

Step 3: Closely examine the remaining answer choices. Choose the one that best matches the main ideas and points of view of both passages.

Quantitative Information
Concept & Strategy Lesson

Quantitative information questions involve the use of graphs, tables, charts, and other graphics. Using the evidence available in the passage and the graphic, you must draw conclusions in order to answer quantitative information questions.

ADDRESSING QUANTITATIVE INFORMATION QUESTIONS

Quantitative information questions require synthesis, meaning that you must combine information from two sources. This means that no matter what the answer to the question is, it must agree with both the passage and the graphic. Having two sources of information to draw from can help you to eliminate answer choices more easily.

TO ANSWER QUANTITATIVE INFORMATION QUESTIONS:

Step 1: Carefully examine the graphic. Eliminate any answer choices that don't reflect the graphic. Be careful to look for specific units of measurement -- some answer choices might seem accurate at first glance, but do not actually describe what is measured by the graphic.

Step 2: Find the relevant portion of the passage. Eliminate any answer choices that disagree with information in the passage.

Step 3: Of the remaining answer choices, choose the one that best reflects both the graphic and the passage.

Evidence-Based Reading Practice
Practice Passages and Questions

Practice Passage 1

This passages details one way in which scientists are trying to meet the challenges caused by global climate change.

People around the world depend on food crops adapted to an array of temperature and precipitation regimes, but those conditions are in
Line flux because of global climate change. Among
(5) the climate changes we can expect in the future are rising temperatures and increases in greenhouse gases such as methane and carbon dioxide (CO_2). So scientists want to identify plant traits that could be used to develop food-
(10) crop cultivars that thrive despite—or perhaps because of—shifts in CO_2 levels, water availability, and air temperature.

As part of this effort, plant physiologist Lewis Ziska and colleagues conducted a study
(15) of several rice cultivars (varieties) to determine whether changes of temperature and CO_2 levels affected seed yields. They also looked for visible traits that could signal whether a plant cultivar has the genetic potential for adapting
(20) successfully to elevated CO_2 levels.

For their study, the scientists included weedy red rice, a breed normally known as more of a pest than a food crop. Weedy red rice often infests cultivated rice cropland, pushing out the
(25) generally more desirable cultivars. Despite the plant's downside, previous assessments indicated that weedy rice growing under elevated CO_2 levels had higher seed yields than cultivated rice growing under the same
(30) conditions.

The scientists used environmental growth chambers to study genetically diverse rice cultivars at current and future projections of atmospheric CO_2 and a range of day/night air
(35) temperatures. They observed that all the rice cultivars put out more biomass at elevated CO_2 levels, although this diminished as air temperatures rose.

To farmers, biomass is less important than
(40) its seed yield. By this metric, which measures the amount of edible plant produced, only weedy rice and one other cultivar responded positively to elevated CO_2 levels when grown at today's normal air temperatures. The researchers were
(45) also intrigued that only weedy rice showed significant increases of biomass and seed yield under elevated CO_2 levels at the higher temperatures expected for rice-growing regions by the middle of the century.

(50) When Ziska and colleagues analyzed the study data for the weedy rice, they observed that seed yield increases under elevated CO_2 resulted from an increase in seed head and tiller production. Tillers are stalks put out by a
(55) growing rice plant; as the plant matures, the seed heads—where the edible part of the rice grain is produced—develop at the end of the tillers.

Since rice tiller production is determined in part by a plant's genetic makeup, crop breeders
(60) might someday be able to use this weedy rice trait to develop commercial rice cultivars that can convert rising CO_2 levels into higher seed yields. In essence, they would be taking the advantageous traits of weedy rice and combining
(65) them with the favorable taste and size of other rice cultivars to make a type of rice that is perfectly suited to the future climate. To the researchers, these findings also suggest that the weedy, feral cousins of cultivated cereals could
(70) have other traits that would be useful in adapting to the environmental challenges that may come with climate change.

"We know that atmospheric CO_2 and air temperatures will increase together," says Ziska.
(75) "Ideally, we can develop plants that respond well, not just to elevated CO_2 levels, but also to higher temperatures and other effects of global climate change."

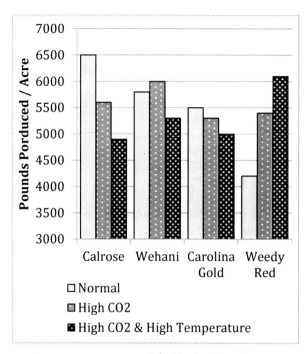

Figure 1: Average seed yields for four rice varieties grown under normal CO_2 and temperature conditions; high-CO_2, normal temperature conditions; and high-CO_2, high-temperature conditions.

1. Based on evidence in the passage, if Figure 1 showed the total biomass, rather than the seed yield, produced by the rice varieties, which of the following would most likely be true?

   A) The left bar would be higher than the middle and right bars for all four varieties.
   B) The left would be higher than the middle bar for only the Weedy Red variety.
   C) The middle bar would be higher than the left bar for all four varieties.
   D) The right bar would be higher than the middle bar for only the Weedy Red variety.

2. As used in line 3, "regimes" most nearly means

   A) conditions.
   B) schemes.
   C) governments.
   D) therapies.

3. How does the phrase "more of a pest than a food crop" in lines 22-23 affect the author's portrayal of the weedy red rice variety?

   A) It hints that any potential benefits of weedy red rice should be dismissed.
   B) It indicates that many people unfairly believe weedy red rice has no value.
   C) It foreshadows the damage that weedy red rice will cause as the climate changes.
   D) It emphasizes that rice is often grown for uses other than food.

4. It can be reasonably inferred from the passage that "biomass is less important than its seed yield" (lines 39-40) as a measure of rice production because

   A) fertilizer can be used to improve biomass but not seed yield.
   B) high-biomass crops are expensive to harvest.
   C) some farmers prefer low-biomass plants.
   D) not all of a rice plant's biomass is edible.

5. Which choice most effectively supports the answer to the previous question?

   A) Lines 17-20 ("They also… CO_2 levels.")
   B) Lines 25-30 ("Despite the… same conditions.")
   C) Lines 35-38 ("They observed… temperatures rose.")
   D) Lines 40-44 ("By this… air temperatures.")

6. Based on information in the passage and the figure, what is the "one other cultivar" referred to in line 42?

   A) Calrose
   B) Wehani
   C) Carolina Gold
   D) Weedy Red

7. As used in line 59, "makeup" most nearly means

   A) temperament.
   B) fiction.
   C) cosmetics.
   D) characteristics.

8. Information in the passage implies that the "advantageous traits of weedy rice" (lines 64) are

A) unlikely to be useful to future rice growers.
B) used to improve the size and flavor of other rice varieties.
C) largely related to tiller and seed-head production.
D) limited to current carbon dioxide and temperature levels.

9. Which choice provides the best evidence to support the answer to the previous question?

A) Lines 44-49 ("The researchers… the century.")
B) Lines 50-54 ("When Ziska… tiller production.")
C) Lines 63-67 ("In essence… future climate.")
D) Lines 75-78 ("'Ideally, we… climate change.'")

10. The passage's overall structure can best be described as

A) comparing and contrasting two alternative techniques.
B) describing a principle followed by several examples of that principle at work.
C) presenting a problem and one potential solution to that problem.
D) telling a chronological history of an innovation.

Practice Passage 2

This passage examines a unique approach to gathering data for scientific research.

It's the season of dramatic weather, when everyone from the National Weather Service to farmers and insurers monitors predictions of
Line weather conditions—and assessments of where
(5) severe weather and its impacts are greatest. In this environment, a citizen science project called CoCoRaHS—the Community Collaborative Rain, Hail and Snow Network—is helpful. This program makes possible a detailed view of
(10) rainfall, snowfall, and hail in regions around the country. The organizers have found that precipitation is often highly variable; in extreme cases, it can vary by inches at locations just a few blocks from each other.

(15) CoCoRaHS was first envisioned in 1997, after an intense rainstorm in Fort Collins, Colorado, caused massive flooding and more than $200 million in damage. Nothing in the forecast indicated that the storm would cause as
(20) much damage as it did. In addition, there was incredible variation in the amount of rainfall within the affected area—from less than 2 inches to more than 14 inches (which nearly equals that area's average *yearly* rainfall) over a
(25) distance of just 5 miles.

The unexpected severity of the storm and its uneven impacts suggested to researchers that enlisting individuals and families to report on precipitation from their locations could provide
(30) a more accurate and useful picture of rainfall and snowfall around the state and the country. Thus, in 1998, CoCoRaHS was born. Since the program started, 46,000 people, including participants from every state in the nation, have
(35) signed up through the CoCoRaHS website. To participate in the network, each citizen scientist must invest in a high-capacity 4-inch-diameter rain gauge (at a cost of about $30). All new participants in the CoCoRaHS network receive
(40) training in how to place their gauges and take accurate readings. Then, each time a rain, hail, or snow storm crosses their area, volunteers take measurements of precipitation.

Their reports are then recorded on the
(45) CoCoRaHS website. The data are displayed and organized for a range of end users—from the National Weather Service to the U.S. Department of Agriculture to emergency managers, hydrologists, farmers, ranchers,
(50) research scientists, educators, and the general public.

During 2014, there were more than 19,000 active users who set out rain gauges and sent in reports. More than 11,000 reports come in every
(55) day. Just as an image is sharper the more pixels it contains, having citizen scientists report precipitation data from thousands of locations provides a detailed picture valuable for predictions, emergency planning, insurance
(60) estimates, and a number of other uses.

Beyond its value to the consumers of the data, CoCoRaHS is engaging non-scientists in the kind of observation, reporting and analysis done by scientists. The educational aspects of
(65) their work are particularly important to members of the CoCoRaHS community. In addition to coordinating the volunteer reporting, CoCoRaHS sponsors webinars every month featuring experts discussing some aspect of
(70) weather or climate. Topics such as cloud formation, lightning, and atmospheric rivers of Pacific water vapor aiming at the west coast have been popular with the volunteers.

Many of the program's volunteers report
(75) being surprised that precipitation varies so much. This sort of learning is valuable to many of the volunteers for many reasons. Some enjoy returning to scientific topics that they have not studied since college. Others say that they wish
(80) they'd pursued a scientific career, and that the CoCoRaHS experience is giving them a scientific outlet. Still others just enjoy being a part of a communal project.

Being able to contribute scientific data to a
(85) network and see the impact of your observations is a powerful experience. The researchers are particularly excited to see volunteers from different age groups (including many high school students), different backgrounds, and
(90) different parts of the country taking part in the project. What volunteers are finding is fascinating, and it helps both scientists and ordinary people better understand rain, hail, and snow—phenomena that we've all experienced
(95) but that most of us take for granted.

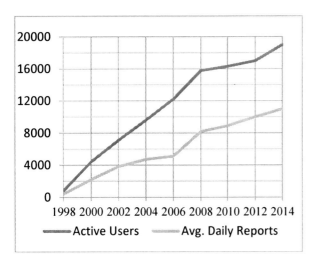

Figure 1: The number of active users and the average number of daily reports during each year of the CoCoRaHS program.

1. It can be reasonably inferred from the passage and the figure that which of the following is true regarding the "46,000 people" (line 33)?

   A) Nearly all are active users, although most of them do not submit daily reports.
   B) Many of them are not currently active users.
   C) Most signed up during the program's first two years.
   D) Nearly all of them provide daily reports on the precipitation in their areas.

2. Based on the figure, which of the following statements is accurate regarding CoCoRaHS?

   A) The program has grown in size during each year of its existence.
   B) The program experienced its largest increase in size between 2010 and 2012.
   C) The number of daily reports has little or no correlation with the number of active users.
   D) If trends continue, the average number of daily reports will reach 20,000 by 2016.

3. Information in the passage implies that the CoCoRaHS program was founded in large part to

   A) teach scientific concepts to students.
   B) better prepare for the impact of severe weather.
   C) help a city recover from a damaging flood.
   D) save money on the collection of weather data.

4. Which choice provides the most effective evidence to support the previous question's answer?

   A) Lines 5-8 ("In this… is helpful.")
   B) Lines 20-25 ("In addition… 5 miles.")
   C) Lines 26-31 ("The unexpected… the country.")
   D) Lines 45-51 ("The data… general public.")

5. The author uses which of the following to explain the significance of having thousands of daily precipitation reports?

   A) A quote from an expert who uses the data
   B) Examples from two contrasting ways of collecting data
   C) An analogy to another topic
   D) Profiles of several of the data collectors

6. As used in line 55, "sharper" most nearly means

   A) harsher.
   B) more sudden.
   C) more intelligent.
   D) clearer.

7. In the context of line 82, "outlet" most nearly means

   A) practice.
   B) store.
   C) exit.
   D) stream.

8. Based on information in the passage, the CoCoRaHS volunteers can best be described as

   A) professional.
   B) youthful.
   C) diverse.
   D) selfish.

9. Which choice best supports the answer to the previous question?

   A) Lines 61-64 ("Beyond its… by scientists.")
   B) Lines 70-73 ("Topics such… the volunteers.")
   C) Lines 79-82 ("Others say… scientific outlet.")
   D) Lines 86-91 ("The researchers… the project.")

10. In the context of the passage's discussion of the CoCoRaHS program, the seventh paragraph (lines 74-83) primarily serves to

A) reveal the motivations of some of those involved with the program.
B) provide evidence that the program has helped advance weather prediction.
C) acknowledge an argument that some critics make against the program.
D) predict the ways that the program will change in the future.

11. The tone of the passage indicates that the relationship between the CoCoRaHS researchers and volunteers can best be characterized as

A) a fun way to teach volunteers, but not a scientifically valuable one.
B) a mutually beneficial collaboration.
C) an example of scientists taking advantage of non-scientists.
D) a well-intentioned failure for both groups.

Practice Passage 3

The following passage examines the history of a well-known political tradition.

On January 8, 1790, President George Washington delivered a speech at Federal Hall in New York City. This speech, called his first
Line annual message to Congress (which we now
(5) refer to as the State of the Union), was short—in fact, it remains the shortest one ever.

In it, Washington touched on several subjects to which he recommended that Congress give its attention, including national
(10) defense, naturalization, uniform weights and measures, promotion of education, and support of the public credit.

The new leaders were fully aware of the enormity of the task in front of them.
(15) Washington's last sentence speaks to the heart of their endeavor: "The welfare of our country is the great object to which our cares and efforts ought to be directed.—And I shall derive great satisfaction from a co-operation with you, in the
(20) pleasing though arduous task of ensuring to our fellow citizens the blessings, which they have a right to expect, from a free, efficient and equal Government."

Washington gave this speech to fulfill the
(25) President's obligation outlined in Article II, Section 3, Clause 1, of the Constitution. It says that the President "shall from time to time give to the Congress Information of the State of the Union, and recommend to their Consideration
(30) such measures as he shall judge necessary and expedient."

The Constitution does not specify how frequently the President should share this information. As he did on so many other issues,
(35) Washington set the precedent that this message would be delivered to Congress once a year.

Washington's actions in another respect were not precedent-setting, however. Washington appeared before a joint session of
(40) Congress to deliver his annual messages in a speech. Second President John Adams followed suit. However, the Third President, Thomas Jefferson, set a new tradition when he sent his messages in writing and did not appear before
(45) Congress.

That precedent stuck until 1913, when President Woodrow Wilson addressed a joint session of Congress. Before Wilson, the annual messages were mostly a report to Congress of
(50) the activities of the Executive branch. After the increased attention Wilson's speech received, the State of the Union became a launching pad for Presidential initiatives and was used to raise

support for the President's legislative agenda.
(55) During Harry Truman's Presidency, the speech came to be widely known as the State of the Union address instead of the annual message.

President Abraham Lincoln was known for
(60) words that reverberate through the decades. His December 1, 1862, message became known as the "Fiery Trial" message, in which he acknowledged that "We of this Congress and this administration, will be remembered in spite
(65) of ourselves... The fiery trial through which we pass, will light us down, in honor or dishonor, to the latest generation."

This message was delivered exactly one month before the Emancipation Proclamation
(70) went into effect. Lincoln ended the message on the subject of slavery: "In giving freedom to the slave, we assure freedom to the free—honorable alike in what we give, and what we preserve. We shall nobly save, or meanly lose, the last
(75) best, hope of earth."

President Ronald Reagan's 1986 State of the Union address was originally scheduled for January 28, 1986. However, that day the Challenger space shuttle exploded. Reagan
(80) postponed his speech for a week in response to the accident. On February 4, Reagan began his message by paying tribute to "the brave seven" Challenger crew members. Later, he addressed the broader implications of the tragedy: "This
(85) nation remains fully committed to America's space program. We're going forward with our shuttle flights. We're going forward to build our space station."

These examples show the resilience of the
(90) State of the Union address. Since Washington's time, the Constitution's command that "from time to time" the President shall share information with Congress has meant, and continues to mean, the delivery of the State of
(95) the Union message once a year. This tradition is now firmly ensconced, and seems likely to continue as long as the union itself continues.

1. In the context of line 17, "object" most nearly means

A) recipient.
B) complaint.
C) article.
D) goal.

2. Information in the passage implies that which of the following is true regarding George Washington?

    A) He referred to his annual speech as a "State of the Union address."
    B) He tended to give longer and more elaborate speeches than later presidents.
    C) Many of the actions that he took have since become presidential traditions.
    D) He focused his speeches predominantly on the issue of slavery.

3. Which choice provides the best evidence to support the answer to the previous question?

    A) Lines 3-6 ("This speech… one ever.")
    B) Lines 13-14 ("The new… of them.")
    C) Lines 24-26 ("Washington gave… the Constitution.")
    D) Lines 34-36 ("As he did… a year.")

4. It can be reasonably inferred from information in the passage that Lincoln's words "reverberate through the decades" (lines 60) at least in part because he

    A) was the first president to use the State of the Union to promote his initiatives.
    B) emphasized cooperating with Congress rather than fighting with them.
    C) was concerned with how his and others' actions would be remembered.
    D) paid tribute to those who lost their lives in a tragedy.

5. Which choice provides the best evidence to support the answer to the previous question?

    A) Lines 50-54 ("After the… legislative agenda.")
    B) Lines 65-67 ("The fiery… latest generation.'")
    C) Lines 78-81 ("However, that… the accident.")
    D) Lines 89-90 ("These examples… Union address.")

6. One of the dominant themes of Lincoln's "'Fiery Trial' message" (line 62) was

    A) the need to create new traditions.
    B) the consequences of a moral choice.
    C) the importance of efficient government.
    D) the tragedy of a continuing war.

7. As used in line 74, "meanly" most nearly means

    A) shamefully.
    B) humbly.
    C) on average.
    D) as required.

8. The final paragraph of the passage is primarily focused on the State of the Union's

    A) influence on popular culture.
    B) enduring appeal.
    C) evolution over time.
    D) use of colorful language.

9. Which two presidents are cited in the passage for helping to evolve the State of the Union into its current form?

    A) Adams and Jefferson
    B) Jefferson and Obama
    C) Wilson and Truman
    D) Lincoln and Reagan

10. The passage's overall structure can best be characterized as moving from

    A) origins to current form.
    B) effects to causes.
    C) similarities to differences.
    D) broad trends to specific instances.

Practice Passage 4

These passages discuss issues related to diversity in computer science education.

Passage 1:

Meet Maddie, a Maryland high-school freshman who has a passion for computing. Eager to continue on her path, she hopes to take
Line a computer science, or CS, course. However, her
(5) school no longer offers this course because it does not count toward students' graduation requirements.

According to computer science professor Marie desJardins, Maddie's story is all too
(10) common. A recent survey revealed several factors at play, including the lack of a unified curriculum and inadequate teacher certification programs. Furthermore, CS classes are less likely to be offered in rural and urban school
(15) districts than in suburban ones. Regardless of the reasons, the results are the same: A disproportionately low number of girls, students of non-white ethnicities, and persons with disabilities are taking CS classes.

(20) DesJardins has been working to change the status quo by training of a wide swath of high school teachers to teach CS. She believes that CS should be included throughout the K-12 curriculum as a set of basic skills and knowledge
(25) for today's world. All citizens of the 21st century, especially the next generation of knowledge-based workers, will benefit greatly from learning about computational thinking, she says.

(30) DesJardins' approach involves getting CS high-school teachers together to write a curriculum for a new Advanced Placement (AP) course called CS Principles. This differs from efforts that use professional curriculum writers
(35) since it integrates the perspectives, pedagogical expertise, and classroom experiences of a diverse group of teachers. The teachers are currently capturing the experiences of real teachers using the material so as to improve the
(40) course.

To scale up these efforts across the nation, desJardins says, we should be focusing on four immediate goals: creating appealing and engaging curricula, training teachers to deliver
(45) this material effectively to a diverse population, providing all students with access to these courses, and making sure that CS counts towards high school math or science requirements.

If desJardins' efforts succeed, computer
(50) science education will become much more accessible in schools across the country, making stories like Maddie's less common.

Passage 2:

The United States is in the middle of a vital time in computing. However, women are
(55) underrepresented, and diverse talent is needed to fill the 1.2 million U.S. computing job openings expected by 2022. At the current rate, U.S. computing undergraduates will only fill 39 percent of these jobs.

(60) Girls represent a valuable, mostly untapped, talent pool, and their lack of participation has serious consequences for future technical innovation. According to the National Center for Women & Information Technology (NCWIT), if
(65) technology is designed by only half our population, we're missing out on the solutions and creations that the other 50 percent could bring.

Another obstacle: half of the United States
(70) doesn't allow computer science to count as a math or science graduation requirement, and the number of high schools offering Advanced Placement (AP) computer science (CS) is down 35 percent since 2005. This lack of informal
(75) introductions to CS impacts all students, especially girls and other underrepresented groups who have fewer occasions to gain experience.

Throughout the year, NCWIT members
(80) work to build a national female talent pipeline for computing. All of NCWIT's efforts are backed by researched-based practices for implementing change and raising awareness for women in technology.

(85) The NCWIT Aspirations in Computing program is one exemplary effort that engages the rapidly growing coalition of NCWIT members and young women from 5th grade through graduate school. In the program,
(90) sponsors provide structured, long-term support for young women entering technical fields. They offer scholarships and internships, host award events, and more.

Additionally, NCWIT has recognized more
(95) than 3,300 young women with its Award for Aspirations in Computing since 2007. Award recipients consistently report greater confidence in their technical abilities, increased enthusiasm about computing, and greater awareness of
(100) career opportunities.

The power of ongoing encouragement shouldn't be underestimated. Research shows it is one of the most influential factors in girls' decisions to pursue computing education and
(105) careers. In a world where technology

increasingly permeates every aspect of society, capitalizing on the benefits of women's participation results in innovation that is as broad as the population it serves.

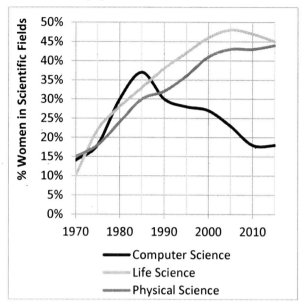

Figure 1: The percentage of graduate student positions held by women in three broad categories of science, according to national surveys.

1. In Passage 1, Maddie primarily functions as

   A) a person whose experiences contrast with those of Marie desJardins.
   B) proof that the methods described in the passage are effective.
   C) an expert whose opinions support the passage's arguments.
   D) an example of a trend that the passage argues should be reversed.

2. In the context of line 44, "engaging" most nearly means

   A) appointing.
   B) engrossing.
   C) combating.
   D) interlocking.

3. Information in Passage 1 implies that most current high school CS texts

   A) were written by developers with little classroom experience.
   B) are too difficult for most high school students.
   C) meet state high school graduation standards.
   D) contain discriminatory language intended to appeal only to male students.

4. Which choice provides the best evidence for the answer to the previous question?

   A) Lines 13-15 ("Furthermore, CS… suburban ones.")
   B) Lines 22-25 ("She believes… today's world.")
   C) Lines 33-37 ("This differs… of teachers.")
   D) Lines 49-52 ("If desJardins'… less common.")

5. In context, the first three paragraphs of Passage 2 are primarily focused on

   A) identifying a problem, several potential solutions for which are presented in the rest of the passage.
   B) discussing specific examples that are then connected to draw broad conclusions later in the passage.
   C) comparing two concepts that are contrasted in the rest of the passage.
   D) providing background information on events that are described later in the passage.

6. As used in line 74, "informal" most nearly means

   A) off-the-record.
   B) casual.
   C) non-professional.
   D) colloquial.

7. Information in Passage 2 implies that, without an increase in female participation in computer science, which of the following will occur?

A) Top technology firms leaving the United States
B) A shortage of qualified computing workers
C) An end to high school-level computer science courses
D) A corresponding drop-off in female participation in other scientific fields

8. Which choice provides the most effective support for the answer to the previous question?

A) Lines 54-57 ("However, women… by 2022.")
B) Lines 74-78 ("This lack… gain experience.")
C) Lines 81-84 ("All of… in technology.")
D) Lines 94-96 ("Additionally, NCWIT… since 2007.")

9. The authors of both passages would most likely agree that which of the following techniques would improve diversity in computer science?

A) Giving awards to young female computer science students.
B) Eliminating Advanced Placement computer science courses.
C) Having active teachers create and test a new computer science curriculum.
D) Allowing more computer science courses to meet high school graduation requirements.

10. How do the approaches of Marie desJardins in Passage 1 and the NCWIT in Passage 2 differ?

A) DesJardins' work focuses more on teachers; the NCWIT's work focuses more on students.
B) DesJardins' work is based on proven research; the NCWIT's work is not.
C) DesJardins' work targets female college students; the NCWIT's work targets grade-school students.
D) DesJardins' work emphasizes computing; the NCWIT's work is broader, emphasizing several areas of the sciences.

11. According to information in the figure, the under-representation of women in computer science, as described in both passages, could potentially be improved upon by examining

A) the state of computer science before 1970.
B) female-dominated fields such as nursing and elementary education.
C) changes made in other scientific fields since 1970.
D) common practices used in computer science during the late 1980s.

Practice Passage 5

The following passage, adapted from Lucy Maud Montgomery's short story "The Finished Letter," describes the relationship between a young girl and an older woman.

She always sat in a corner of the west veranda at the hotel, knitting something white and fluffy, or pink and fluffy, or pale blue and
Line fluffy—always fluffy, at least, and always
(5) dainty. When she finished one she gave it to some girl and began another. Every girl at Harbor Light that summer wore some distracting thing that had been fashioned by Miss Sylvia's slim, tireless, white fingers.

(10) She was old, with that serene old age that is as beautiful in its way as youth. Her girlhood and womanhood must have been very lovely to have ripened into such a beauty of sixty years. It was a surprise to everyone who heard that she
(15) had never had children. She looked so like a woman who ought to have stalwart, grown sons and dimpled little grandchildren.

For the first two days after the arrival at the hotel she sat in her corner. There was always a
(20) circle of young people around her; old folks and middle-aged people would have liked to join it, but Miss Sylvia, while she was gracious to all, let it be distinctly understood that her sympathies were with youth. She sat among the
(25) boys and girls, young men and women, like a queen. Her dress was always the same and somewhat old-fashioned, but nothing else would have suited her half so well. She knitted continually and talked a good deal, but listened
(30) more. We sat around her at all hours of the day and told her everything.

When you were first introduced to her, you called her Miss Stanleymain. Her endurance of that was limited to twenty-four hours. Then she
(35) begged you to call her Miss Sylvia, and as Miss Sylvia you spoke and thought of her forevermore.

Miss Sylvia liked us all, but I was her favorite. She told us so frankly and let it be
(40) understood that when I was talking to her, we were not to be interrupted. I was as vain of her favor as any lovelorn suitor, not knowing, as I came to know later, the reason for it.

Although Miss Sylvia had an unlimited
(45) capacity for receiving confidences, she never gave any. We were all sure that there must be some romance in her life, but our efforts to discover it were unsuccessful. Miss Sylvia parried tentative questions so skillfully that we

(50) knew she had something to defend. But one evening, when I had known her a month, she revealed to me some of her story. The last chapter was missing.

We were sitting together on the veranda at
(55) sunset. Most of the hotel people had gone sailing. I was reading one of my stories to Miss Sylvia. In my own defense, I must allege that she tempted me to do it. I did not go around with manuscripts under my arm, inflicting them on
(60) defenseless people. But Miss Sylvia had discovered that I was a writer, and moreover, that I had shut myself up in my room that very morning and perpetrated a short story. Nothing would do but that I read it to her.

(65) It was a rather sad little story. The hero loved the heroine, and she loved him. There was no reason he should not love her, but there was a reason he could not marry her. When he found that he loved her, he knew that he must go away.
(70) But might he not, at least, tell her his love? Might he not, at least, find out for his consolation if she cared for him? In the end, he went away without a word, believing it to be the more dignified course. When I began to read,
(75) Miss Sylvia was knitting, a pale green something this time. After a little her knitting slipped unheeded to her lap and her hands folded idly above it. It was the most subtle compliment I had ever received.

(80) When I turned the last page of the manuscript and looked up, Miss Sylvia's soft brown eyes were full of tears. She lifted her hands, clasped them together and said in an agitated voice:

(85) "Oh, no, no; don't let him go away without telling her—Don't let him do it!"

"But, you see, Miss Sylvia," I explained, flattered beyond measure that my characters had seemed so real to her, "that would spoil the
(90) story. It would have no reason for existence then. Its motif is his mastery over self. He believes it to be the nobler course."

"No, no, it wasn't—if he loved her he should have told her. Think of her—she loved
(95) him, and he went without a word and she could never know he cared for her. Oh, you must change it! I cannot bear to think of her suffering what I have suffered."

Miss Sylvia broke down and sobbed. To
(100) appease her, I promised that I would remodel the story, although I knew that doing so would leave it absolutely pointless.

1. According to the passage, Miss Sylvia's interactions with "the boys and girls" (line 25) are

   A) stern and judgmental.
   B) generous and informal.
   C) crude and rebellious.
   D) personal and revealing.

2. Which example from the passage best supports the answer to the previous question?

   A) Lines 15-17 ("She looked… little grandchildren.")
   B) Lines 26-28 ("Her dress… so well.")
   C) Lines 28-31 ("She knitted… her everything.")
   D) Lines 39-41 ("She told… be interrupted.")

3. In the context of line 41, "vain" most nearly means

   A) prideful.
   B) idle.
   C) insignificant.
   D) futile.

4. As used in line 45, "confidences" most nearly means

   A) scams.
   B) self-assurances.
   C) beliefs.
   D) secrets.

5. It can be reasonably inferred from information in the passage that "the reason for" (line 43) Miss Sylvia's preference toward the narrator is that Miss Sylvia

   A) hopes to convince the narrator to follow a profession other than writing.
   B) feels comfortable revealing personal details to the narrator and no one else.
   C) sees a similarity between her daughter and the narrator.
   D) shares the narrator's belief that love is not necessary for young people.

6. Which choice most effectively supports the answer to the previous question?

   A) Lines 51-53 ("But one… was missing.")
   B) Lines 66-68 ("There was… marry her.")
   C) Lines 82-84 ("She lifted… agitated voice.")
   D) Lines 97-98 ("I cannot… have suffered.")

7. The author's use of the word "perpetrated" in line 63 is most likely intended to convey which of the following?

   A) That the narrator's story was secretly written with Miss Sylvia in mind
   B) That the narrator is not entirely confident in her writing abilities
   C) That the story prominently features a famous real-life crime
   D) That the narrator believes her story is immoral or even illegal

8. The passage's narrator agrees to "remodel" (line 100) her story primarily out of

   A) pity and affection for a mentor figure.
   B) a desire to make the story more likely to be published.
   C) concern for the story's literary merit.
   D) an intention to improve the story's realism.

9. The primary purpose of the passage is most nearly to

   A) argue that all children should have older role models.
   B) reveal a character to be more sinister than she at first appears.
   C) compare and contrast two approaches to writing fiction.
   D) subtly hint at the tragic past of a character.

10. The passage's tone when describing Miss Sylvia can best be characterized as

   A) satirical.
   B) defiant.
   C) reverential.
   D) disappointed.

The following passage discusses several lines of research intended to help the United States' rainbow trout populations.

Each year, the rainbow trout industry suffers significant economic losses due to bacterial cold-water disease, caused by the
Line bacterium *Flavobacterium psychrophilum*. The
(5) disease also affects salmon and other cold-water fish species. It first occurs when fish are small, often leading to rapid death. Larger fish can become chronically infected and consequently have lesions and impaired growth and yield.
(10) At the Agricultural Research Service's National Center for Cool and Cold Water Aquaculture (NCCCWA) in Leetown, West Virginia, scientists have developed a new line of trout that is resistant to bacterial cold-water
(15) disease. They've also developed a susceptible line and a control line to use in studies of how breeding changes disease-resistance properties in trout. They have identified regions on several chromosomes that are responsible for disease
(20) resistance and have developed a test that detects *F. psychrophilum* after infection.
Molecular biologist Greg Wiens and geneticist Timothy Leeds recently completed a field performance evaluation in collaboration
(25) with industry and government stakeholders. In a 2013 study, Wiens measured performance of the control, disease-susceptible, and disease-resistant lines of fish under farm conditions before and after natural exposure to the
(30) pathogen.
After exposure, the disease-resistant line had a higher rate of survival than the control or susceptible lines. In addition, during the outbreak, fewer disease-resistant fish harbored
(35) the pathogen in their internal tissues, compared to the control and susceptible fish.
Wiens and fellow scientist David Marancik developed a highly sensitive real-time test that accurately measures small amounts of *F.*
(40) *psychrophilum* in fish tissue. The test recognizes a unique gene sequence that is only found in that pathogen. In the study, more than 200 different strains of *F. psychrophilum* were detected. These strains were all collected at farms where
(45) fish suffered from the disease.
No other species of environmental bacteria or fish pathogens were recognized by the test, which demonstrates its high specificity. At the conclusion of the farm trial, the test confirmed
(50) that the resistant-line fish did not harbor detectable levels of pathogen.

Scientists at NCCCWA are also investigating the mechanisms that cause fish to be disease resistant. After finding a correlation
(55) between disease resistance and larger spleen size in rainbow trout, Wiens and geneticist Yniv Palti searched for common genetic regions that influence both spleen size and disease resistance.
(60) In their study, they mapped regions in the trout genome that determine spleen size and found links to chromosomes 19, 16, and 5. They also mapped disease resistance and found a closely linked region on chromosome 19 that
(65) had a major effect on bacterial cold-water disease resistance. This is the first study to identify a genetic link between a physical trait—spleen size—and specific disease resistance in fish. The researchers are now working to
(70) identify genes and mechanisms of resistance.
Based on the results of several field trials and laboratory-evaluation data, disease-resistant rainbow trout eggs were released in small numbers to stakeholders, who are propagating
(75) the line and continuing to evaluate its performance in large-scale trials in conjunction with NCCCWA scientists. If these evaluations continue to show results, the new trout line may soon appear at the seafood counter nearest you.

1. According to information in the passage, which of the following is most likely true regarding *Flavobacterium psychrophilum*?

   A) It infects only rainbow trout.
   B) It is found mainly in the spleens of infected fish.
   C) It has different effects on older and younger fish.
   D) It will soon be eliminated from fish farms.

2. Which choice best supports the answer to the previous question?

   A) Lines 6-9 ("It first... and yield.")
   B) Lines 18-21 ("They have... after infection.")
   C) Lines 31-33 ("After exposure... susceptible lines.")
   D) Lines 37-40 ("Wiens and... fish tissue.")

3. The "susceptible line" and "control line" (lines 15-16) primarily serve as

A) examples of what the resistant line could become.
B) other trout types that can be compared to the new disease-resistant line.
C) previous attempts to solve the problem that the resistant line is trying to solve.
D) evidence that the resistant line will have little effect.

4. In line 9, "yield" most nearly means

A) amount produced.
B) surrender.
C) investment.
D) explosive force.

5. Which of the following does the author use to support the claim that the scientists' test for *F. psychrophilum* is "highly sensitive" (line 38)?

A) Data comparing the effectiveness of this test to that of other common tests
B) A quote from a famous scientist vouching for the test's efficacy
C) An extended explanation of how the test works on a molecular level
D) Evidence that the test identifies many strains of the bacterium—and nothing else

6. As used in line 44, "strains" most nearly means

A) tunes.
B) injuries.
C) exertions.
D) varieties.

7. Based on the passage, which of the following most accurately characterizes what scientists currently know about the link between large spleens and disease resistance?

A) They have not yet identified which genes increase resistance or how the resistance is increased.
B) They know which genes affect both spleen size and disease resistance in humans, but not in fish.
C) They considered such a link, but data has so far shown there to be no correlation between spleen size and disease resistance.
D) They have hypothesized that there is such a link but have yet to find any evidence to support it.

8. Which choice most clearly provides supporting evidence for the previous question's answer?

A) Lines 46-48 ("No other… high specificity.")
B) Lines 54-59 ("After finding… disease resistance.")
C) Lines 69-70 ("The researchers… of resistance.")
D) Lines 77-79 ("If these… nearest you.")

9. It can be reasonably inferred from information in the passage that the "stakeholders" in line 74 are

A) genetic scientists.
B) seafood eaters.
C) trout farmers.
D) government officials.

10. The passage's tone can best be described as

A) whimsical.
B) factual.
C) argumentative.
D) pessimistic.

Practice Passage 7

This passage discusses the development of SONAR technology and its use in marine biological research.

During the twentieth century, the use of acoustics to study life in the oceans was developed into a significant tool for research in Line marine biology. The general pattern was the (5) development of acoustic technology for nonbiological research uses, navigation and military operations to name two and then the application of that technology to the detection and study of marine life.

(10) Many historians cite the sinking of the RMS Titanic as the immediate stimulus for the development of underwater acoustic ranging technology. In response to this event, Reginald Fessenden developed the "Fessenden (15) oscillator" to detect icebergs and the sea floor. This device was first used on the US Coast Guard Cutter *Miami* in 1914. The threat of German submarines during the First World War led to significant advances in underwater (20) acoustic technology.

The period from 1939 to 1945, World War II, saw an extremely rapid development of our understanding of the physics of sound propagation in the sea. The acronym, SONAR (25) (SOund Navigation And Ranging), was proposed by F. V. (Ted) Hunt of Harvard University in 1942 and is the term most commonly applied to acoustic detection devices, both active and passive. This (30) newfound knowledge was quickly applied to more peaceful enterprises, the commercial whaling and fishing industries in particular.

Following the end of World War II, 1946, surplus military SONAR units were fitted onto (35) some whale catcher vessels of European nations and were used to hunt whales in the Southern Ocean. The use of this equipment greatly improved the efficiency of the whalers' efforts in killing whales. In the case of baleen (40) whales, the SONAR pings frightened the whales, resulting in an escape behavior in which the animals swam at high speed near the surface in a straight line away from the sound source. This caused them to tire more quickly (45) and made it easier to follow a whale and kill it.

During the "Cold War," 1948 to 1990, the reliance on passive acoustic methods to detect and track submarines gained favor and resulted in the expenditure of $15 billion over 40 years

(50) by the American defense establishment to develop and deploy the SOund SUrveillance System (SOSUS). During World War II, it had been discovered that, at the depth in the ocean where sound velocity is minimized, sound (55) energy becomes trapped and can travel a great distance without dissipating. This "sound channel" or SOFAR level would allow a listener to hear sounds from great distances, tens of thousands of kilometers. In the 1950s, (60) the US Navy began building a network of listening stations from which Soviet submarines could be located and tracked even if they were thousands of miles away.

In 1991, the navy largely decommissioned (65) the SOSUS but left a small number of monitoring posts, three in the North Pacific Ocean, operational and made these available to the scientific community. The decommissioned SOSUS listening posts allowed biologists to (70) track migrating whales in the North Pacific Ocean. Different marine mammals produce vocalizations which are characteristic of each species, allowing them to be tracked and identified at significant distances. An (75) individual blue whale was tracked for 43 days using the SOSUS network.

The study of anthropogenic effects, wind farms, ship traffic, and military activity on marine mammals and fish is an increasingly (80) important field of bioacoustic research. This is leading to an increased understanding of the role of acoustics in marine life as well as the effects of acoustic pollution in an increasingly noisy ocean. Of particular interest to scientists (85) is the effect of acoustic pollution on whale foraging behavior and communication. Blue whales produce characteristic low-frequency (less than 100 Hz) "D-calls," believed to communicate the location of a food source to (90) other whales. Anthropogenic noise has been shown to significantly disrupt whales' D-call patterns, although the long-term implications of this disruption for whale foraging and other behaviors are still unknown.

(95) By the last quarter of the twentieth century, acoustic technology had become a significant tool in the study of marine life comparable in significance to molecular biology techniques and other leading-edge

(100) research technologies. Bioacoustics, by the end of the twentieth century, had become a mature independent discipline, thus setting the stage for significant new advances in this area of research in the twenty-first century.

Effect of Sound on Blue Whale Calls

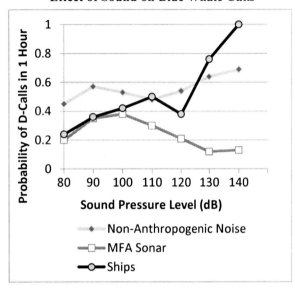

(Adapted from Mariana Melcón et al., "Blue Whales Respond to Anthropogenic Noise," *PLOS ONE*, February 2012)

1. As used in line 11, "stimulus" most nearly means

   A) catalyst.
   B) encouragement.
   C) instigation.
   D) subsidy.

2. The author indicates that the first efforts to invent underwater acoustic technology

   A) greatly aided the study of marine life.
   B) resulted from a desire to protect ships from natural hazards.
   C) were undertaken by the U.S. Coast Guard.
   D) quickly led to the invention of SONAR.

3. Which choice provides the best evidence for the answer to the previous question?

   A) Lines 1-4 ("During... marine biology.")
   B) Lines 10-13 ("Many historians... technology.")
   C) Lines 16-17 ("This device... in 1914.")
   D) Lines 21-29 ("The period... passive.")

4. The author of the passage would most likely agree that technology developed by the military

   A) is the primary source of scientific progress in the modern world.
   B) is extremely expensive and would be more lucrative if its development were left to the private sector.
   C) may become available for civilian applications in the years following the conclusion of major conflicts.
   D) should be restricted in its use on account of the risks it poses to marine wildlife.

5. Which choice provides the best evidence for the answer to the previous question?

   A) Lines 21-24 ("The period... in the sea.")
   B) Lines 46-50 ("During... defense establishment")
   C) Lines 64-68 ("In 1991... scientific community.")
   D) Lines 80-84 ("This is leading... noisy ocean.")

6. As used in line 85, "pollution" most nearly means

   A) contamination.
   B) corruption.
   C) disturbance.
   D) impurity.

7. The author most likely mentions "molecular biology techniques" (lines 98-99) in order to

   A) predict a likely area in which "significant new advances" (line 103) will be realized.
   B) favorably compare a technology that might wrongly be considered old-fashioned to one considered cutting-edge.
   C) identify molecular biology as an area of study in which acoustic sensing technologies are used.
   D) convey the relative importance of a set of research tools and methods.

8. Which of the following is an accurate statement based on the graph that follows the passage?

A) Whales produce more D-calls in the presence of ship noise than in that of sonar regardless of the decibel level of the noise.
B) Whales produce more D-calls in the presence of human-generated noise than in that of natural noise.
C) Increasing the decibel level of sound pressure from SONAR can consistently be predicted to result in decreasing frequency of whale D-calls.
D) Whales in the presence of a ship producing 140 decibels of noise can be predicted to average one D-call per hour.

9. Compared to the first five paragraphs (lines 1-63), the 6th, 7th, and 8th paragraphs constitute a shift toward emphasizing a technology's use

A) for peaceful rather than violent ends.
B) for research rather than commercial and military applications.
C) for civilian rather than military purposes.
D) in ways that are potentially harmful rather than strictly helpful.

10. Which of the following is a valid inference from information in both the passage and the graph?

A) Blue whales emit fewer D-calls in the presence of SONAR because they are frightened by the sound.
B) In the presence of SONAR, blue whale pods are entirely unable to forage effectively.
C) Ships constitute the largest source of noise pollution in the ocean and the greatest threat to whales.
D) The ability of whales to communicate with each other in the search for food is likely impaired by the presence of SONAR.

11. The author's primary purpose in writing this passage was most likely to

A) evaluate the level of risk posed by the use of SONAR to marine mammals.
B) defend the role of the military in inventing technologies later used for civilian research.
C) provide a historical overview of how a technology has developed and become an important tool in a particular scientific field.
D) weigh the beneficial and harmful effects of a major invention over the course of the twentieth century.

Practice Passage 8

This passage discusses the history of an unusual invented language.

Johann Schleyer was a German priest whose irrational passion for umlauts may have been his undoing. During one sleepless night in
Line 1879, he felt a divine presence telling him to
(5) create a universal language. The result was Volapük. It was designed to be easy to learn, with a system of simple roots derived from European languages, and regular affixes which attached to the roots to make new words.
(10) Volapük was the first invented language to gain widespread success. By the end of the 1880s there were more than 200 Volapük societies and clubs around the world and 25 Volapük journals. Over 1500 diplomas in
(15) Volapük had been awarded. In 1889, when the third international Volapük congress was held in Paris, the proceedings were entirely in Volapük. Everyone had at least heard of it. President Grover Cleveland's wife even named
(20) her dog Volapük.

Though Schleyer was German, a large part of the Volapük vocabulary was based on English. "Volapük" was a compound formed from two roots, *vol* (from "world") and *pük*
(25) (from "speak"). However, it was often hard to spot the source of a Volapük word because of the way Schleyer had set up the sound system of the language. "Paper" was *pöp*, "beer" *bil*, "proof" *blöf* and "love" *löf*. He had rational
(30) reasons for most of the phonological choices he made. For simplicity, he tried to limit all word roots to one syllable. He avoided the 'r' sound, "for the sake of children and old people, also for some Asiatic nations." The umlauts,
(35) however, were there for *löf*.

"A language without umlauts," he wrote, "sounds monotonous, harsh, and boring." He decried the "endlessly gloomy u and o," the "broad a" and the "sharp i" of umlautless
(40) languages. Though many members of the growing Volapük community may have agreed with his aesthetic judgment, many others thought that for Volapük to have a serious chance at being a world language, the umlauts
(45) had to go.

Indeed, in the United States especially, those umlauts added a threatening and/or ridiculous air of foreignness to the language. Much fun was had at the expense of Volapük
(50) on account of those umlauts in local papers such as the *Milwaukee Sentinel*:

A charming young student of Grük
Once tried to acquire Volapük
(55) But it sounded so bad
That her friends called her mad,
And she quit it in less than a wük.

By 1890 the Volapük movement was
(60) falling apart due to arguments about umlauts and other reforms. Meanwhile Esperanto, another language that had been rapidly growing since its introduction in 1887, was scooping up all the new recruits to the
(65) universal language idea.

Schleyer decried Esperanto as "an ugly-sounding hodgepodge." He criticized its use of "unnecessary" and "difficult to pronounce" sounds like "sh" and "ch." He scoffed at it for
(70) allowing diphthongs ("Ugly!"), "harsh sound combinations," and the "rattling, hard, bony 'r'". Also, it had no umlauts. According to Schleyer, if you compared Esperanto to Volapük it was clear that one "was created by a
(75) Pole" (the Bialystok-born Ludovic Zamenhof), and the other by "a music connoisseur, composer, and poet."

Every language has its lumpy bits, and beauty is in the ear of the beholder. You like
(80) potato; I like potahto, and Schleyer preferred *pötet*. It wasn't really the umlauts that killed Volapük, but a combination of factors, the most important probably being that the chances of any artificial language gaining a following
(85) are slim to none. There were hundreds of invented languages that came before Volapük and hundreds that came after, and almost no one has heard of any of them. Esperanto is the rare exception, but its success (relative as it is)
(95) has less to do with its linguistic features than with the luck of timing and circumstances.

Volapük didn't die out completely. It has a bit of life today; there are a few online lessons and discussion boards. There is even a Volapük
(100) Wikipedia with over 100,000 articles. And its name lives on in the Danish expression *det er det rene volapyk* – "It's pure Volapük," or, in other words "It's Greek to me."

1. According to the passage, the ease of learning Volapük resulted from its

   A) similarity to German.
   B) small vocabulary.
   C) pleasant, smoothly-flowing sound.
   D) systematic construction of words from simple building blocks.

2. Which choice provides the best evidence for the answer to the previous question?

   A) Lines 6-9 ("It was designed… new words.")
   B) Lines 21-28 ("Though Schleyer…. the language.")
   C) Lines 31-32 ("For simplicity…one syllable.")
   D) Lines 72-77 ("According to… 'and poet.'")

3. As used in line 16, "congress" most nearly means

   A) delegation.
   B) legislature.
   C) summit.
   D) union.

4. By this statement in lines 34-35 ("The umlauts, however, were there for *löf*."), the author most nearly means that

   A) Volapük's heavy use of umlauts was due to Schleyer's personal preferences rather than a rational, pragmatic motivation.
   B) Schleyer felt that umlaut-altered vowel sounds were easier for people of all ages to pronounce.
   C) Schleyer found himself unable to achieve the simplicity he desired for Volapük without the use of umlauts.
   D) the umlauts in Volapük provided a distinctly Germanic influence to an otherwise English-based language.

5. The author most likely included the *Milwaukee Sentinel*'s poem (lines 53-57) to illustrate

   A) a common criticism of Volapük made by American linguistic scholars.
   B) the universal hostility with which Volapük was received by its intended audience.
   C) the apparent strangeness to an English speaker of Volapük's rules of pronunciation.
   D) how nineteenth-century Americans' prejudice against foreigners hindered the adoption of Volapük in America.

6. The author would most likely agree that, compared to Johann Schleyer, Ludovic Zamenhof was

   A) formally trained in music and poetry.
   B) more successful in creating a language of lasting popularity.
   C) far less interested in the aesthetic or musical qualities of language.
   D) inspired more by Romance languages than by Germanic ones in his creation of an invented language.

7. As used in line 94, "relative" most nearly means

   A) analogous.
   B) contingent.
   C) measured.
   D) pertinent.

8. The author would most likely agree that Volapük failed to attain greater popularity because of

   A) the inherent difficulty of achieving widespread adoption of an invented language.
   B) its ugly phonetic features.
   C) widespread ridicule by the mass media.
   D) its lack of appeal to non-English speakers.

9. Which choice provides the best evidence for the answer to the previous question?

   A) Lines 21-23 ("Though Schleyer… on English.")
   B) Lines 49-51 ("Much fun... *Sentinel*.")
   C) Lines 66-72 ("Schleyer decried… umlauts.")
   D) Lines 81-85 ("It wasn't really… to none.")

10. The author's overall attitude toward Schleyer is most nearly one of

    A) marked ambivalence.
    B) disillusioned admiration.
    C) dismissive ridicule.
    D) good-natured amusement.

Practice Passage 9

The following excerpt is from Vanity Fair, *by the English novelist William Makepeace Thackeray. It was first published in 1847.*

Cuff's fight with Dobbin, and the unexpected issue of that contest, will long be remembered by every man who was educated at
Line Dr. Swishtail's famous school. The latter Youth
(5) (who used to be called Heigh-ho Dobbin, Gee-ho Dobbin, and by many other names indicative of puerile contempt) was the quietest, the clumsiest, and, as it seemed, the dullest of all Dr. Swishtail's young gentlemen. His father
(10) was a grocer in the city: and it was bruited abroad that he was admitted into Dr. Swishtail's academy upon what are called "mutual principles"—that is to say, the expenses of his board and schooling were defrayed by his
(15) father in goods, not money; and he stood there—most at the bottom of the school—in his scraggy corduroys and jacket, through the seams of which his great big bones were bursting—as the representative of so many
(20) pounds of tea, candles, sugar, mottled-soap, plums (of which a very mild proportion was supplied for the puddings of the establishment), and other commodities. A dreadful day it was for young Dobbin when one of the youngsters
(25) of the school, having run into the town upon a poaching excursion for hardbake and polonies, espied the cart of Dobbin & Rudge, Grocers and Oilmen, Thames Street, London, at the Doctor's door, discharging a cargo of the wares
(30) in which the firm dealt.

Young Dobbin had no peace after that. The jokes were frightful, and merciless against him. One boy would set a sum—"If a pound of mutton-candles cost sevenpence-halfpenny,
(35) how much must Dobbin cost?" and a roar would follow from all the circle of young knaves, usher and all, who rightly considered that the selling of goods by retail is a shameful and infamous practice, meriting the contempt
(40) and scorn of all real gentlemen.

"Your father's only a merchant, Osborne," Dobbin said in private to the little boy who had brought down the storm upon him. At which the latter replied haughtily, "My father's a
(45) gentleman, and keeps his carriage"; and Mr. William Dobbin retreated to a remote outhouse in the playground, where he passed a half-holiday in the bitterest sadness and woe. Who amongst us is there that does not recollect

(50) similar hours of bitter, bitter childish grief? Who feels injustice; who shrinks before a slight; who has a sense of wrong so acute, and so glowing a gratitude for kindness, as a generous boy? and how many of those gentle
(55) souls do you degrade, estrange, torture, for the sake of a little loose arithmetic, and miserable dog-Latin?

Now, William Dobbin, from an incapacity to acquire the rudiments of the above language,
(60) as they are propounded in that wonderful book the Eton Latin Grammar, was compelled to remain among the very last of Doctor Swishtail's scholars, and was "taken down" continually by little fellows with pink faces and
(65) pinafores when he marched up with his downcast, stupefied look, his dog's-eared primer, and his tight corduroys. High and low, all made fun of him. They sewed up those corduroys, tight as they were. They cut his bed-
(70) strings. They upset buckets and benches, so that he might break his shins over them, which he never failed to do. They sent him parcels, which, when opened, were found to contain the paternal soap and candles. There was no little
(75) fellow but had his jeer and joke at Dobbin; and he bore everything quite patiently, and was entirely dumb and miserable.

Cuff, on the contrary, was the great chief and dandy of the Swishtail Seminary. He
(80) smuggled wine in. He fought the town-boys. Ponies used to come for him to ride home on Saturdays. He had a gold repeater and took snuff like the Doctor. He had been to the Opera, and knew the merits of the principal actors,
(85) preferring Mr. Kean to Mr. Kemble. He could knock you off forty Latin verses in an hour. He could make French poetry. What else didn't he know, or couldn't he do? They said even the Doctor himself was afraid of him.
(90) Cuff, the unquestioned king of the school, ruled over his subjects, and bullied them, with splendid superiority. This one blacked his shoes: that toasted his bread, others would give him balls at cricket during whole summer
(95) afternoons. "Figs" was the fellow whom he despised most, and with whom, though always abusing him, and sneering at him, he scarcely ever condescended to hold personal communication.

1. The phrase "mutual principles" in lines 12-13 refers to

   A) ideals of fairness.
   B) an exchange of favors or services.
   C) a prior agreement that must be honored.
   D) implied bribery.

2. Which choice provides the best evidence for the answer to the previous question?

   A) Lines 4-9 ("The latter… young gentlemen.")
   B) Lines 13-15 ("…that is... not money")
   C) Lines 33-35 ("One boy…must Dobbin cost?'")
   D) Lines 37-40 ("…who rightly considered… real gentlemen.")

3. According to the passage, which of the following is NOT a way in which Dobbin differs from most other students at his school?

   A) He is more intelligent and studious.
   B) He does not come from an upper-class background.
   C) He is quiet and reserved.
   D) He is teased and bullied because of his father's occupation.

4. Which choice provides the best evidence for the answer to the previous question?

   A) Lines 4-9 ("The latter… young gentlemen.")
   B) Lines 41-43 ("'Your father...upon him.")
   C) Lines 45-48 ("Mr. William… and woe.")
   D) Lines 58-63 ("Now, William… scholars")

5. The "Doctor" referred to throughout the passage is

   A) a physician.
   B) the head of a boys' school.
   C) the nickname of another boy who is bullied by Cuff.
   D) Dobbin's father.

6. The passage suggests that the first incident in which Dobbin is teased about his family background is especially unfair because

   A) no other student at the school is bullied.
   B) being a grocer is normally considered a respectable career.
   C) the boy teasing him is not upper-class either.
   D) his father provides much of the food that the boys at school eat.

7. In the context of the passage as a whole, lines 48-57 ("Who amongst us…dog-Latin?") serve to

   A) suggest the existence of a moral gray area.
   B) acknowledge the narrator's personal connection to the events of the story.
   C) clarify a character's motivation.
   D) directly encourage the reader to empathize with a particular character.

8. As used in line 77, "dumb" most nearly means

   A) foolish.
   B) incoherent.
   C) speechless.
   D) unintelligent.

9. The choice of the words "splendid superiority" (line 92) to describe Cuff is most likely intended to convey that Cuff is

   A) intimidating and impressive.
   B) narcissistic and delusional.
   C) charismatic and likable.
   D) deserving of his social status.

10. As used in line 98, "condescended" most nearly means

   A) acquiesced.
   B) agreed.
   C) consented.
   D) stooped.

The following pair of passages presents two different viewpoints regarding the future of a federally funded particle physics laboratory near Chicago.

Passage 1:

Fermilab was once the pre-eminent facility for high energy physics. However, the Large Hadron Collider (LHC) on the border of
Line France and Switzerland dwarfs the accelerator
(5) at Fermilab in terms of size, energy and ability to discover particles. It's only currently operating at half of its design energy, but has already set records. It is a dazzling facility.

We need to get beyond the "gee-whiz" and
(10) determine whether or not spending on Fermilab is prudent. There are two basic types of scientific research: theoretical and practical. In theoretical research, the scientists at Fermilab have introduced us to top quarks, bottom
(15) quarks, charm quarks, tao neutrinos and numerous others. The question to be asked is how the discovery of these particles will enhance our lives. Even if you could deliver a tangible answer to that question, how would
(20) Fermilab be able to do a better job than the LHC?

If you look at Fermilab's website or look for the answer to the question "What has high-energy particle physics done for us?", most of
(25) the answers are not so exciting. The "discoveries" most often mentioned are powerful instruments created for use at Fermilab, not as a result of discoveries made at Fermilab. The World Wide Web is also
(30) mentioned. Because scientists needed to transfer large amounts of data, they created the precursor to the Internet, and that is somehow justification for the particle accelerators. Because scientists needed to measure really
(35) small particles, they invented sophisticated instruments now used in medical imaging. But to say that medical imaging wouldn't have advanced otherwise is a dubious claim. I am guessing that if we had just put the money
(40) directly into research on supercomputers, medical imaging, etc., we could have come to the same discoveries at a fraction of the cost.

We could keep Fermilab going for a while. It could limp along for years doing minor
(45) research, but why? Are we going to make the case that budgets are tight right now and in a few years when we have more money we'll

ramp back up? I don't see any hope in the medium or short range that we will get to big
(50) budget surpluses any time soon. If we think that Fermilab will have a big mission in a couple of years, we are only kidding ourselves. It's time to cut the cord.

Passage 2:

Particle physics research pushes the
(55) frontiers of knowledge and technology. The development and construction of particle accelerators, particle detectors and other research tools has led to many benefits to society.
(60) The invention of the World Wide Web and contributions to the development of medical imaging techniques are among the better known particle physics innovations. But particle physics has myriad lesser-known
(65) impacts. For example, few people have probably heard that low-energy electron beams from particle accelerators provide an environmentally friendly way of sterilizing food packaging.
(70) There are more than 30,000 particle accelerators in operation around the world today. They shrink tumors, make better tires, spot suspicious cargo, clean dirty drinking water, help design drugs, discover the building
(75) blocks of matter, and do much more.

Every major medical center in the nation uses accelerators producing x-rays, protons, neutrons or heavy ions for the diagnosis and treatment of disease. Positron emission
(80) tomography, the technology of PET scans, came directly from light-sensing detectors initially designed for particle physics experiments. Gamma-ray detectors designed by particle physicists now reveal tumors in
(85) dense tissue.

Biomedical scientists use the intense light emitted by synchrotron accelerators to decipher the structure of proteins, information that is key to understanding biological processes and
(90) healing disease. A clearer understanding of protein structure allows for the development of more effective drugs, such as Kaletra, one of the world's most-prescribed drugs to fight AIDS.
(95) Cables made of superconducting material can carry far more electricity than conventional cables, with only nominal power loss. They offer an opportunity to meet increasing power needs in urban areas where copper

(100) transmission lines are near their capacity. Fermilab's partnership with industry to develop the mass production of superconducting wire for the Tevatron accelerator jump-started this industry.

(105) Particle physicists developed the World Wide Web to share information quickly and effectively with colleagues around the world. Few other technological advances in history have more profoundly affected the global

(110) economy and societal interactions than the Web. In 1992, Fermilab launched the third web server in the United States. In 2001, revenues from the World Wide Web exceeded one trillion dollars, with exponential growth

(115) continuing.

1. The statement in lines 6-8 of Passage 1 ("It's only… dazzling facility.") is most likely included in order to

   A) acknowledge the technological feat of constructing a particle accelerator even while dismissing the practical value of ever doing so.
   B) indicate that a newer facility has rendered Fermilab obsolete.
   C) suggest that the author would support massive government investment in a particle accelerator if it were state-of-the-art.
   D) state a claim made by opponents of the author's position, with which the author does not actually agree.

2. Which choice provides the best evidence for the answer to the previous question?

   A) Lines 1-2 ("Fermilab was once… physics.")
   B) Lines 16-18 ("The question… our lives.")
   C) Lines 18-21 ("Even if... the LHC?")
   D) Lines 22-25 ("If you… not so exciting.")

3. The use of "gee-whiz" in quotation marks in line 9 suggests that the author of Passage 1

   A) is alluding to a previously stated opinion on Fermilab by a public figure.
   B) believes that less childish, more respectable arguments are needed to settle the debate at hand.
   C) hopes that the Large Hadron Collider's existence will not diminish general interest in the still-valuable, though less glamorous, technology available at Fermilab.
   D) believes some people are irrationally attached to Fermilab because of a sense of awe at the technology it represents.

4. As used in line 19, "tangible" most nearly means

   A) appreciable.
   B) concrete.
   C) palpable.
   D) physical.

5. The critique presented in paragraph 3 of Passage 1 (lines 22-42) is most nearly that Fermilab's defenders

   A) fail to make a distinction between the purpose of an invention and the reason that invention came to be.
   B) overstate the value beyond particle physics of technologies invented for use at Fermilab.
   C) advocate for research investments that are not likely to prove cost-effective.
   D) fail to demonstrate any direct benefit to society from particle physics itself.

6. In response to the assertion in lines 25-29 of Passage 1 ("The discoveries… at Fermilab."), the author of Passage 2 would most likely point out that

   A) particle accelerators are used directly in a wide variety of fields.
   B) the World Wide Web has contributed an enormous amount of value to the global economy since its creation.
   C) Calling these innovations "not so exciting" serves to demonstrate the clear bias of Passage 1's author.
   D) these discoveries are valuable whether or not they would have come to pass even without Fermilab.

7. Which choice provides the best evidence for the answer to the previous question?

A) Lines 55-59 ("The development… society.")
B) Lines 60-65 ("The invention… impacts.")
C) Lines 70-75 ("There are… much more.")
D) Lines 108-115 ("Few other… continuing.")

8. Which of the following is an example cited by Passage 2 of "powerful instruments created for use at Fermilab, not as a result of discoveries made at Fermilab" (lines 27-29)?

A) "the World Wide Web" (line 60)
B) "30,000 particle accelerators" (lines 70-71)
C) "Positron emission tomography" (lines 79-80)
D) "more effective drugs" (line 92)

9. As used in line 97, "nominal" most nearly means

A) insignificant.
B) ostensible.
C) stated.
D) symbolic.

10. Unlike Passage 1, Passage 2

A) is supportive of extending government funding for Fermilab.
B) does not explicitly advocate a course of action.
C) asserts that technologies developed at Fermilab have provided economic and societal benefits.
D) is likely written by a particle physicist.

11. With which of the following statements would the authors of Passage 1 and Passage 2 likely both agree?

A) Fermilab is no longer suited for cutting-edge research, which can be done more effectively at the Large Hadron Collider.
B) The World Wide Web likely would not have been developed if particle physicists had not needed to invent its precursor technology for their purposes.
C) Theoretical research is of less value to society than practical research.
D) Government-funded scientific endeavors have the potential to deliver broad benefits to society.

Page 54

The following report, from the research division of the U.S. Department of Education, addresses the gender gap in mathematical and scientific fields.

Although there is a general perception that men do better than women in math and science, researchers have found that the differences
Line between women's and men's math- and
(5) science-related abilities and choices are much more subtle and complex than a simple "men are better than women in math and science." In fact, experts disagree among themselves on the degree to which women and men differ in their
(10) math- and science-related abilities. A quick review of the postsecondary paths pursued by women and men highlights the areas in math and science in which women are not attaining degrees at the same rate as men.

(15)   In 2004, women earned 58 percent of all bachelor's degrees. In general, women earn substantial proportions of the bachelor's degrees in math and the sciences, except in computer sciences, physics, and engineering.
(20) The pattern at the master's degree level is similar. At the doctoral level, however, gender imbalances become more prevalent, including in math and chemistry. Women earned 45 percent of all doctoral degrees, but they earn
(25) less than one-third of all doctoral degrees in chemistry, computer sciences, math, physics, and engineering. In contrast, women earn 67 percent of the doctoral degrees in psychology and 44 percent in other social sciences. This
(30) disproportionate representation in math and science graduate degrees is also reflected in math and science career pathways. While women make up nearly half of the U.S. workforce, they make up only 26 percent of the
(35) science and engineering workforce. The question many are asking is why women are choosing not to pursue degrees and careers in the physical sciences, engineering, or computer science.

(40)   An explanation for the observed differences in college and occupational choices may be that males and females have variant math and science abilities, as measured by standardized tests. Although girls generally do
(45) as well as, or better than, boys on homework assignments and course grades in math and science classes, boys tend to outscore girls when tested on the same content in high-

pressure situations, such as standardized tests
(50) with time limits. These tests are typically not linked to instructed curriculum, and so can be understood to be measures of more general abilities in math and science. For example, on the 2005 NAEP math and science assessments,
(55) girls scored lower than boys when controlling for highest course completed at all levels, except the lowest level. Performance differences on timed standardized tests do not necessarily mean that girls are not as capable as
(60) boys in math or science. Researchers have found, for instance, that SAT math scores underpredict young women's performance in college math courses. This suggests that it is not ability, per se, that hinders girls and women
(65) from pursuing careers in math and science. If not ability, then what?

Areas where consistent gender differences have emerged are children's and adolescents' beliefs about their abilities in math and science,
(70) their interest in math and science, and their perceptions of the importance of math and science for their futures. In general, researchers have found that girls and women have less confidence in their math abilities than males do
(75) and that from early adolescence, girls show less interest in math or science careers. This gender difference is interesting, and somewhat puzzling, given that males and females generally enroll in similar courses and display
(80) similar abilities (at least as measured by course grades). In other words, girls, particularly as they move out of elementary school and into middle and high school and beyond, often discount their own abilities in mathematics and
(85) science. However, it is important to note that girls who have a strong self-concept regarding their abilities in math or science are more likely to choose and perform well in elective math and science courses and to select math- and
(90) science-related college majors and careers. This is noteworthy because it suggests that improving girls' beliefs about their abilities could alter their choices and performance. Theory and empirical research suggest that
(95) children's beliefs about their abilities are central to determining their interest and performance in different subjects.

**Gender Disparities by Academic Degree
(Bachelor's and Master's Degrees)**

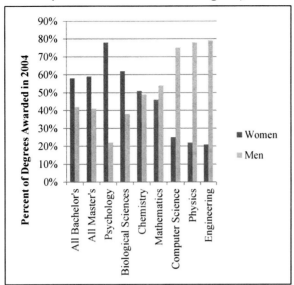

(Source: Diane Halpern et al., "Encouraging Girls in Math and Science", for the *What Works Clearinghouse* initiative, Institute of Education Sciences, U.S. Department of Education)

1. Which of the following observations, discussed in the passage, about the relationship between gender and math and science ability does NOT help support the authors' claim that this relationship is "subtle and complex" (line 6)?

   A) The size and nature of the gender gap varies at different ages and academic levels.
   B) The size and nature of the gender gap varies based on the type of evaluation used to measure it.
   C) Men and women obtain advanced degrees in computer science and engineering at dramatically different rates.
   D) There is a disparity between adolescent girls' self-assessments of their math and science ability and their performance in math and science classes.

2. Based on information in the passage and/or the associated graph, the percentage of doctoral degrees in psychology awarded to men is

   A) greater than the percentage of bachelor's and master's degrees in psychology awarded to men.
   B) greater than the percentage of bachelor's and master's degrees in mathematics awarded to women.
   C) greater than the percentage of bachelor's and master's degrees in biology awarded to men.
   D) less than the percentage of the science and engineering workforce that consists of women.

3. In context of the passage as a whole, the function of the third paragraph (lines 40-66) is most nearly to

   A) propose a novel interpretation of a familiar trend.
   B) summarize the existing data pertaining to an ongoing controversy.
   C) present and cast doubt upon a standard explanation for a sociological phenomenon.
   D) argue against the validity of a common measure of math and science ability.

4. As used in lines 55-56, "controlling for" most nearly means

   A) accounting for.
   B) instructing.
   C) manipulating.
   D) supervising.

5. The authors would most likely agree that standardized tests

   A) are intended to measure innate talent rather than book learning.
   B) do not produce meaningful or consistent predictions of students' performance in math and science.
   C) are an assessment format that is inherently biased in favor of male students.
   D) are an important but imperfect measure of math and science ability.

6. Which choice provides the best evidence for the answer to the previous question?

A) Lines 44-50 ("Although… time limits.")
B) Lines 50-53 ("These tests… math and science.")
C) Lines 57-63 ("Performance differences… math courses.")
D) Lines 63-66 ("This suggests… then what?")

7. It can be inferred from the passage that girls' "self-concept regarding their abilities in math or science" (lines 86-87)

A) does not affect their actual performance in math and science classes or activities.
B) tends to diverge increasingly from their actual abilities from adolescence onward.
C) can be improved by choosing to take elective classes in math or science.
D) is negatively influenced by poor performance on math and science tests.

8. Which choice provides the best evidence for the answer to the previous question?

A) Lines 76-80 ("This gender… similar abilities")
B) Lines 81-85 ("In other words… and science.")
C) Lines 85-90 ("However… and careers.")
D) Lines 90-93 ("This is… performance.")

9. As used in line 84, "discount" most nearly means

A) forget.
B) rebate.
C) subtract.
D) underrate.

10. Which of the following must necessarily be an accurate statement, according to information in the passage and/or the accompanying graph?

A) More women received bachelor's degrees in 2004 than received doctoral degrees.
B) In 2004, more bachelor's degrees were awarded to women in math than in computer science.
C) Approximately 26 percent of women in the U.S. work force hold science and engineering jobs.
D) More than three times as many women as men received bachelor's or master's degrees in psychology in 2004.

Practice Passage 12

An Analysis of "Democracy"

Written in 1949, in the midst of civil rights tensions that had yet to form into a full-blown movement, Langston Hughes's poem Line "Democracy" argues that those without (5) freedom should not wait for it. This worthy message is one few readers would argue with, and the fact that it comes from one of America's greatest poets endows it with even more weight. Yet, few readers would call (10) "Democracy" the best poem Langston Hughes ever wrote. Just the opposite may be true, in fact. This is due mainly to two contrary approaches within the simple, twenty-one line poem. It is marred both by unsophisticated or (15) even silly rhymes used to express high-minded ideals and by end rhyme that is mixed in a jarring way with free verse.

"Democracy" begins with a four-line stanza that says that freedom will not come (20) "this year" by means of "compromise and fear." That is, the speaker, who clearly identifies as a person without freedom or democracy, dismisses the policy of accommodation that some African American leaders were (25) advocating at the time the poem was written. Although the message of the four lines is exactly clear, the problems of the free-verse poem begin here. The four lines completely lack meter, yet they present the end rhymes (30) "year" and "fear." These simple rhymes make serious ideas sound singsong and dilute the gravity of the message.

The same problem occurs in the second stanza. There the speaker says he has the right (35) "to stand" and to "own the land." Again the idea is powerful, but the simple rhymes, this time embedded in a five-line stanza, sound silly in the service of such a noble idea—or at least inadequate to it. The cliché in this stanza about (40) standing on one's own feet also diminishes the power of the message. Finally, there is the unpredictable rhyme, which also undercuts the stanza. Lines 3 and 5 rhyme; lines 1, 2, and 4 do not. This mixture of free verse and rhyme, (45) for no apparent literary effect, is discordant. And while it might be argued that the mixing of free verse and exact rhyme is as contradictory as the coexistence of free and the not free within a so-called "democracy," the poem does (50) not seem to be about such complexity. Instead, it says more simply, "No more waiting: I want freedom, now."

The third stanza, which consists of five lines, is more powerful because its rhymes

(55) seem less weak or contrived. Although Hughes uses yet another cliché, that tomorrow is another day, he strongly conveys the idea that waiting for tomorrow is tiring advice that ignores the needs of the present moment. (60) Furthermore, it could be argued that Hughes incorporates clichés because the advice to wait for freedom had become a kind of cliché by 1949. Consistent with the cliché that might just work for that reason, the rhymes in this stanza, (65) which has a final sophisticated last line, seem less forced and more appropriate to the message of refusing to wait for what is necessary and right. They also seem more appropriate to the overall message of wanting and deserving (70) democracy.

The last two stanzas, which consist of four lines and three lines respectively, each line no longer than four words, also express strong ideas about freedom. Nevertheless, they again (75) seem tossed off and singsong. Freedom is called a "strong seed," which does not make a lot of sense in the context, and, worse, seems to be used for the sake of rhyming with "need." As if to intensify the poem's problems, this (80) stanza also switches suddenly, disturbingly, and just this once to regular meter. The last stanza, which calls for equality, also does so in a too-simple way. It uses three lines to rhyme "too" and "you." Perhaps this drives home the idea (85) that freedom can, after all, be a simple matter. More likely, it leaves readers with a sense that this highly regarded poet, who most likely, like his speaker, cannot wait for democracy, unfortunately did not have the patience or take (90) the time to make "Democracy" a better poem.

1. Which of the following is a claim the author makes early and supports throughout the passage?

   A) Langston Hughes uses rhyme and rhythm as metaphors for freedom and oppression.
   B) Although written by a superior American poet, "Democracy" is an inferior poem.
   C) The speaker in "Democracy" relies on common clichés to support a theme about common ground.
   D) Because the concept of democracy is such a simple idea, it demands a simple poem to do it justice.

2. Which choice provides the best evidence for the answer to the previous question?

A) Lines 1–5 ("Written . . . wait for it")
B) Lines 5–9 ("This worthy . . . more weight")
C) Lines 12–14 ("This is due . . . poem")
D) Lines 14–17 ("It is . . . free verse")

3. Which of the following best summarizes paragraph 2?

A) The poem's shortcomings begin in the first verse.
B) The principles of compromise and hope become the main ideas in the poem.
C) African American leaders in 1949 wanted people to accommodate the laws of the time.
D) The concept of democracy is naturally complex.

4. In paragraph 3, the author implies the claim that

A) "Democracy" is ultimately a poem about impatience.
B) grand ideas should be expressed in an appropriately grand manner.
C) free verse creates a tone of discordance and contradiction.
D) owning land was the goal of many African Americans in the mid-twentieth century.

5. Which choice provides the best evidence for the answer to the previous question?

A) Lines 33–34 ("The same problem . . . stanza")
B) Lines 34–35 ("There the . . . the land'")
C) Lines 35–39 ("Again the . . . to it")
D) Lines 41–44 ("Finally . . . do not")

6. As it is used in line 32, "gravity" most nearly means

A) consequence.
B) seriousness.
C) attraction.
D) pressure.

7. As it is used in line 57, "conveys" most nearly means

A) makes.
B) carries.
C) transfers.
D) communicates.

8. What claim does the author make in paragraph 4 about the line in the poem that states, "Tomorrow is another day"?

A) The author most likely chose it because so many words rhyme with "day."
B) "Tomorrow" would have been a better title for the poem because this is its most important line.
C) Although it is a worn out expression, it adequately suggests that the fight for democracy had become tiresome.
D) The line is the weakest and most unfortunate line in the poem because it is such a common saying.

9. Which of the following does the author imply in the last paragraph?

A) Even great poets sometimes get impatient or careless.
B) Great poetry can be surprising in its simplicity.
C) The best lines of poetry are no longer than four words.
D) Calling freedom a "strong seed" is a powerful metaphor.

10. Based on information in the passage, which of the following would you expect the author to admire?

A) A haiku about world history
B) A nursery rhyme about life and death
C) A long, epic poem about a quest for power
D) A free verse poem about the order of the universe

Reading Practice Answer Key

Explanations can be found online at http://www.tpgenius.com/

Practice Passage 1	Practice Passage 2	Practice Passage 3	Practice Passage 4	Practice Passage 5	Practice Passage 6
1. C	1. B	1. D	1. D	1. B	1. C
2. A	2. A	2. C	2. B	2. C	2. A
3. B	3. B	3. D	3. A	3. A	3. B
4. D	4. C	4. C	4. C	4. D	4. A
5. D	5. C	5. B	5. A	5. B	5. D
6. B	6. D	6. B	6. C	6. A	6. D
7. D	7. A	7. A	7. B	7. B	7. A
8. C	8. C	8. B	8. A	8. A	8. C
9. B	9. D	9. C	9. D	9. D	9. C
10. C	10. A	10. A	10. A	10. C	10. B
	11. B		11. C		

Practice Passage 7	Practice Passage 8	Practice Passage 9	Practice Passage 10	Practice Passage 11	Practice Passage 12
1. A	1. D	1. B	1. B	1. C	1. B
2. B	2. A	2. B	2. C	2. A	2. D
3. B	3. C	3. A	3. D	3. C	3. A
4. C	4. A	4. A	4. B	4. A	4. A
5. C	5. C	5. B	5. A	5. D	5. A
6. C	6. B	6. C	6. A	6. C	6. B
7. D	7. C	7. D	7. C	7. B	7. B
8. A	8. A	8. C	8. C	8. B	8. C
9. B	9. D	9. A	9. A	9. D	9. C
10. D	10. D	10. D	10. B	10. D	10. D
11. C			11. D		

Explanations can be found online at http://www.tpgenius.com/

Section 3
Evidence-based Writing

Subjects and Verbs
Sentence Formation
Punctuation
Pronouns
Frequently Confused Words
Parallelism
Modifiers
Logical Comparisons
Organization
Style and Tone
Proposition, Support, Focus
Quantitative Information
Words in Context

Subjects and Verbs
Concept & Strategy Lesson

All complete sentences must have a subject and a verb. The subject is the noun or pronoun performing the action. The verb is the action being performed.

SUBJECT-VERB AGREEMENT

One of the types of errors common to the PSAT 10/11 is subject-verb agreement. Subjects and verbs must agree in number – plural subjects get plural verbs, and singular subjects get singular verbs.

IDENTIFYING SUBJECTS AND VERBS

The first step to identifying a subject-verb agreement error is to identify the subject and the verb of the sentence. Let's use an example to help identify tricky subjects or verbs:

All of the children, including Rob, cared for their pets.

In this sentence, there are several nouns or pronouns that might be the subject, including *all*, *children*, *Rob*, and *pets*. We begin by identifying the subject:

Step 1:   Cross out phrases that are set apart inside of commas or dashes.

All of the children, ~~including Rob,~~ cared for their pets.

Step 2:   Cross out prepositional phrases. These are phrases that begin with a preposition like of, for, under, etc.

All ~~of the children, including Rob,~~ cared ~~for their pets~~.

In this sentence, the subject is "all," which is a pronoun that is referring to *the children*. Now we can identify the verb:

Step 3:   Identify the action taking place. If there is no clear action, look for helping verbs like is/are, was/were, or has/have. This is the verb.

In this sentence, the verb is *cared*.

SUBJECT-VERB AGREEMENT ERRORS

There are several primary rules governing subject-verb agreement. Knowing these rules allows you to identify and correct subject-verb agreement errors.

Rule 1: Plural subjects take plural verbs, and singular subjects take singular verbs.

> **Correct:** Each of the rivers was overflowing.
> **Incorrect:** Each of the rivers were overflowing.

Rule 2: "Here" and "there" are not subjects. In sentences that begin with these words, the subject generally follows the verb.

> **Correct:** There are sandbags along the riverbank.
> **Incorrect:** There is sandbags along the riverbank.

Rule 3: Compound subjects connected by "and" take plural verbs.

> **Correct:** Joanna and Grace want to go see a movie.
> **Incorrect:** Joanna and Grace wants to go see a movie.

Rule 4: Compound subjects connected by "nor" or "or" could require either a singular or a plural verb. The subject that is closer to the verb determines whether the verb should be singular or plural.

> **Correct:** The students or the teacher needs to vacuum the classroom.
> **Incorrect:** The students or the teacher need to vacuum the classroom.

Rule 5: When the subject is an indefinite pronoun, a pronoun that does not refer to specific person, place, or thing, the subject might be singular or plural depending on the context. The chart below identifies indefinite pronouns as singular or plural.

Singular Indefinite Pronouns		Plural Indefinite Pronouns	Variable Indefinite Pronouns
Somebody	Everybody	Both	Any
Something	Everything	A number	Some
Someone	Everyone	Fewer	More
Anybody	Each	Few	Most
Anything	Neither	Many	All
Anyone	Either	Several	None
Nobody	Much		
No one	One		
Nothing	The number		

VERB TENSE, MOOD, AND VOICE

In addition to testing subject-verb agreement, the PSAT 10/11 will also test errors in verb tens, mood, and voice. A verb's tense tells us when an action occurs. A verb's mood tells us the attitude of the speaker. In addition, a verb's voice tells us the relationship between the verb and the participants in the action described by the verb.

VERB TENSES

Tenses tell us when the action of a verb occurs – past, present, or future. See the chart below for a detailed description of various verb tenses.

Past	Present	Future
Simple Past: Actions that took place at a specific time in the past. *I rode the bus home on Tuesday.*	Simple Present: Actions that take place at the present moment. *I ride the bus home every day.*	Simple Future: Actions that will happen at a point in time in the future. *I will ride the bus home on Friday.*
Past Progressive: Actions that occurred over a period of time in the past and were interrupted by another action. *I was riding the bus when it started snowing.*	Present Progressive: Actions that occur over a period of time that includes the present moment. *I am riding the bus.*	Future Progressive: Actions that will occur over a period of time in the future. *I will be riding the bus every day next week.*
Past Perfect: Actions that occurred before another event in the past. *I had been riding the bus before my brother started driving me to school.*	Present Perfect: Actions that occurred in the past and include the present moment. *I have been riding the bus all year.*	Future Present: Actions that will occur in the future but before another event in the future. *By the time I graduate, I will have been riding the bus for four years.*

On the PSAT 10/11, it will be important to use context clues from the passage to determine the correct verb tense for a given sentence. Remember that sometimes the clues might come from sentences that come before or after the sentence in which the error has been underlined.

To address verb tense errors, follow these steps:

Step 1:   Identify the time at which the action takes place and determine whether there are other actions or events that might affect the verb tense.

Step 2:   Eliminate answer choices that clearly provide the wrong verb tense.

Step 3:   Select the answer that best identifies the time at which the action takes place.

VERB MOODS

Most sentences us the *indicative mood*, including questions and statements of fact or opinion. The *imperative mood* is used to give commands. In these sentences, the subject is usually assumed to be "you," or the person being addressed by the sentence. Finally, the *subjunctive mood* expresses states of unreality, such as hypothetical situations, requests, hopes, and wishes.

Sentences that use the subjunctive mood will often include some form of the verb *to be* – either *was* or *were*. When a sentence is expressing something that isn't true, the sentence should use *were*. Such sentences will often begin with the word "if," as in, "If I were in charge…"

Indicative Mood: I **will win** the lottery this week.
Imperative Mood: Please **go buy** a lottery ticket for me.
Subjunctive Mood: I wish I **would win** the lottery jackpot.

VERB VOICE

Verb voice is either passive or active. A verb is in the active voice if the action is being performed by the subject. A verb is in the passive voice if a party other than the subject is performing the action.

Active Voice: I **watched** a movie last night.
Passive Voice: A movie **was watched** last night.

Generally, active voice is considered to be more correct for stylistic reasons. The only exceptions to this rule are when the thing being acted upon is more important in the sentence than the actor or when the author does not know who performed the action. This is rare, so it is usually best to choose active voice over passive voice when selecting the best answer on the PSAT 10/11.

VERB ERRORS

Verb tense, mood, and voice questions will always include a verb in the underlined portion of the sentence. If the underlined portion of the question and the answer choices include verbs, examine the rest of the sentence to determine whether there is an error in verb tense, mood, or voice.

TO ANSWER SUBJECT AND VERB QUESTIONS:

Step 1: Identify the subject and the verb. Determine whether the verb agrees with the subject. If the verb and the subject do not agree, then the error is a subject-verb agreement error. Eliminate any answer choices that disagree with the subject.

Step 2: Examine the context of the sentence to determine whether the correct verb tense is used. Eliminate any answer choices that do not use the correct tense.

Step 3: Examine the rest of the sentence to determine the correct verb mood. Eliminate any answer choices that are not in the correct mood.

Step 4: If more than one answer choice remains, choose the one that best suits the rest of the sentence.

Subjects and Verbs

Sample Questions

The most well-known of all ghost ship (1)<u>stories are</u> that of *The Flying Dutchman*. Although much of its story is mere legend, it is based on a real ship captained by Hendrick Vanderdecken, who sct sail in 1680 from Amsterdam. According to legend, Vanderdecken's ship (2) <u>encountered</u> a severe storm as it was rounding the Cape of Good Hope. Vanderdecken ignored the dangers and kept sailing, but the ship sank, killing everyone on board. As punishment, the legend says, Vanderdecken and his crew are doomed to sail the waters near the Cape for all eternity. Sightings of the mysterious ship have continued for hundreds of years since the ship's sinking.

1. A) NO CHANGE
   B) stories is
   C) stories were
   D) stories was

Step 1: The subject of the sentence is "most well-known," not "stories," so the underlined verb ("are") does not agree with the subject. Since the subject is singular, we can eliminate choices A and C, which have plural verbs.

Step 2: The next sentence uses the present tense in regard to the story of The Flying Dutchman, so this sentence should also use the present tense. We can eliminate choice D.

We can now skip the remaining steps because we have only one answer choice remaining. Choice B is the correct answer.

2. A) NO CHANGE
   B) will have encountered
   C) will encounter
   D) encounters

Step 1: None of the answer choices disagree with the subject.

Step 2: We know that the action took place in the past, so we can eliminate choices B, C, and D.

We can skip the remaining steps because we are left with only one answer choice remaining. Choice A is the correct answer.

Sentence Formation
Concept & Strategy Lesson

Complete sentences must have a subject and a verb, and they must express a complete idea. Sentences that don't meet these requirements are sentence fragments. Sentences that contain multiple subjects and verbs without being properly connect to each other are either run-on sentences or comma splices. It is important to know what makes a complete sentence and how to combine sentences in order to succeed on the PSAT 10/11.

Sentences are made up of clauses. A clause is a series of words that includes a subject and a verb. A *dependent clause* cannot stand on its own as a sentence, and an *independent clause* can stand on its own as a sentence. All sentences are made up of clauses. There are four basic types of sentences:

Simple Sentence:	Lois likes to watch movies about ghosts and monsters.
Compound Sentence:	These movies are often scary, but she thinks they are fun.
Complex Sentence:	Because all of her friends refuse to watch scary movies, she watches them alone.
Compound-Complex Sentence:	Although that makes them even scarier, Lois still enjoys horror movies; they will always be her favorite kind of movie.

A *simple sentence* has just one independent clause. A *compound sentence* has two independent clauses connected by either a semicolon or a comma and a coordinating conjunction. A *complex sentence* has a dependent clause and an independent clause. And a *compound-complex sentence* contains two independent clauses and one dependent clause.

FRAGMENTS, RUN-ONS, AND COMMA SPLICES

Sentence fragments are incomplete sentences. They are missing a subject or a verb, or they do not express a complete idea. In other words, a sentence fragment is a sentence that is missing an independent clause.

Fragment: After the movie is over.
Complete Sentence: The movie is over.

The sentence fragment and the complete sentence differ by just one word, but that word is enough to make the first sentence a fragment because it creates an incomplete idea.

Run-ons and comma splices represent an opposite error to a sentence fragment. In these errors, too many clauses occur in the sentence without being properly connected.

Run-On: The movie is over so Lois went home.
Comma Splice: The movie is over, Lois went home.
Correct Sentence: The movie is over, so Lois went home.

Correcting fragments, run-ons, and comma splices can often be done by combining sentences properly.

COMBINING SENTENCES
There are several ways to properly combine sentences: Coordination, subordination, semicolons, and colons.

COORDINATION
Coordination is used to combine two independent clauses with a comma and a coordinating conjunction. There are seven coordinating conjunctions that you can remember using the acronym FANBOYS: For, And, Nor, But, Or, Yet, So.

Incorrect: The movie is over, or Lois went home.
Incorrect: The movie is over so Lois went home.
Correct: The movie is over, so Lois went home.

There are two common errors when dealing with coordination. The first, as seen above, is to use a conjunction that doesn't properly communicate the relationship between the two clauses. In this case, "or" does not express any logical relationship between the first and second clauses. The second is to use a coordinating conjunction without a comma. Coordination requires both a comma and a conjunction.

SUBORDINATION
Subordination is slightly more complicated than coordination. With subordination, one clause becomes a dependent clause while the other remains an independent clause. Dependent clauses can be formed by either omitting the subject or verb, or by adding a subordinating conjunction. There are many subordinating conjunctions, including:

Subordinating Conjunctions

After	Although	As
Because	Before	Even
How	If	In order that
Now that	Once	Provided
Rather than	Since	So that
Than	That	Though
Unless	Until	When
Whenever	Where	Whereas
Wherever	Whether	While

As with coordination, it is important to choose a conjunction that properly expresses the relationship between the two ideas. However, the rules for punctuation with subordination are different from those with coordination. With subordination, we use a comma only when the clause with the subordinating conjunction comes first. If the clause with the subordinating conjunction comes second, no comma is needed.

Incorrect: Although the movie is over Lois has not yet gone home.
Incorrect: Lois has not yet gone home, although the movie is over.
Incorrect: Whether the movie is over, Lois has not yet gone home.

Correct: Although the movie is over, Lois has not yet gone home.
Correct: Lois has not yet gone home although the movie is over.

In the first sentence, the clause containing the subordinating conjunction "although" should have a comma after it. In the second sentence, the clauses should not be divided by a comma because the clause containing the subordinating conjunction comes last. In the third sentence, the subordinating conjunction "whether" does not describe a logical relationship between the two clauses.

SEMICOLONS AND COLONS

Sentences can also be combined without conjunctions by using a semicolon or a colon.

Semicolons are used to combine two independent clauses that are very closely related. Since we can't use a conjunction when we use a semicolon to combine independent clauses, the relationship between the two clauses has to be clear enough that no conjunction is necessary.

Colons are used to combine two independent clauses when the second clause clarifies or illustrates the first. As with semicolons, the relationship between the two independent clauses needs to be close enough that no conjunction is necessary. Colons can also be used to introduce a list of items, but even when used in this way, the clause before the colon needs to be an independent clause.

Incorrect: My favorite types of movies are: comedy, fantasy, and horror.
Incorrect: My favorite types of movies are comedies and fantasies; but I also like horror movies.

Correct: My favorite types of movies are comedies and fantasies; I also like horror movies.
Correct: I have three favorite types of movies: comedy, fantasy, and horror.

The first sentence uses a colon incorrectly because the clause preceding the colon is not an independent clause. The second sentence uses a subordinating conjunction with a semicolon, but sentences connected with semicolons should not use conjunctions.

SENTENCE FORMATION ERRORS

Sometimes, the PSAT 10/11 will specifically ask which of the following answer choices best combines two sentences. In this case, it is easy to tell that you will need to combine two sentences using punctuation, coordination, or subordination. In most cases, the test will simply provide an underlined portion of one or two sentences, and the underlined portion will contain the part of the sentence that should be altered in order to correct a sentence formation error.

TO ANSWER SENTENCE FORMATION QUESTIONS:

Step One: Identify the error by looking at the underlined portion and the sentences immediately before and after the underlined portion.

Step Two: Eliminate any answer choices that fail to solve the error.

Step Three: Examine the remaining answer choices to ensure that they do not create new errors.

Step Four: Choose the answer that addresses the original error without creating any new errors.

Sentence Formation
Sample Questions

The Kinetoscope is an early motion picture exhibition device. It was designed for films to be viewed by one person at a time through a peephole window at the top of the device. The Kinetoscope was first described by Thomas Edison, but it was largely developed by his employee William Kennedy Laurie Dickson. (1)<u>The device was very popular in the U.S., it had even greater influence abroad.</u> Edison had chosen to patent the (2) <u>device only in the U.S. so inventors abroad were free</u> to alter and improve the technology.

1. A) NO CHANGE
   B) Unless the device was very popular in the U.S., it had even greater influence abroad.
   C) The device was very popular in the U.S. but it had even greater influence abroad.
   D) Although the device was very popular in the U.S., it had even greater influence abroad.

Step 1: The original sentence is a comma splice because it contains two independent clauses connected by nothing but a comma. We can eliminate choice A.

Step 2: Choice C does not solve the error because it creates another run-on (this time due to a lack of a comma). We can eliminate choice C.

Step 3: Choice B creates a new error because the conjunction "unless" does not describe a logical relationship between the two clauses. We can eliminate choice B.

Step 4: The correct answer is choice D.

2. A) NO CHANGE
   B) device. Only in the U.S., so inventors abroad were free
   C) device only in the U.S., so inventors abroad were free
   D) device only in the U.S.; so inventors abroad were free

Step 1: The original sentence is a run-on sentence. We can eliminate choice A.

Step 2: None of the other answer choices are run-ons.

Step 3: Choice B creates a new error by creating a sentence fragment. Choice D creates an error by using both a semicolon and a conjunction.

Step 4: Choice C is the correct answer.

Punctuation
Concept & Strategy Lesson

There are many different types of punctuation common to the English language. The PSAT 10/11 will test your knowledge of punctuation rules.

PARENTHETICAL ELEMENTS
Parenthetical elements, also sometimes referred to as nonessential elements, are parts of a sentence that are unnecessary to the primary meaning of the sentence. They need to be set off by punctuation in order to help the clarity of the sentence.

PARENTHESES
Parentheses are used to set off something that seems out of place in the sentence or that would otherwise interrupt the flow of the sentence. Parenthesis must always be used in pairs.

> **Incorrect:** The television show (that aired last night) was pretty good.
> **Correct:** VE Day (Victory in Europe Day) was a national holiday.

In the first sentence, the information inside the parentheses is important to the sentence because it defines which television show is being discussed. In the second sentence, there is a pair of parentheses and the information contained within them simply clarifies what "VE Day" is an abbreviation for, which is good information but would interrupt the flow of the sentence otherwise.

DASHES
Dashes are often used to add drama or emphasis to the information contained within them. Unlike parentheses, which minimize the information inside them, dashes highlight the information inside them.

> **Incorrect:** My birthday – April 15 – is an inauspicious day in history.

> **Correct:** April 15 is the date on which Abraham Lincoln was killed, the *Titanic* sank, and the Boston Marathon was bombed – it's also my birthday.
> **Correct:** April 15 – an inauspicious day – is the date of many tragic events in history.

The first sentence is incorrect because there are no reasons to emphasize the date since it is not a key point in the sentence. Both the second and third sentences are good examples of correct use of dashes. The information that follows the dash is unexpected, and the dash emphasizes that information. Note that there is only one dash in the second sentence, but two in the third sentence. Only one dash is needed when the parenthetical element is at the end of the sentence; otherwise, two are needed.

COMMAS & PARENTHETICAL ELEMENTS

Commas do not interrupt the flow of the sentence the way that parentheses or dashes do, so commas are generally use commas to set off information that feels like a natural part of the sentence.

Incorrect: The Centers for Disease Control, also known as the CDC, is a federal agency in charge of protecting public health through disease research and prevention.
Correct: The CDC, a federal agency, is also a founding member of the International Association of Public Health Institutes.

In the first sentence, the information inside the commas interrupts the flow of the sentence without adding important information. Parentheses would be more appropriate in this case. The second sentence is an example of correct use of commas to offset a parenthetical element. Note that there are two commas; as with dashes, when the parenthetical element is in the middle of the sentence, two commas are needed, but when the parenthetical element comes at the end of the sentence, only one comma is needed.

COMMAS – OTHER RULES

Commas serve many functions in sentences. In addition to setting off parenthetical elements, commas are commonly used to separate clauses within a sentence or to separate items in a series.

COMMAS WITH COORDINATION AND SUBORDINATION

For a thorough overview of coordination and subordination, review the lesson on Sentence Formation. Remember that the rules for comma usage with coordination and subordination are:

Rule 1: When combining clauses using coordination, you must use a comma and a coordinating conjunction.

Incorrect: Jason went to the store and Jessica went to her friend's house.
Correct: Jason went to the store, and Jessica went to her friend's house.

Rule 2: When combining clauses using subordination, use a comma when the subordinating clause comes first.

Incorrect: Although they are not home you can wait for them here.
Correct: Although they are not home, you can wait for them here.

Rule 3: When combining clauses using subordination, do NOT use a comma when the subordinating clause comes second.

Incorrect: You can wait for them here, although they are not home.
Correct: You can wait for them here although they are not home.

ITEMS IN A SERIES

Commas are also used to separate items in a series when those items do not already contain commas. When the items in the series already contain commas or are particularly lengthy, semicolons are used to separate the items.

SEMICOLONS

There are several rules for proper semicolon use:

Rule 1: Semicolons can be used to combine two independent clauses when those clauses are closely a clearly related to one another.

Incorrect: I need to buy some more notebook paper; all of my pens have gone missing.
Incorrect: I need to buy some more notebook paper; because my sister used my last sheet.
Correct: I need to buy some more notebook paper; my sister used my last sheet.

Rule 2: Semicolons can be used to separate items in a series when those items contain commas.

Incorrect: When you go to the store, please get apples; milk; and eggs.
Incorrect: When we go on vacation, we will visit Atlanta, Georgia, Orlando, Florida, and Charleston, South Carolina.
Correct: When we go on vacation, we will visit Atlanta, Georgia; Orlando, Florida; and Charleston, South Carolina.

Rule 3: Though semicolons should generally not be used with conjunctions, they can be used with conjunctive adverbs (such as therefore or however) and with transitional phrases (such as for example).

Incorrect: There are many exceptions to grammar rules; and this makes English grammar difficult to master.
Correct: There are many exceptions to grammar rules; therefore, English grammar is difficult to master.

COLONS

Unlike semicolons, colons are only used to combine sentences when the second sentence clarifies, explains, or otherwise expands upon the first sentence. Colons are also used to introduce items in a series, but only when the clause preceding the colon is an independent clause.

Incorrect: When you go to the store, please get: apples, milk, and eggs.
Correct: When you go to the store, please pick up these items: apples, milk, and eggs.

PUNCTUATION RULES

1. Parenthetical Elements: Parentheses minimize information, dashes emphasize information, and commas are most commonly used to offset parenthetical elements. Parentheses must always come in pairs, but dashes and commas can sometimes be used singly.

2. Commas: Use a comma with a coordinating conjunction when combining independent clauses. Only use a comma with a subordinating conjunction when the subordinating clause comes first. Use commas to separate items in a series when those items do not already contain commas.

3. Semicolons: Use semicolons to combine sentences when those sentences are clearly related. Semicolons very rarely require a conjunction. Semicolons are also used to separate items in a series when those items already contain commas.

4. Colons: Use colons to combine sentences when the second sentence expands upon the ideas in the first sentence. Colons can also introduce items in a series, but the clause before the colon must always be an independent clause.

TO ANSWER PUNCTUATION QUESTIONS:

Step 1: Identify the punctuation error.

Step 2: Eliminate any answer choices that fail to correct the error.

Step 3: Eliminate answer choices that create new punctuation errors or that create sentence boundary errors.

Punctuation
Sample Questions

Although many people believe that *The Star-Spangled Banner* is about the (1)<u>Revolutionary War the</u> lyrics were actually written in 1814 following the Battle of Fort McHenry during the War of 1812. *The Star-Spangled Banner*(2) <u>– which was officially used by the Navy beginning in 1889,</u>became the official national anthem of the United States in 1931. Prior to that, several other songs were commonly used as anthems of **(3)** <u>the U.S. including:</u> *Hail Columbia; Yankee Doodle;* and *My Country, 'Tis of Thee.*

1. A) NO CHANGE
    B) Revolutionary War. The
    C) Revolutionary War; the
    D) Revolutionary War, the

The first clause in this sentence is a subordinating clause because of the conjunction *although*. When a subordinating clause comes at the beginning of the sentence, it must be followed by a comma, therefore D is the correct answer. Choice A creates a run-on sentence. Choice B creates a sentence fragment. Choice C is an improper use of a semicolon.

2. A) NO CHANGE
    B) , which was used by the Navy beginning in 1889,
    C) which was officially used by the Navy beginning in 1889
    D) – which was officially used by the Navy beginning in 1889 –

Choice A uses both a dash and a comma, which is improper use of punctuation. Although dashes and commas do not always come in pairs, they should not be paired with each other. Choice C has no punctuation separating the parenthetical element from the rest of the sentence, creating an unnecessarily confusing sentence. Nothing about the information in the parenthetical element is surprising or dramatic, so dashes are not necessary. Choice B is the correct answer because it properly offsets the parenthetical element with a pair of commas.

3. A) NO CHANGE
    B) the U.S., including:
    C) the U.S.: these included
    D) the U.S. including;

The word *including* makes the clause preceding the colon a fragment, so both choice A and choice B are incorrect. Choice D is an incorrect use of a semicolon. Choice C makes the clause preceding the colon an independent clause, which makes the use of the colon correct. Choice C is the correct answer.

Pronouns
Concept & Strategy Lesson

Pronouns take the place of nouns in sentences to make writing less repetitive. The noun that a pronoun replaces is called its antecedent.

PRONOUN-ANTECEDENT AGREEMENT

Just as subjects and verbs must agree, so must pronouns and their antecedents. When a pronoun takes the place of singular noun, the pronoun must be singular; when a pronoun takes the place of a plural noun, the pronoun must be plural.

Incorrect: Each student must turn in their homework.
Correct: Each student must turn in his or her homework.

In the sentences above, the incorrect sentence replaces *each student*, which is singular, with the plural pronoun *their*. The error is corrected in the second sentence, where *each student* is replaced by *his or her*.

It can be tempting to use *they* or *their* as a singular pronoun because *they* is gender-neutral. Although it might feel awkward to use *he or she* instead, it is more correct to do so because *they* is really plural.

PRONOUN CASES

The case of a pronoun refers to whether the pronoun is acting as a subject or an object in the sentence. Look at the table below for information about pronoun cases:

SUBJECT CASE

	singular	plural
1st person	I	We
2nd person	You	You
3rd person	He/she/it/one	They

OBJECT CASE

	singular	plural
1st person	Me	Us
2nd person	You	You
3rd person	Him/her/it/one	Them

When dealing with questions involving pronouns on the PSAT 10/11, it is important to determine whether the pronoun is acting as a subject or an object in order to determine whether the appropriate pronoun is being used. Remember that the subject of the sentence performs the action, and the object is acted upon.

Determining pronoun case is often straightforward, but can be tricky with compound subjects and objects.

> **Incorrect:** My dad will give the car to my sister and I when we graduate.
> **Correct:** My dad will give the car to my sister and me when we graduate.

In this example, *my sister and I* functions as an indirect object, so it would be correct to say *my sister and me*. The best way to determine which pronoun to use in situations like this is to eliminate the first person in the sentence and see which pronoun sounds better. In this case, the sentence would then read, "My dad will give the car to I" or "My dad will give the car to me." Since we would say *me* in the sentence without "my sister," *me* is the correct pronoun.

AMBIGUOUS PRONOUN REFERENCES

In good writing, it is important that pronouns and their antecedents must be clearly related. The reader should be able to tell what a pronoun refers to.

> **Incorrect:** When we went to the museum, the guide told my sister that she knew a lot about art history.
> **Correct:** When we went to the museum, the guide told my sister that my sister knew a lot about art history.

In the first sentence, we have no way of knowing whether the guide said that *my sister* knew a lot about art history or that *the guide* knew a lot about art history. Although the second sentence seems repetitive, it correctly clarifies who knew a lot about art history.

Another common error with ambiguous pronoun references occurs when there is no antecedent at all.

> **Incorrect:** If you want to work in a museum, they require that you have a degree in art history.
> **Correct:** If you want to work in a museum, the management requires that you have a degree in art history.

In the first sentence, the pronoun *they* does not actually refer to anyone at all – it has no antecedent. The sentence must be rewritten to clarify who *they* are.

RELATIVE PRONOUNS

Relative pronouns introduce certain types of dependent clauses called relative clauses. The following chart lists relative pronouns:

	Subject	Object	Possessive
Animate/Human restrictive	Who/that	Whom/that	Whose
Animate/Human nonrestrictive	Who	Whom	
Inanimate/Nonhuman restrictive	Which/that	Which/that	Whose/of which
Inanimate/Nonhuman nonrestrictive	Which	Which	

The two types of relative clauses are restrictive (defining the antecedent and giving necessary information) and non-restrictive (giving extra, unnecessary information), and each type of clause has its own specific pronouns. In addition, when choosing relative pronouns, a distinction is made between human and non-human antecedents. For people (and other beings that can think like people, like characters), you use the pronoun *who*, and for everything else you should use the pronoun *which*.

PRONOUN RULES

1. Pronouns must agree with their antecedents in number – plural antecedents get plural pronouns, and singular antecedents get singular pronouns.
2. Pronouns must be in the correct case. Pronouns that act as subjects should be in the subject case, and pronouns that act as objects should be in the object case.
3. Pronouns must have clear antecedents.
4. In relative clauses, use "who" to refer to people and "which" to refer to things.

TO ANSWER PRONOUN QUESTIONS:

Step 1: If the underlined portion of the sentence contains either a pronoun or an antecedent, identify any pronoun errors in the sentence.

Step 2: Eliminate answer choices that fail to correct the pronoun error.

Step 3: Eliminate answer choices that create new pronoun errors or that fail to identify a clear relationship between the pronoun and antecedent.

Step 4: Choose the answer that corrects the original error without introducing any new errors.

Pronouns
Sample Questions

In early 2015, two probes that had spent the past year orbiting the moon on a NASA mission slammed into **(1)**<u>its</u> surface, destroying **(2)**<u>it</u>. This wasn't an accident. Such crash-landings are a typical method of bringing unmanned space missions to an end. As a result, **(3)**<u>us</u> and our space programs have littered our solar system with debris. In fact, the moon now hosts nearly 400,000 pounds of man-made material.

1. A) NO CHANGE
   B) the moon's
   C) their
   D) the probes'

In this sentence, "its" refers to the moon's surface – after all, the probes couldn't crash into their own surfaces. We can therefore eliminate choices C and D. Between A and B, B is the better answer because "its" is an unclear pronoun reference and "the moon's" clarifies the sentence's meaning.

2. A) NO CHANGE
   B) itself
   C) themselves
   D) ourselves

The probes wouldn't have destroyed the moon, so "it" must be referring to the probes. Since "probes" is plural, we can eliminate choices A and B. "Ourselves" wouldn't refer to the probes, so C is the correct answer.

3. A) NO CHANGE
   B) we
   C) people
   D) ourselves

To clarify whether the pronoun should be in the object or subject case, we should drop "and our space programs." If we do this, we see that "we" works better than "us." B is the correct answer.

Frequently Confused Words
Concept & Strategy Lesson

The PSAT 10/11 will test your knowledge of frequently confused words, including possessive determiners and pairs or groups of words that are commonly confused.

The following is a list of some of the most commonly confused words that might appear on the PSAT 10/11:

accede exceed	**Accede** means "to agree or allow": The county *acceded* to our request for speed bumps on our road.
	Exceed means "to go beyond": My perfect test score *exceeded* my expectations.
accept except	**Accept** means "to take willingly": I had to sign in order to *accept* the package.
	Except means "excluding": The package contained everything *except* batteries.
adapt adept adopt	**Adapt** means "to adjust": You must float fish in the tank before releasing them in order to allow them to *adapt* to the water temperature.
	Adept means "skilled": Fish are *adept* at swimming.
	Adopt means "to accept as your own": Though I was nervous, I *adopted* a self-assured posture.
adverse averse	**Adverse** means "unfavorable": A low test score will *adversely* affect your grade.
	Averse means "unwilling": I am averse to jumping from high heights.
advice advise	**Advice** means "an opinion intended to be helpful": My sister loves to give me *advice* about my clothes.
	Advise means "to give advice": My sister loves to *advise* me about my clothes.
affect effect	**Affect** means "to influence": The temperature can *affect* the growth rate of plants.
	Effect is usually a noun meaning "a result": The temperature can have an *effect* on the growth rate of plants.
alternately alternatively	**Alternately** means "taking turns": This afternoon, the weather has been *alternately* sunny and rainy.
	Alternatively means "as an option: An umbrella is useful because it can protect you from rain; *alternatively*, it can shield you from the sun.
among between	**Among** is used for things that are not distinct or individuals: Gina is choosing *among* her top colleges.
	Between is used for things that are distinct or individual: She had trouble deciding *between* American College and U.S. University.

assure ensure insure	**Assure** means "to guarantee": The doctor *assured* me that it was just a cold.
	Ensure means "to make sure": The medicine will *ensure* that I get over the cold quickly.
	Insure means "to provide insurance against loss or injury": Luckily, I am *insured*, so the doctor's bill will be small.
bare bear	**Bare** usually means "to reveal": When his private emails were leaked, the Senator was forced to *bare* his secrets to the world.
	Bear usually means "to carry": Now he must *bear* the burden of public shame.
breadth breath breathe	**Breadth** means "width" or "extent": The *breadth* of the damage was irreversible.
	Breath means "the air that you breathe": I ran until I had no more *breath*.
	Breathe means "to take air into your lungs": He couldn't *breathe* when the rock fell on his chest.
censor sensor censure	**Censor** is to prohibit free expression: It is wrong to *censor* the press.
	A **sensor** is something that interprets stimulation: Our security system includes a motion *sensor*.
	Censure means "to harshly criticize": They will *censure* the lawyer for his misbehavior.
complement compliment	**Complement** means "to make complete" or "to supplement": The upholstery *complements* the wall color by making it seem richer.
	Compliment means "to express admiration": My mom *compliments* my speaking abilities after every debate tournament.
conscience conscious	**Conscience** means "knowing right from wrong": The lie weighed on my *conscience*.
	Conscious means "being awake or aware": I became *conscious* when Bobby dumped ice water on my face.
device devise	A **device** is an instrument used to complete a task: I need a sharp *device* to open the box.
	To **devise** is "to create": I will *devise* a way to open the box.
disinterested uninterested	**Disinterested** means "unbiased or impartial": The judge serves as a *disinterested* party.
	Uninterested means "not interested": Harry was *uninterested* in the movie, so he spent the whole time reading a book.
elicit illicit	**Elicit** means "to draw out": The knock on the door did not *elicit* a response.
	Illicit means "illegal or illegitimate": The locker search turned up no *illicit* materials.
emanate eminent	**Emanate** means "to issue or spread": The old, rotting broccoli caused a stench to *emanate* from the fridge.

imminent	**Eminent** means "prestigious": An *eminent* attorney spoke at the graduation ceremony.
	Imminent means "about to happen": The thunder suggests that the storm is *imminent*.
explicit implicit	**Explicit** means "clear and direct": The teacher's detailed instructions were *explicit*.
	Implicit means "indirectly" or "implied": Her tone of voice suggested an *implicit* meaning hidden in her words.
figuratively literally	**Figuratively** means metaphorical, not realistic or exact: To say that I am turning over a new leaf is to speak *figuratively*.
	Literally means exactly as it happened: After all, *literally* turning over a new leaf wouldn't actually accomplish anything.
lay lie	**Lay** means "to set or put down flat": Please *lay* the book on the table.
	Lie means "to rest supine or remain in a certain place": I will lie down and read.
noisome noisy	**Noisome** means "disgusting, offensive, annoying": A *noisome* odor alerts us that the baby's diaper is dirty.
	Noisy means "making a lot of sound": The baby tends to be *noisy* when he needs to be changed.
peek pique peak	**Peek** means to look quickly without someone knowing: A *peek* through the curtains revealed an eerie sight.
	Pique can either mean "to provoke" or "resentment": Any noise outside will *pique* my curiosity. OR I am in a state of *pique* over the loud noises my neighbors make.
	Peak means "the highest point": The mountain's *peak* offered a fantastic view.
perspective prospective	A **perspective** is a point of view: My sister shares my *perspective* on curfews.
	Prospective means "possible or likely to happen": I am going to visit my *prospective* colleges.
precede proceed	**Precede** means "to come before": Studying should *precede* test day.
	Proceed means "to move forward": Once you read the directions, you may *proceed*.
restive restful	**Restive** means "impatient, nervous, or restless": Sally is *restive* when she has sat still too long.
	Restful means "full of rest, calm, quiet": The week after graduation promises to be *restful*.
than then	**Than** is used to compare: This test is harder *than* any other test I've taken.
	Then is used to describe a time that is not now: Sharpen your pencil and *then* begin the test.

By becoming familiar with the words in this chart, you will be better able to recognize frequently confused words on the PSAT 10/11. Whenever you see answer choices that are spelled or pronounced very similarly, the question is likely a frequently confused words question, and you should pay careful attention to the minute differences between the answer choices.

POSSESSIVE DETERMINERS
Another category of frequently confused words is possessive determiners.

Possessive determiners tell us who possesses something. Examples include *my* and *her.* Some possessive determiners, like *your, their,* and *its* fall under the category of frequently confused words that might appear on the PSAT 10/11.

Your vs. You're: "Your" is a possessive determiner, as in, "Your hair looks nice today." "You're" is a contraction that means "you are," as in, "You're going to the store."

Their vs. There vs. They're: "Their" is a possessive determiner, as in, "Their dog ran away." "There" is most frequently used to show the existence or position of something, as in, "There is a dog over there." "They're" is a contraction that means "they are," as in, "They're going on vacation."

Its vs. It's: "Its" is a possessive determiner, as in "The dog licked its injured foot." "It's" is a contraction that means "it is," as in, "It's cold in here."

> **TO ANSWER FREQUENTLY CONFUSED WORDS QUESTIONS:**
>
> **Step 1:** Look for answer choices that are spelled or pronounced similarly.
>
> **Step 2:** Carefully examine the context of the sentence to identify the correct word choice.

Frequently Confused Words
Sample Questions

Among all music formats, only online streaming and vinyl saw growth in 2014. Both digital downloads and CD sales declined. The resurgence of vinyl, a music format many have believed to be all but extinct, is surprising. The reason for its resurgence depends on one's **(1)** prospective. Some fans of vinyl believe that music simply sounds better on a record, but since many vinyl albums are reproduced from CDs, this is unlikely to be true. In truth, the resurgence of vinyl is likely about nostalgia and identity, as vinyl allows people to own and display **(2)** there musical tastes.

1. A) NO CHANGE
    B) prospect
    C) persecute
    D) perspective

All four answer choices are pronounced similarly. Based on the context of the sentence, we know that the correct word choice means "point of view." The only answer choice that matches this is choice D.

2. A) NO CHANGE
    B) they're
    C) their
    D) your

All four answer choices are possessive determiners. Based on the context of the sentence, we know that we need a plural possessive pronoun. Choice C is the only answer choice that fits.

Parallelism
Concept & Strategy Lesson

Parallelism requires that elements in a sentence (or in related sentences) share the same form. This creates a better overall writing style by making writing clearer and preventing awkwardness.

PARALLELISM WITH COORDINATING CONJUNCTIONS
When elements of a sentence are joined by a coordinating conjunction, those elements must be in the same form.

> **Incorrect:** I like to read and playing computer games.
> **Correct:** I like to read and play computer games.
> **Correct:** I like reading and playing computer games.

In the first sentence, "to read" and "playing" serve the same purpose, so they need to be in the same form. The second and third sentences correct this error.

PARALLELISM WITH ITEMS IN A SERIES
The same rules apply to items in a series: items in a series must be in the same form.

> **Incorrect:** Today I need to go to the store, picking up the dry cleaning, and stop by the post office.
> **Correct:** Today I need to go to the store, pick up the dry cleaning, and stop by the post office.

In the first sentence, the second item in the series (*picking up the dry cleaning*) is in a different form from the other two items. To correct the error, the item must match the form of the other items.

PARALLELISM IN COMPARISONS
When two things are being compared, both items must be in the same form.

> **Incorrect:** Driving across the country takes more time than to fly.

> **Correct:** Driving across the country takes more time than flying.
> **Correct:** To drive across the country takes more time than to fly.

In the first sentence, the verbs *driving* and *to fly* are not in the same form. This error is corrected in the second and third sentences.

Parallelism
Sample Questions

New research shows that babies learn best before they sleep. The researchers tested 6- and 12-month old babies to see whether learning right before a nap would improve memory. During the experiment, researchers showed a baby **(1)** <u>how to remove a mitten from a puppet, ring a bell, and replacing the mitten</u>. They then tested whether the babies could perform those actions after 4 hours and after 24 hours. The 216 babies were split into groups. **(2)**<u>One group naps for at least 30 consecutive minutes,</u> one group did not nap during the four hour period following the demonstration, and one group did not receive a demonstration in order to act as a baseline. The babies who napped performed far better than those who didn't when compared to the baseline group, suggesting that sleep helps to improve learning in babies.

1. A) NO CHANGE
   B) how to remove a mitten from a puppet, how to ring a bell, and replace the mitten
   C) how to remove a mitten from a puppet, ring a bell, and replace the mitten
   D) removing a mitten from a puppet, ringing a bell, and replaced the mitten

The original sentence lacks parallelism because the verbs "remove," "ring," and "replacing" are not in the same form. Only choice C puts all three verbs into the same form.

2. A) NO CHANGE
   B) One group napped for at least 30 consecutive minutes
   C) One group had napped for at least 30 consecutive minutes
   D) One group has napped for at least 30 consecutive minutes

The original sentence uses the present tense verb "naps," while the other two items in the series use the past tense. Only choice B uses the same simple past tense as the other items in the series.

Modifiers
Concept & Strategy Lesson

MODIFIER ERRORS
A modifier is a word or phrase that describes, clarifies, or otherwise modifies something else in a sentence. Modifier errors typically occur when the object being modified is either missing or does not appear immediately before or after the modifier. The PSAT 10/11 will test your ability to identify and correct modifier errors.

FIXING MISPLACED MODIFIERS
If you suspect that a question might contain a misplaced modifier, the first step is identifying the modifying word or phrase. Modifiers are usually adjectives, adverbs, or phrases such as prepositional phrases. They are often, but certainly not always, set apart by commas. In the sample sentences below, the modifiers are underlined:

Sample 1: The woman <u>with brown hair</u> walked to her car.

Sample 2: Her <u>brand-new</u> car was cherry red.

Sample 3: <u>Parked crookedly</u>, the car was <u>already</u> dented.

In the first sentence, *with brown hair* modifies *woman*. In the second sentence, *brand-new* modifies car. And in the final sentence, *parked crookedly* modifies *car* and *already* modifies *dented*.

The placement of modifiers can change the meaning of a sentence. Look at these sample sentences:

Sample 1: Miss Jones waved at Evan <u>just</u> as she came in.

Sample 2: Miss Jones waved <u>just</u> at Evan as she came in.

Sample 3: Miss Jones <u>just</u> waved at Evan as she came in.

These sentences are all virtually identical with the exception of the placement of *just*. By placing this modifier in different parts of the sentence, we can change the sentence's meaning. In the first sentence, the modifier tells us when Miss Jones waved at Evan because it modifies *as she came in*. In the second sentence, the modifier tells us that Miss Jones did not wave at anyone except for Evan because it modifies *at Evan*. And in the third sentence, the modifier tells us that Miss Jones only waved at Evan and did not greet him in any other way because it modifies *waved at*.

Since the placement of a modifier can change a sentence's meaning, misplaced modifiers can create unintended meanings. For example:

Incorrect: Thundering down the hill, Isaac was worried that the rocks would land on his campsite.
Correct: Isaac was worried that the rocks, which were thundering down the hill, would land on his campsite.

The incorrect sentence includes a misplaced modifier. *Thundering down the hill* is modifying Isaac. This makes little sense – why would Isaac be worried about rocks landing on his campsite if he was the one thundering down the hill? The corrected sentence ensures that *thundering down the hill* modifies rocks. This sentence makes much more sense.

The best way to fix a misplaced modifier is to ensure that the modifier is located as close to the intended object as possible.

TO ANSWER MISPLACED MODIFIER QUESTIONS:
Step 1: Identify the modifier.

Step 2: Identify the word/phrase being modified.

Step 3: Identify the word/phrase that *should* be modified. If this word/phrase is not the same as the word/phrase identified in step two, the error is a misplaced modifier.

Step 4: Eliminate any answer choices that fail to address the misplaced modifier error or that create new errors.

Step 5: Of the remaining answer choices, choose the one that places the modifier closest to the word/phrase being modified.

SPOTTING AND FIXING DANGLING MODIFIERS

A similar type of error occurs when a modifier describes something that isn't actually mentioned in a sentence – this is called a dangling modifier. As with misplaced modifiers, it's important to first identify the modifier and then identify the thing being modified. Let's look at an example:

<u>Walking near the river</u>, the fish jumped.

In this sentence, the modifier, *walking near the river*, is modifying *fish*. This doesn't make logical sense. As an intelligent reader, we know that it is highly unlikely that the fish jumped while they were walking near the river; we can assume that the actual subject of the sentence is a person who was walking near the river. However, good writing never makes the reader assume something like that. To fix this dangling modifier, we need to rewrite the sentence to include the proper subject:

<u>Walking near the river</u>, *I watched as* the fish jumped.

In this corrected version of the sentence, the modifier clearly describes *I*. The sentence makes more sense and the modifier error is solved.

> **TO ANSWER DANGLING MODIFIER QUESTIONS:**
> **Step 1:** Identify the modifier.
>
> **Step 2:** Identify the word/phrase being modified.
>
> **Step 3:** Decide what word/phrase should be modified. If it is missing, the error is a dangling modifier.
>
> **Step 4:** Eliminate answer choices that fail to solve the dangling modifier error or that create new errors. Pay particular attention to those that create misplaced modifiers.
>
> **Step 5:** Of the remaining answers, choose the one that creates the most logical relationship between the modifier and the word/phrase that should be modified.

Modifiers
Sample Questions

Growing cities have nowhere to go but up, leading to taller and taller buildings. The most efficient way to build new homes, skyscrapers cast long shadows, putting the people living and working below in near-permanent darkness. Attempting to solve the problem, **(1)** pairs of skyscrapers that work together to reflect sunlight in order to minimize shade have been designed by architects. **(2)** Using specially designed software, the buildings are curved to allow one building to reflect sunlight into the shade of the other building.

1. A) NO CHANGE
    B) working together to reflect sunlight in order to minimize shade, pairs of skyscrapers have been designed by architects
    C) architects have designed pairs of skyscrapers that work together to reflect sunlight in order to minimize shade
    D) architects, working together to reflect sunlight in order to minimize shade, have designed pairs of skyscrapers

First we must identify the modifier in the sentence. The first modifier in the sentence is "Attempting to solve the problem." Next we identify the thing being modified. As written, "Attempting to solve the problem" modifies "pairs of skyscrapers." This is illogical. Our next step is to identify what should be modified. It is the architects that are attempting to solve the problem, so architects should be modified. We can eliminate choice B because it fails to place architects near the modifier. We can also eliminate choice D because it creates a new modifier error by making "working together...minimize shade" modify architects. This leaves us choice C, which solves the original error without creating new ones.

2. A) NO CHANGE
    B) Architects designed curved buildings that use specially designed software
    C) The buildings are curved using specially designed software
    D) Using specially designed software, architects designed curved buildings

The underlined portion of the sentence includes the modifier "Using specially designed software." As written, the modifier modifies "the buildings." Obviously the buildings didn't use specially designed software, so we know there is a modifier error. When we look for the word/phrase that should be modified, there does not seem to be a clear answer in the sentence. This means that we are looking at a dangling modifier. We can eliminate choice B because we already know that the buildings aren't using software. We can also eliminate C because the software wouldn't actually curve the buildings – buildings are built by people, not by software. This leaves choice D, which correctly places "architects" immediately after the modifier, as the correct answer.

Logical Comparisons
Concept & Strategy Lesson

On the PSAT 10/11, some questions test our ability to recognize and correct incomplete, inconsistent, or unclear comparisons. As readers, we often use logic to make sense of what we read, so sometimes illogical comparisons aren't immediately clear. This can make logical comparison questions somewhat difficult.

INCOMPLETE COMPARISONS

For a comparison to be complete, at least two things have to be compared. Incomplete comparisons make the reader guess which two things are being compared. Let's look at an example:

Incorrect: That school has a longer waiting list this year.

This sentence doesn't answer a fundamental question: A longer waiting list this year *than what*? Longer than last year? Longer than the other school? We have only one item here to compare, so we need to guess. The comparison needs to be completed in order to make sense:

Correct: That school has a longer waiting list this year *than the school down the street does.*
Correct: That school has a longer waiting list this year *than last year.*
Correct: That school has a longer waiting list this year *than in any year prior.*

Each of these sentences clarifies the comparison by providing a second item to compare. Some incomplete comparisons can be harder to spot. For example:

Incorrect: Sue got a higher PSAT 10/11 score than anyone in her class.

At first glance, this seems to be a complete comparison: The two things being compared are "Sue" and "anyone in her class." But since Sue is presumably in her class, the sentence actually compares Sue to herself. There is a very simple way to fix this:

Correct: Sue got a higher PSAT 10/11 score than anyone *else* in her class.

INCONSISTENT COMPARISONS

Not only must comparisons be complete, but they must also be consistent. This means that a comparison needs to compare apples to apples, not apples to oranges. For instance:

Incorrect: Sue's PSAT 10/11 score was not as high as the valedictorian.

This sentence compares Sue's PSAT 10/11 score with the valedictorian. A test score and a person are not similar enough for the comparison to be considered consistent. There are two ways to correct this problem:

Correct: Sue's PSAT 10/11 score was not as high as the valedictorian's PSAT 10/11 score.
Correct: Sue's PSAT 10/11 score was not as high as the valedictorian's.

Both of these examples create a complete comparison by ensuring that the items being compared are both PSAT 10/11 scores. Notice that the second correct sentence simply makes "valedictorian" possessive. Inconsistent comparisons can often – though not always – be solved this way.

UNCLEAR COMPARISONS

The last type of logical comparison error is an unclear comparison. For a comparison to be clear, the reader needs to be able to easily tell which items are being compared. For example:

Incorrect: I usually help my sister with her homework more than my brother.

This sentence could mean more than one thing, as you can see in the corrected versions:

Correct: I usually help my sister with her homework more than I help my brother with his.
Correct: I usually help my sister with her homework more than my brother does.

Unclear comparisons can usually be solved in more than one way. You must rely on the context of the passage to determine which interpretation is correct. For instance, if the incorrect sentence above had been in a paragraph that discussed the author's much older brother and much younger sister, then the correct version of the sentence would most likely be the second version.

TO ANSWER LOGICAL COMPARISON QUESTIONS:

Step 1: Identify the items being compared and figure out whether the error is because of an incomplete, inconsistent, or unclear comparison.

Step 2: Eliminate any answer choices that fail to solve the error or that create a new error. Look out for answer choices that create another logical comparison error.

Step 3: Of the remaining answer choices, choose the one that best fits the context of the paragraph.

Logical Comparisons
Sample Questions

Tom Petty and Bruce Springsteen have something interesting in common: Although both are very well-known rock artists with decades' long careers, they are not known for their number one hits. Surprisingly, Bruce Springsteen has **1)** <u>fewer number one hits.</u> In fact, he has never had a number one hit. In that regard, Tom Petty's musical career has been slightly more successful **2)**<u>than Bruce Springsteen</u>. After a 38-year long career, Tom Petty finally landed his first number one album, yet he still has never had a number one hit song.

1. A) NO CHANGE
    B) fewer number one hits than Tom Petty does.
    C) fewer number one hits than any artist.
    D) fewer number one hits than Tom Petty's.

First we must identify the items being compared and the type of error. In this sentence, Bruce Springsteen's number of top hits is being compared to…nothing. This means we have an incomplete comparison. Based on the context of the paragraph, we can figure out that the writer meant to compare Bruce Springsteen's number of top hits and Tom Petty's number of top hits. We can eliminate A since it creates the incomplete comparison; C also creates an incomplete comparison by comparing Bruce Springsteen to himself (and it fails to complete the comparison in a logical manner based on the context of the passage). This leaves us with choices B and D. Although an apostrophe can often correct an illogical comparison, in this case, it creates a new error by ruining the sentence's parallelism. Choice B is the correct answer.

2. A) NO CHANGE
    B) than Bruce Springsteen has.
    C) than Bruce Springsteen's.
    D) than Bruce Springsteen's success.

In this sentence, Tom Petty's career is being compared to Bruce Springsteen. This is an illogical comparison because we can't compare a career and a person, so we can eliminate choice A. Choice B is also illogical because it compares Tom Petty's career with "Bruce Springsteen has." Choice D compares Tom Petty's career with Bruce Springsteen's success, which is also illogical. This leaves us with choice C as the correct answer.

Organization
Concept & Strategy Lesson

The PSAT 10/11 has several types of question that test your ability to improve the organization or a paragraph or passage. These include questions that ask you to determine the most logical sequence of sentences within a paragraph or paragraphs within a passage; questions that ask you to add an introduction or conclusion that suits the passage or that accomplishes a particular goal; and questions that ask you to improve the transitions or transitional sentences in the passage.

LOGICAL SEQUENCE

Logical sequence questions ask you to put ideas in the most logical order, whether by rearranging sentences within a paragraph, deciding the most appropriate place to add a sentence, or rearranging paragraphs within a passage. Answering logical sequence questions requires that you pay close attention to context, relationships between ideas, and use of transitions in order to determine the most logical order of ideas.

LOGICAL SEQUENCE OF SENTENCES

Logical sequence questions that focus on sentences will either require that you rearrange the sentences within a paragraph or add a sentence in the most appropriate place in a paragraph. The most logical order of sentences in any given paragraph depends on the content of the individual sentences, so these questions require much closer reading than many other writing questions.

Concepts that are closely related to one another should appear close together in the paragraph, and if there is a cause and effect relationship within the paragraph, the cause usually should come before the effect. Pay close attention to transitional words and phrases because these can often provide clues to help determine the most logical sequence of sentences.

TO ANSWER LOGICAL SEQUENCE OF SENTENCES QUESTIONS:

Step 1: Look for transitional words or phrases that don't seem to make sense. Eliminate any answer choices that don't address these illogical transitions.

Step 2: Look for sentences that contain closely related ideas but that are not placed close together in the paragraph. Eliminate any answer choices that do not place closely related ideas together.

Step 3: Look for sentences that relate to the paragraph immediately preceding or following the paragraph in question. Eliminate answer choices that do not place these sentences nearest this paragraph.

Step 4: Of the remaining answer choices, choose the one that seems to place the sentences in the most logical order. Reread the paragraph as it should be based on the answer choice you selected. If the paragraph now makes logical sense, move on to the next question.

LOGICAL SEQUENCE OF PARAGRAPHS

Logical sequence questions that focus on paragraphs require that you arrange the paragraphs within the passage in the most logical order. Often, these questions ask where a certain paragraph should be placed.

Understanding the basic structure of a well-written passage is helpful when answering these questions. Remember that the first paragraph usually serves as an introduction and the final paragraph usually serves as a conclusion. The body paragraphs provide supporting information and should flow logically from one idea to the next. As with logical sequence of sentences questions, transitions can be very helpful in determining the best order of the paragraphs.

TO ANSWER LOGICAL SEQUENCE OF PARAGRAPHS QUESTIONS:

Step 1: Look for transitional words, phrases, or sentences that seem out of place. Eliminate any answer choices that fail to solve this problem.

Step 2: Look for paragraphs that contain closely related ideas that are not placed near each other. Eliminate any answer choices that do not place closely related paragraphs near one another.

Step 3: Of the remaining answer choices, choose the one that seems to place the paragraphs in the most logical order.

Step 4: Quickly skim the passage with the paragraphs in the order indicated by the answer you selected. If the new version of the passage makes good sense, move on to the next question.

INTRODUCTIONS AND CONCLUSIONS

Introduction questions usually ask you to either add a sentence to the beginning of the passage or to change a sentence that already appears in the beginning of the passage. Remember that a good introductory sentence will introduce the main topic of the passage without explicitly outlining all of the details of the passage.

Much like introduction questions, conclusion questions also ask you to either add or change a sentence, this time at the end of the passage. Remember that a good conclusion should emphasize the main point of the passage.

TO ANSWER INTRODUCTION AND CONCLUSION QUESTIONS:

Step 1: Consider the style and tone of the passage and eliminate any answer choices that don't suit the style or tone.

Step 2: Eliminate any answer choices that refer to information that is not related to or disagrees with the main ideas of the passage.

Step 3: Eliminate answer choices that focus on a detail of the passage rather than the main claim/idea of the passage.

Step 4: Examine the remaining answer choices. Choose the one that best suits the introductory or concluding paragraph.

Step 5: Reread the beginning or end of the passage with your chosen answer inserted. If the new introduction/conclusion flows naturally and makes logical sense, move on to the next question.

TRANSITIONS

Transition questions require that you use transitional strategies to create a smooth progression of ideas within a passage. The easiest transition questions will simply ask you which transitional word or phrase best links two ideas, but many transition questions go beyond basic transitional words and phrases to include transitional sentences.

TRANSITIONAL WORDS AND PHRASES

The following is a table containing frequently used transitions and transitional phrases and the relationships they demonstrate:

FUNCTION	TRANSITIONAL WORDS AND PHRASES			
Sequence	First Second Third Next Then	Finally After Afterward At last Before	Currently During Earlier Immediately Later	Meanwhile Now Recently Simultaneously Subsequently
Conclusion	Finally In a word In brief In conclusion	In the end In the final analysis On the whole	Thus To conclude To summarize	In sum To sum up In summary
Example	For example To illustrate	For instance	Namely	Specifically
Position	Above Adjacent Below	Beyond Here	In front In back	Nearby There
Cause/Effect	Therefore Accordingly	Consequently Thus	Hence	So
Emphasis	Even Truly	Indeed	In fact	Of course
Similarity	Also Just as	In the same way Similarly	Likewise	Much as
Contrast	But Nonetheless Still	However Notwithstanding Yet	In spite of In contrast	Nevertheless On the contrary

It is important to know the functions of different transitions in order to identify the best transition to use in the context of the passage. For example:

Incorrect: Animal welfare and human welfare are closely connected. *Nevertheless,* failure to embrace spay and neuter programs has led to animal overpopulation in many communities, causing the spread of certain diseases and a rise in minor car accidents.

Correct: Animal welfare and human welfare are closely connected. *For example,* failure to embrace spay and neuter programs has led to animal overpopulation in many communities, causing the spread of certain diseases and a rise in minor car accidents.

The transition used in the first example incorrectly identifies the relationship between the two sentences as a contrasting relationship. But the information in the second sentence doesn't contrast with the information in the first sentence; instead it clarifies the information by providing an example. *For example* provides a transition that properly identifies this relationship.

TO ANSWER TRANSITIONAL WORDS AND PHRASES QUESTIONS:

Step 1: Read the sentence containing the transition as well as the sentences immediately before and after. Determine which two sentences are connected by the transition.

Step 2: Identify the relationship between the two sentences. Eliminate any answer choices that don't reflect that relationship.

Step 3: Of the remaining choices, choose the one that best reflects the relationship between the two sentences.

TRANSITIONAL SENTENCES

Transitional sentences perform the same function as transitional words and phrases, but there are an infinite number of possible permutations of transitional sentences. This is because transitional sentences more thoroughly articulate the relationship between two ideas. Transitional sentences usually link paragraphs, so they can generally be found at the beginning or end of a paragraph. When a transitional sentence appears at the beginning of a paragraph, it is connecting that paragraph with the one preceding it. When a transitional sentence appears at the end of a paragraph, it is connecting that paragraph with the one following it. As with introduction and conclusion questions, transitional sentence questions require that you pay close attention to the context of the passage, particularly the two paragraphs being linked.

TO ANSWER TRANSITIONAL SENTENCES QUESTIONS:

Step 1: Identify the two paragraphs being linked by the transition sentence.

Step 2: Identify the main idea of each paragraph. Eliminate any answer choices that either disagree with these main ideas or are not related to them.

Step 3: Determine the relationship between the two paragraphs. Eliminate any answer choices that create a relationship that is not reflected by the passage.

Step 4: Eliminate any answer choices that reference information found in paragraphs other than the ones referenced by the question.

Step 5: Of the remaining options, choose the one that most logically and clearly connects the information in the paragraphs while maintaining the appropriate style and tone.

Style and Tone
Concept & Strategy Lesson

Authors use a specific style and tone to convey their intended meanings. Style is the way in which an author writes, including word choice or sentence patterns. Tone is the emotion that the author conveys through his writing. Style and tone can both be determined by the author's purpose. For instance, if the author is writing to a group of friends to convince them to do something, the style will likely be informal (since the intended audience is a group of friends) and the tone would likely be passionate (in order to persuade).

IDENTIFYING STYLE AND TONE

The author's purpose will often determine the tone of a passage. An author might be writing to explain, persuade, or tell a story. An author who intends to persuade an audience will often use a passionate tone, whereas an author writing simply to inform will often use an objective tone.

Style can sometimes be easier to determine simply by reading the passage. An author who uses slang and avoids high-level vocabulary is usually using an informal style, whereas an author who uses technical terms and high-level vocabulary is usually using a formal style. Style should generally remain consistent throughout a passage, so stylistically correct answer choices will generally suit the rest of the passage.

TO ANSWER STYLE AND TONE QUESTIONS:

Step 1: Quickly examine the passage for clues regarding the passage's style and tone. In particular, look for the author's word choice and purpose.

Step 2: Eliminate any answer choices that are inconsistent with the style or tone of the passage as a whole.

Step 3: Closely examine the paragraph that contains the part of the passage referenced by the question. Eliminate any answer choices that do not suit the style and tone of the surrounding sentences.

Step 4: Of the remaining answer choices, choose the one that best reflects the style and tone of the passage as a whole.

Proposition, Support, Focus
Concept & Strategy Lesson

In addition to testing your knowledge of grammar and usage, the PSAT 10/11 will also test your ability to edit a passage to improve its content. The main question types used to test this skill are proposition, support, and focus questions.

PROPOSITION

Proposition questions test your ability to identify the main idea of a passage or paragraph. These questions will typically ask you to add or replace a sentence in order to provide a better thesis statement or topic sentence.

To answer these questions, it is important to exercise active reading skills. While reading the passage, make notes in the margins regarding the main idea of the passage as a whole and of each individual paragraph.

TO ANSWER PROPOSITION QUESTIONS:

Step 1: If the question is about a thesis statement, look at your notes regarding the main ideas of each paragraph in order to determine the main idea of the passage; summarize the main idea of the passage in your own words. If the question is about a specific paragraph, carefully reread the paragraph; summarize the main idea of the paragraph in your own words.

Step 2: Eliminate any answer choices that seem to focus on a specific detail rather than on the main idea. Likewise, eliminate answer choices that are overly generalized.

Step 3: Eliminate any answer choices that do not suit the style or tone of the passage.

Step 4: Of the remaining answer choices, choose the one that most closely matches your summary of the main idea.

SUPPORT

Support questions test your ability to identify appropriate evidence in support of a particular claim. These questions will generally ask you to add, remove, or revise supporting evidence in order to improve the claims made in the text.

TO ANSWER SUPPORT QUESTIONS:

Step 1: Carefully read the paragraph or sentence referenced in the question in order to determine the argument or main idea.

Step 2: Eliminate any answer choices that are irrelevant, only loosely connected, or more closely linked to arguments or ideas found elsewhere in the passage.

Step 3: Eliminate any answer choices that contradict the information found in the passage.

Step 4: Of the remaining choices, choose the one that provides the strongest and clearest support for the argument or main idea.

FOCUS

Good writing requires that each paragraph be focused on a single main idea. Focus questions test your ability to eliminate unnecessary information in order to improve the focus of a paragraph. As with proposition and support questions, it is helpful if you make notes regarding the main ideas of the paragraphs in a passage.

TO ANSWER FOCUS QUESTIONS:

Step 1: Carefully read the paragraph or sentence referenced in the question in order to determine the argument or main idea.

Step 2: Without looking at the answer choices, try to identify the sentence that is least related to the main idea of the paragraph.

Step 3: Examine the answer choices. If the sentence you identified in step two is listed as an answer choice, that is most likely the correct answer. If not, move on to step 4.

Step 4: Work through the answer choices one at a time. Reread the paragraph without the sentence identified by each answer choice. Choose the answer choice that creates the clearest and most concise paragraph.

Quantitative Information
Concept & Strategy Lesson

Each writing section will include at least one passage that is accompanied by a graphic such as a table, chart, graph, or map. Several questions will reference these graphics.

ADDRESSING QUANTITATIVE INFORMATION QUESTIONS

Quantitative information questions require that you add, remove, or revise information in the passage to reflect information in the graphic. Other quantitative information questions may ask what you can tell from both the passage and the graphic.

Answering these questions requires synthesizing information from both the passage and the graphic -- the correct answer choice will never contradict information found in either the passage or the graphic.

TO ANSWER QUANTITATIVE INFORMATION QUESTIONS:

Step 1: Carefully examine the graphic. Pay particular attention to units of measurement. Eliminate any answer choices that disagree with the information in the graphic.

Step 2: Eliminate any answer choices that disagree with information found in the passage.

Step 3: Examine the remaining answer choices carefully. Choose the one that most closely reflects information from the passage and the graphic.

Words in Context
Concept & Strategy Lesson

The writing section tests your understanding of vocabulary and word choice through questions that require that you revise the passage for precision and concision. Precision questions test your ability to choose the most appropriate word or phrase for a particular context. Concision questions test your ability to recognize and correct wordiness and redundancy.

PRECISION

Precision questions may be presented in one of two ways. The question may ask you to choose the most precise word for a particular sentence, or it may simply offer an underlined word or phrase accompanied by three alternative choices. Regardless of the question's presentation, precision questions require you to understand the slight differences in the meanings of similar words. There are a few basic concepts that must be understood in order to answer these questions.

First, it is important to recognize the difference between an accurate word choice and a precise word choice. Consider this example:

Accurate: She really enjoys reading *books*, particularly those in the science fiction and fantasy genres.
Precise: She really enjoys reading *novels*, particularly those in the science fiction and fantasy genres.

In the first sentence, the use of *books* is accurate, but the use of *novels* in the second sentence is more precise. *Books* is very general -- it includes a whole host of bound pages. *Novels* is more specific -- it narrows things down to fictional stories. It is important to use the context of the sentence or paragraph in which the word in question appears in order to choose the answer that reaches the ideal level of specificity.

The second concept to consider when answering precision questions is the idea of connotation. A word's connotation is its implied meaning. For example, all of these words are synonyms for "smile": beam, grin, laugh, smirk, and simper. Some of these words suggest extreme happiness or joy (beam, grin, laugh), while others have more negative connotations (smirk, simper). It is important to use the context of the sentence or paragraph in which a given word appears in order to determine whether you should choose a word with a positive or negative connotation.

TO ANSWER PRECISION QUESTIONS:

Step 1: Without looking at the answer choices, cover up the underlined word and come up with your own word choice for the sentence. Try to be as specific as you can based on the given context.

Step 2: Eliminate any answer choices that disagree with the word you selected.

Step 3: Use the context of the passage to eliminate any additional answer choices that are too general, too specific, or have the wrong connotation.

Step 4: Of the remaining answer choices, choose the one that best completes the sentence.

CONCISION

Like precision questions, concision questions may either specifically ask which answer choice is most concise or offer an underlined portion of the sentence and three alternative choices. Unlike precision questions, concision questions that don't include a specific question can be hard to spot because they will often include a rather lengthy underlined portion. You must first rule out other possible errors before determining whether the question is a concision question.

As with precision questions, concision questions require a thorough understanding of a couple of concepts: wordiness and redundancy.

WORDINESS

When answering a concision question, you will usually choose the answer that includes the fewest words without losing any meaning. The most common mistakes that lead to wordiness include:

Passive Voice
It is usually best to use active voice in writing, in part due to the wordiness created by passive voice. For example:

Passive: The birthday gift was given to Sarah by her aunt and uncle.
Active: Her aunt and uncle gave Sarah a birthday gift.

"There is," "There are," and "It is"

These often unnecessary phrases simply add word count. For example:

Wordy: There are too many people in this room.
Better: This room has too many people.

This and That

Sentences can often be combined or shortened to reduce wordiness by eliminating words like "this," "that," and "which." For example:

Wordy: I enjoy cooking, which is because my grandmother taught me.
Concise: I enjoy cooking because my grandmother taught me.

REDUNDANCY

Redundancy occurs when there is needless repetition of words, phrases, or ideas within a given sentence or paragraph. For example:

Redundant: Many uneducated citizens who *never graduated from school* continue to vote for education improvements.
Concise: Many uneducated citizens continue to vote for education improvements.

TO ANSWER CONCISION QUESTIONS:

Step 1: Read the sentence containing the underlined portion and the surrounding sentences. Identify any redundancies in the underlined portion

.

Step 2: Examine the answer choices. Eliminate any answer choices that are overly lengthy or redundant.

Step 3: Eliminate any answer choices that lose important meaning by cutting out too many words.

Step 4: Of the remaining choices, choose the one that conveys the same information in the fewest words. Reread the sentence with your chosen answer to ensure that no new redundancies are created.

Evidence-based Writing Practice
Practice Passages and Questions

Practice Passage 1

Helping Small Farmers Cope with Climate Change

Last year, I served as a Peace Corps agribusiness **(1)** <u>advisor in Bluefields a small farming and</u> fishing village in Westmoreland parish in southwest Jamaica. I worked primarily with a group of organic farmers, **(2)** <u>promoting</u> sustainable agriculture and introducing climate change adaptation strategies through community engagement. I also conducted research on the vulnerability of local agricultural livelihoods to climate change.

(3) <u>Despite</u> the community integration and learning process, I facilitated an assessment with the Westmoreland Organic Farmers Society, a local organization engaged in production agriculture and home economics. The results of the assessment helped us to better understand factors affecting the economic and environmental sustainability of their livelihoods. Through informal discussions with farmers, I also **(4)** <u>gained a sense of awareness</u> of how changing weather patterns, such as variable rainfall, increased risk for these small-scale farm families.

In October 2012, Bluefields community organizations were given the opportunity to apply for small grants to support the development of livelihood opportunities more resilient to climate change. Designing a project and submitting a successful proposal **(5)** <u>was easier</u> because we had already collectively identified and prioritized the needs and interests of the organization.

1. A) NO CHANGE
    B) advisor, in Bluefields a small farming and
    C) advisor in Bluefields, a small farming and
    D) advisor in Bluefields a small farming, and

2. Which choice most precisely conveys the intended meaning?

    A) NO CHANGE
    B) propagandizing
    C) demanding
    D) wishing for

3. Which transitional phrase is most appropriate here?

    A) NO CHANGE
    B) Without
    C) As part of
    D) Prior to

4. A) NO CHANGE
    B) sensed a gain in awareness
    C) gained awareness
    D) grew aware of

5. A) NO CHANGE
    B) were easier
    C) were more easy
    D) was more easy

Among other things, the funds went toward establishing an organic demonstration farm. {6} The farm was also used to host a Farmer Field School where community members learned about organic farming practices, **(7)** <u>the potential impacts of</u> climate change, and possible adaptation and mitigation strategies. The group was also able to purchase improved processing equipment and receive food safety training, important steps toward establishing a formal agribusiness.

(8) <u>The group continues to develop and improve the farm, as well as its processing capacity.</u> More importantly, the Jamaican farmers are increasing resiliency by adapting new technology to their own cultural norms and practices. Working side-by-side with my Jamaican friends to establish the demonstration **(9)** <u>farm, one</u> of the joys of my life; it also showed me how difficult it is to cultivate marginal lands with simple hand tools—a reality for millions of men and women around the world.

[1] The data I collected can also be used to measure changes in vulnerability over time. [2] During my service, I designed a study to assess the vulnerability of local agricultural livelihoods to climate change. [3] My hope is that the results will illuminate areas where targeted programs can improve farmers' resiliency and increase incomes. {10}

6. Which true detail, if added here, best in the context of the passage?

   A) Groups in Chile and Malawi also received grant funds.
   B) The group's first addition was a structure to catch and store rain for irrigation.
   C) Organic farms do not use synthetic pesticides or fertilizers.
   D) In ten years, farmers hope to raise enough funds to build a larger demonstration farm.

7. A) NO CHANGE
   B) potentially impacted by
   C) impacting potentially by
   D) an impact potentially from

8. Which choice best states the paragraph's main theme?

   A) NO CHANGE
   B) Around the world, climates vary, but many challenges are shared.
   C) Scientists predict that sea levels will rise by at least 3 feet over the next century due to climate change.
   D) Most Jamaican farmers work on a small scale of 1 to 5 acres.

9. A) NO CHANGE
   B) farm; one
   C) farm, and one
   D) farm was one

10. The sentences in the preceding paragraph would be most logically placed in which order?

    A) As they are now
    B) 1, 3, 2
    C) 2, 3, 1
    D) 3, 1, 2

I hope the change **(11)** <u>we've seen</u> in Bluefields will be that of more sustainable livelihoods through environmental stewardship and human empowerment. This is a very possible outcome if the Jamaican men and women I worked with in the farmers group are any indication.

11. A) NO CHANGE
B) we'd seen
C) we're seeing
D) we'll see

Practice Passage 2

Healthy Nails, Healthy Workers

(1) <u>There are hundreds of thousands of Vietnamese Americans living in the U.S.</u> After learning about the nail salon industry from friends in my English class, I became a manicurist. The work offered a flexible schedule for mothers of small children, like me, and the required training wasn't as long as for other professions. With determination, I was able to work my way up to eventually become the co-owner of Traci's Nails in Oakland, California. Last year, my business was officially recognized as a "Healthy Nail Salon" by Alameda County, California, for using safer practices and products in my salon. I've been able to do what is best for **(2)** <u>my health, the health of my co-workers, and my customers.</u>

[1] Like **(3)** <u>my industry,</u> I chose to become a manicurist to make women feel beautiful and to provide for my family. [2] Although there are many good things about the job—the glamour, the artistry, the beautiful colors, and the new **(4)** <u>designs—there</u> are also significant hazards. [3] Salon workers are exposed to toxic chemicals and **(5)** <u>repetitive, redundant</u> motions that can cause injuries and illnesses. [4] Many experience health symptoms like breathing difficulty, red and watery eyes, and skin reactions on a daily basis. [5] These symptoms also match with common allergic reactions. [6] We tell ourselves to accept these short-term health problems, but we worry about the possible long-term effects of chemical exposure: cancer, reproductive issues, and asthma. {6}

1. Which sentence best introduces the narrator?

   A) NO CHANGE
   B) My name is Chanh, and I am 5'2" tall.
   C) I immigrated to the United States, along with my young daughter, in 1992.
   D) I speak English much more fluently than I did 30 years ago.

2. A) NO CHANGE
   B) my health, my co-workers, and the health of my customers
   C) healthy me, my co-workers, and my healthy customers
   D) the health of myself, my co-workers, and my customers

3. A) NO CHANGE
   B) others in my industry
   C) my employment in the industry
   D) the industry's employment

4. A) NO CHANGE
   B) designs—and there
   C) designs; there
   D) designs, there

5. A) NO CHANGE
   B) repetitively excessive
   C) repetitive
   D) can also cause repetitive

6. Which sentence in the preceding paragraph can be deleted without losing information relevant to the passage?

   A) Sentence 3
   B) Sentence 4
   C) Sentence 5
   D) Sentence 6

The Occupational Safety and Health Administration (OSHA) has many useful resources for salon workers and owners like me, including a booklet called *Stay Healthy and Safe While Giving Manicures and Pedicures* **(7)** (which is 42 pages long). For the last several years, **(8)** they have been working to empower nonprofit organizations that offer safety training and resources to salon workers and employers. **(9)** OSHA in hair and nail salons also has special webpages about safety, the danger of chemicals like toluene, and how to transition to safer chemicals in the workplace. In California, thanks to the work of the California Healthy Nail Salon Collaborative, several areas have implemented Healthy Nail Salon Recognition Programs, awarding salons that use less-toxic products, improve ventilation, and participate in trainings that encourage healthier workplaces.

As an owner, I have gained greater control over the products and practices used in my workplace. I am hoping that other owners in the industry also adopt safer products and practices. That's why the collaborative work of OSHA, advocacy organizations like the California Healthy Nail Salon Collaborative, and local governments is so **(10)** lively to the lives of salon workers across the country.

(11) Nail salon workers and owners should not have to forego good health in order to make a living!

7. Given the narrator's background, which parenthesized detail fits best in the passage?

A) NO CHANGE
B) (available in Vietnamese, Korean, and Spanish as well as English)
C) (unfortunately not useful for miners or farm workers)
D) (a brochure I have read ten times)

8. A) NO CHANGE
B) organizations have
C) the booklet has
D) OSHA has

9. A) NO CHANGE
B) OSHA about safety in hair and nail salons also has special webpages
C) OSHA also has special webpages in hair and nail salons about safety
D) OSHA also has special webpages about safety in hair and nail salons

10. Which choice most precisely conveys the intended meaning?

A) NO CHANGE
B) alive
C) vital
D) vivid

11. Which statement best summarizes the passage's argument?

A) NO CHANGE
B) Nail salons should be banned from using toluene.
C) Without OSHA, American workplaces would be much less safe.
D) Immigrants, especially those with children, struggle to make ends meet.

Practice Passage 3

What Women Want: Equal Pay

Fifty years ago, when President Kennedy signed the Equal Pay Act into **(1)** <u>law women</u> earned an average of 59 cents on the dollar compared to their male colleagues. At that time, as **(2)** <u>incredible</u> as it seems today, it really was legal to pay a woman less money to do the same work as a man. By signing the Equal Pay Act, Kennedy finally made it illegal to discriminate against women in the payment of wages.

We have seen progress over the past 50 years—but not enough. Today in America, for every dollar paid to a man, a woman is paid about 77 cents when the calculations are based on annual earnings, and more like 81 cents based on weekly wages. For women of color and women with disabilities, the wage gap is even larger. {3}

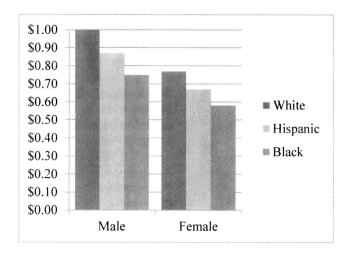

Figure 1:

Annual earnings by gender and ethnicity on a per-dollar basis.

This reality has major implications for **(4)** <u>women's</u> ability to afford essentials like food, housing, and gas. Now more than ever, American families rely on the wages of women. **(5)** <u>In my city alone, there are thousands of single mothers supporting families.</u> Despite this, the wage disparity between women and men has persisted.

1. A) NO CHANGE
   B) law—women
   C) law; women
   D) law, women

2. Which choice fits best with the tone of the passage?

   A) NO CHANGE
   B) spectacular
   C) favorable
   D) unique

3. Which statement, if added here, best supports the passage's argument with accurate information from the figure?

   A) The evidence shows, however, that white females are paid more than black men.
   B) Black females, for instance, earn less than 60 cents compared to each dollar a white male earns.
   C) One exception to this trend is Asian females, who typically ea about as much as white males.
   D) Hispanic females make less, on per-dollar basis, than women of other ethnicities.

4. A) NO CHANGE
   B) womens'
   C) womens
   D) women

5. Which true statement provides the most effective evidence to support the paragraph's claims?

   A) NO CHANGE
   B) Some women even earn higher wages than their male colleagues.
   C) American women today are better educated than they were even 20 years ago.
   D) Women make up nearly half of the U.S. labor force and a growing percentage of household breadwinners.

[1] In 2010, President **(6)** <u>Obama's creation,</u> the National Equal Pay Task Force to ensure that equal pay laws are vigorously enforced throughout the country. [2] As we in the task force chart the equal pay agenda for the next half-century, we look at strategies that empower each worker to know **(7)** <u>their</u> worth. [3] One of the biggest obstacles to combating pay discrimination is that so many women do not know they are being underpaid due to discrimination. [4] To address the policies and norms that result in pay secrecy, the task force continues to focus on the importance of collecting and publicizing better data on pay. {8}

Closing the pay gap once and for all will help millions of women and their families right now, but it also has implications for the economic future of our country. We must enable government worker protection agencies to collaborate and coordinate more effectively, and we must encourage employers to take responsibility for **(9)** <u>the idea that they can offer</u> fair pay to all workers.

[5] Enforcement of existing civil rights laws, including the Equal Pay Act, will help. [6] Those laws, however, also leave gaps that must be filled. [7] That's why it is imperative that Congress address loopholes in existing law, strengthen remedies for pay discrimination, **(10)** <u>increased</u> outreach and education to working women, and provide additional research and resources to fight pay inequity. [8] Unfortunately, rampant gridlock in Congress has prevented any real progress from occurring. [9] Solutions to the problem of pay discrimination must also address the broader framework of practices that limit the full economic participation of women workers. {11}

6. A) NO CHANGE
   B) Obama created
   C) Obama, who created
   D) Obama; he created

7. A) NO CHANGE
   B) your
   C) his or her
   D) its

8. The sentences in the preceding paragraph would be most logically placed in which order?

   A) As they are now
   B) 2, 3, 1, 4
   C) 3, 2, 4, 1
   D) 4, 1, 3, 2

9. A) NO CHANGE
   B) their duty to offer
   C) offering and granting
   D) offering

10. A) NO CHANGE
    B) increases in
    C) increasing
    D) increase

11. Which sentence in the preceding paragraph can most easily be deleted to improve the paragraph's focus?

    A) Sentence 5
    B) Sentence 6
    C) Sentence 8
    D) Sentence 9

Practice Passage 4

The Birdman

[1] Bird artist John Gould captured the essence of his avian subjects with quick, bold lines, but his great success was due to more than a good drawing hand. [2] Just as important was his manner of production, which yielded an incredible fifty oversized volumes between 1830 and 1881. [3] First, Gould would make a rough sketch, jotting notes on the manuscript as to how to fill out the picture and which colors to add. [4] Then, he would pass the image on to other **(1)** artists and colorists, including, his wife Elizabeth. [5] She died in 1841, but John Gould continued producing drawings for another four decades. [6] Gould's beautiful drawings assured his popularity among a wealthy clientele, while the reliable scientific information in his tomes made for a wider commercial success. {2}

Born in Dorset in 1804, **(3)** taxidermy was Gould's passion as a child. He soon turned these skills into a lucrative career. By the time he was twenty, Gould was **(4)** involved in the booming trade and interest in taxidermy. This soon led to an appointment as curator and preserver to the Zoological Society of London's museum. {5}

1. A) NO CHANGE
   B) artists and colorists, including his wife, Elizabeth
   C) artists, and colorists including his wife, Elizabeth
   D) artists, and colorists including, his wife Elizabeth

2. Which sentence in this paragraph should be deleted because it consists entirely of information that is stated elsewhere in the passage?

   A) Sentence 2
   B) Sentence 3
   C) Sentence 4
   D) Sentence 5

3. A) NO CHANGE
   B) Gould became adept at taxidermy
   C) his taxidermy skills were evident
   D) Gould's father taught him taxidermy

4. Which choice most precisely matches the intended meaning?

   A) NO CHANGE
   B) adopted by
   C) capitalizing on
   D) running through

5. Which statement, if added here, best supports the paragraph's ideas about Gould's career?

   A) While in London, Gould witnessed many important events, including Queen Victoria's coronation.
   B) Many of the specimens Gould worked on can still be viewed at the museum today.
   C) Gould lacked a rigorous education; instead, he spent his teenage years working as a gardener.
   D) This prestigious position came with a salary of 100 pounds, a hefty income at the time.

In 1829, Gould married Elizabeth Coxen, a well-bred governess. **(6)** As they raised a family, Elizabeth and John worked together to illustrate his books on birds. The first work John and Elizabeth collaborated on was the massive *A Century of Birds from the Himalaya Mountains*, which was issued in parts between 1830 and 1833. The two collaborated on two more tomes, **(7)** which were about the birds of Europe and Australia, before Elizabeth's death in 1841. Afterward, John Gould continued his work with other collaborators for another 40 years.

[7] More than an artist, Gould was a consummate entrepreneur, as the factory-like production of his art books attests. [8] During the hummingbird craze, which started with England's first glimpses of the unusual animal during the Great Exhibition of 1851, Gould collected well over five thousand hummingbird skins **(8)** in his personal collection. [9] Gould wrote about hummingbirds with admiration after seeing them for the first time: "With what delight did I examine its tiny body and feast my eyes on its glittering plumage."

{**9**}

6. A) NO CHANGE
   B) Because they raised
   C) And raising
   D) If raising

7. A) NO CHANGE
   B) they
   C) in which
   D) in that

8. A) NO CHANGE
   B) in the collection that he personally gathered
   C) for his own personal use
   D) DELETE the underlined portion

9. Where in the preceding paragraph would the following sentence be most logically added?

   However, he was not immune to the fascinations of his era.

   A) Before Sentence 7
   B) After Sentence 7
   C) After Sentence 8
   D) After Sentence 9

(10) Today, Gould's drawings are prized by art aficionados around the world. He helped identify species in the collection of 450 birds that Charles Darwin presented to the museum of the Zoological Society in 1837. This identification played a significant role in developing the theory of evolution. With Gould's help, Darwin was able to develop the concept of divergent evolution, whereby isolated populations can become new species. In addition to **(11)** aiding Darwin, Gould wrote more than three hundred scientific articles.

10. Which choice best articulates the paragraph's main idea?

A) NO CHANGE
B) Despite his many accomplishments, Gould remains little-known outside of ornithology circles.
C) In the course of his work, Gould also made notable contributions to science.
D) Gould's career in many ways parallels that of his American contemporary, John James Audubon.

11. A) NO CHANGE
B) the aid provided to Darwin by him
C) helping and giving aid to Darwin
D) being one of those who aided Darwin

Practice Passage 5

Micro-Plastics: the New Pollution

[1] This is a relatively new but growing global problem, as is trash from plastic products in general. [2] As much as 80 percent of trash in the ocean comes from sources on land, and up to 60 percent of this trash is plastic. [3] Maybe you've heard of "micro-plastics." [4] **(1)** <u>There</u> created when plastic products eventually break down into tiny particles that drift in our ocean waters and can be eaten by fish and other wildlife. {2}

I got an offer from two conservation groups to tag along as they trawled **(3)** <u>the upper Chesapeake Bay waters of plastics pollution to assess the extent</u>. As an oceanographer, I always cherish the days that I get to take my off my tie and get back out on the bay, so I was eager to join them.

I predicted that we wouldn't find much. My theory was that the Chesapeake Bay is too **(4)** <u>dynamic, with its constant tides, winds, and currents, to</u> allow for large concentrations of micro-plastics. That environment contrasts strongly with the relatively quiet open-ocean circulation patterns that concentrate plastics pollution in the worst known instances, such as the **(5)** <u>popular</u> Great Pacific Garbage Patch.

1. A) NO CHANGE
    B) Their
    C) They're
    D) There's

2. The sentences in the preceding paragraph would be most logically placed in which order?

    A) As they are now
    B) 2, 1, 3, 4
    C) 3, 2, 4, 1
    D) 3, 4, 1, 2

3. A) NO CHANGE
    B) the upper Chesapeake Bay waters to assess the extent of plastics pollution
    C) the extent of plastics pollution to assess the upper Chesapeake Bay waters
    D) to assess the extent the upper Chesapeake Bay waters of plastics pollution

4. A) NO CHANGE
    B) dynamic with its constant tides, winds, and currents, to
    C) dynamic, with its constant tides, winds, and currents to
    D) dynamic with its constant tides, winds and currents to

5. Which choice fits best with the passage's context and tone?

    A) NO CHANGE
    B) conspicuous
    C) sleazy
    D) notorious

{6} Unterlined: Unfortunately, my educated guess proved wildly inaccurate. The lead scientist for the sampling efforts was shocked at the amount of plastics that emerged from the sample net. The tiny specs of colored plastics scattered through all the leaves and organic debris captured by the net was among the highest amounts of plastic that he had seen in any ocean water sample.

What we do on land, including how we **(7)** dispose of our trash, impact the quality of our waters and wildlife. As an oceanographer, I was taught that the oceans and coastal waters are the heartbeat of our planet. {8} In addition, seafood is a crucial source of nutrition for many cultures, and oceanic algae are among the top producers of atmospheric oxygen. In short, the oceans make our planet livable. That's why they deserve our respect and protection.

6. Which choice provides the most effective and accurate topic sentence for the paragraph?

A) NO CHANGE
B) Including me, there were 12 people on the expedition—most of them scientists.
C) Scientists estimate that a single plastic soda bottle can break down into thousands of bits of micro-plastic.
D) The ocean was beautiful that day, with no obvious signs of pollution.

7. A) NO CHANGE
B) disposes of our trash, impact
C) disposes of our trash, impacts
D) dispose of our trash, impacts

8. Which true statement, if added here, adds the most effective evidence to support the paragraph's main ideas?

A) They cover two-thirds of the Earth and control our planet's weather patterns, food production, and atmosphere.
B) I have always particularly appreciated the enormous impact Chesapeake Bay has on the culture of the region.
C) They have provided one of the most important means of transportation for humans over the last 2,000 years.
D) Many millions of years ago, the distant ancestors of humans lived in the ocean.

[5] **(9)** <u>Some</u> great efforts underway by government agencies and many dedicated outside organizations to stem the flow of trash into our waters. [6] In one of the more promising of these efforts, the Trash Free Waters program, the Environmental Protection Agency is developing projects **(10)** <u>to support efforts by groups to significantly reduce</u> trash entering our watersheds and oceans. [7] Such federal environmental programs are relatively new; the EPA was not even established until 1970. [8] Let's hope that these efforts are successful and that I see less plastic during future trips on the Chesapeake Bay. {11}

9. A) NO CHANGE
    B) There are some
    C) With some
    D) And some

10. A) NO CHANGE
    B) to support a significant reduction in
    C) to significantly reduce
    D) with groups who support significantly reducing

11. Which sentence in the preceding paragraph should be deleted to improve the passage's focus?

    A) Sentence 5
    B) Sentence 6
    C) Sentence 7
    D) Sentence 8

Practice Passage 6

Ending Deadlocks with the Seventeenth Amendment

When Congress opened its doors under the new Constitution for the first time on March 4, 1789, at Federal Hall in New York City, there were only eight senators present out of 22 expected. The senators from **(1)** the state of New York, which was hosting, were not among them. The day before, the New York state legislature had **(2)** adjourned without electing any senators.

In February and March, **(3)** the State Senate's Federalist controllers, and the State Assembly, controlled by the Anti-Federalists, fought bitterly over their preferred candidates for the U.S. Senate. Since both parties expected to win a majority in each house in New York's upcoming elections in **(4)** April, they were content to allow the state's Senate seats to remain vacant. Therefore, as the First Congress met in New York City, New York itself was not represented in the Senate. The state legislature remained in a deadlock for five months. It was not until July 16, 1789, that Federalists Rufus King and Philip J. Schuyler **(5)** had been chosen as New York's first senators.

[1] The issue of senatorial deadlocks did not end with the First Congress. [2] They are a consequence of the method of selection agreed upon by the Founders. [3] Article I, Section 3, of the Constitution states, "The Senate of the United States shall be composed of two Senators from each State, chosen by the Legislature thereof, for six Years." [4] Indeed, the only direct democracy outlined in the Constitution applies to members of the House of Representatives. {6}

1. A) NO CHANGE
   B) that very state, the host state, New York,
   C) the host state of New York
   D) New York, state of hosting,

2. In context, which choice most precisely conveys the intended meaning?

   A) NO CHANGE
   B) delayed
   C) divorced
   D) prolonged

3. A) NO CHANGE
   B) State Senate, controlled by the Federalists
   C) Federalists who controlled the State Senate
   D) the party that controlled the State Senate, the Federalists,

4. A) NO CHANGE
   B) April; they were content
   C) April; content
   D) April, content

5. A) NO CHANGE
   B) were chosen
   C) were being chosen
   D) have been chosen

6. Which sentence in the preceding paragraph can be deleted without detracting from the passage's focus?

   A) Sentence 1
   B) Sentence 2
   C) Sentence 3
   D) Sentence 4

Since most state legislatures are bicameral (with two houses), deadlocks frequently **(7)** <u>rose</u> when the two houses were controlled by different political parties and could not agree on a candidate. Instead of compromising in these instances, state legislatures would simply not elect any senator for months, or even years. Between 1891 and 1905 alone, 45 deadlocks occurred in 20 different states; in 14 of those cases, no Senate election was held for an entire legislative session. {8}

7. A) NO CHANGE
    B) razed
    C) arose
    D) raised

8. Which true statement, if added here, best characterizes the extent of the problem described in the paragraph?

    A) Today, senatorial seats can sometimes remain vacant for months, pending a special election.
    B) Many legislatures of the era were also corrupt, electing senators in exchange for money or favors.
    C) Many deadlocks were caused by inexperienced legislators in Western states; deadlocks soon became less frequent in these states.
    D) For instance, Delaware had only one senator in the 56th Congress (1899–1901) and no senators at all in the 57th Congress (1901–1903).

[5] As support grew, it eventually led to the ratification of the 17th Amendment to the U.S. Constitution in 1913. [6] This amendment abolished the system of senatorial election by state legislatures and replaced it with direct popular election by citizens. [7] The issue of deadlocks, along with frequent allegations of corrupt senatorial **(9)** elections, and a push for more democratic participation contributed to a surge of support for a constitutional amendment to allow citizens to directly elect senators. [8] **(10)** One hundred and twenty-four years after the first deadlock in New York, the new method for selecting senators finally ensured an end to empty seats in the Senate. {11}

9. A) NO CHANGE
    B) elections and a push for more democratic participation contributed
    C) elections and a push, for more democratic participation, contributed
    D) elections and a push for more democratic participation, contributed

10. Which choice is most effective in the context of the passage as a whole?

    A) NO CHANGE
    B) Over a century ago
    C) Despite the dogged opposition of several states
    D) Whether this was a widespread problem or not

11. The sentences in the preceding paragraph would be most logically placed in which order?

    A) As they are now
    B) 6, 5, 7, 8
    C) 7, 5, 6, 8
    D) 7, 8, 5, 6

Practice Passage 7

A Short-Sighted Speech?

The latest buzzword in the ever-shifting politics of American education is STEM. For the uninitiated, STEM is an acronym for Science, Technology, Engineering, and Math. **(1)** More relatedly, to hear many elected officials and well-meaning school reformers tell it, it's the only thing a young graduate can hope to get a decent job in anymore. An English major, you say? **(2)** You might as well get in line to apply at Burger King.

When it comes to STEM, Florida Governor Rick Scott is a true believer. In a 2011 interview published in the Sarasota Herald-Tribune, **(3)** it sparked controversy as Scott not only said Florida's public universities should devote more money to STEM programs and less to the humanities, but seemingly suggested that experts in less technical fields were not needed in Florida.

"We don't need a lot more anthropologists in the state," said Scott. "It's a great degree if people want to get it, but we don't need them here."

1. A) NO CHANGE
   B) The relevant part being
   C) More to the point
   D) To clarify what is truly meant

2. Which choice for the underlined sentence supports the author's characterization of the views of "many elected officials and… reformers"?

   A) NO CHANGE
   B) That would not qualify as a STEM field.
   C) You will probably need more years of schooling.
   D) Why would anyone want to study something so useless?

3. A) NO CHANGE
   B) Scott sparked controversy as he
   C) sparking controversy, it
   D) he sparked controversy as it

The governor's comments, to no one's surprise, didn't sit well with one group of **(4)** people in particular: anthropologists. Many quickly leapt to their profession's defense, accusing the governor of ignorance of **(5)** their many practical and profitable applications. Brent Weisman, chair of the Department of Anthropology at the University of South Florida (USF), retorted, "Anthropologists at USF work side by side with civil and industrial engineers, cancer researchers, specialists in public health and medicine, chemists, biologists, and others in the science, technology, and engineering fields that the governor so eagerly applauds." {6}

Students in Weisman's department prepared an online **(7)** presentation, in it various anthropologists describe their jobs. One helps doctors understand the cultural issues that complicate improving health care for migrant farm workers. Another advises businesses on cultural differences that affect international negotiations. Yet another, a forensic anthropologist, helps detectives reconstruct the events that led to a crime scene.

4. A) NO CHANGE
   B) people, in particular
   C) people, in particular,
   D) people in particular,

5. A) NO CHANGE
   B) one's many
   C) many of their
   D) its many

6. Which addition to this paragraph would best support the claim that anthropology is a relevant and practical field of study?

   A) A criticism of low salaries for anthropologists
   B) An explanation of how anthropologists use math
   C) A statistic indicating an increasing number of jobs and professions requiring anthropological training
   D) A defense of the idea that anthropology is a valid science

7. A) NO CHANGE
   B) presentation; in which,
   C) presentation where
   D) presentation in which

[1] **(8)** <u>Accordingly,</u> even within the field, not everybody is sold on the virtues of an anthropology degree. [2] And although there are jobs for anthropologists outside of academia, most are available to other social scientists as well. [3] As a practicing anthropologist, **(9)** <u>Governor Scott might have a point, says Janice Harper</u>. [4] She observes that the median age of an anthropology Ph.D. graduate is 36, higher than for any other field of study. [5] For these grads, finding a tenure-track job as a college professor can be a bit like finding a unicorn. {10}

Perhaps the governor's decision to single out the field for criticism above all other less-lucrative majors **(11)** <u>was a personal issue</u>. Critics of Governor Scott's remarks soon noted that his own daughter had recently graduated from a small liberal arts college. Her degree was in—what else?—anthropology.

8. Which choice for the underlined portion provides the most logical transition from the previous paragraph?

A) NO CHANGE
B) Still,
C) In fact,
D) In contrast,

9. A) NO CHANGE
B) Janice Harper says Governor Scott might have a point
C) says, Governor Scott might have a point, according to Janice Harper.
D) Governor Scott, according to Janice Harper, might have a point.

10. In this paragraph, Sentence 2 would most logically and cohesively be placed

A) where it is now.
B) after Sentence 3.
C) after Sentence 4.
D) after Sentence 5.

11. Which choice for the underlined portion is clearest and most precise?

A) NO CHANGE
B) was his personal opinion.
C) had a more personal origin.
D) was a personal one.

Practice Passage 8

Engineers at NASA's Marshall Space Flight Center in Huntsville, Alabama **(1)** <u>has successfully tested</u> the most complex rocket engine parts that it ever has created using additive manufacturing, or 3-D printing. NASA engineers pushed the limits of technology by designing a rocket engine injector – a highly complex part that sends propellant into the engine – with design features that took advantage of 3-D printing technology.

To make the parts, the design was entered into the 3-D printer's computer. The printer then built each part by layering metal powder and fusing it together using a laser, a process known as selective laser melting.

[1] This additive manufacturing process allowed rocket designers to create an **(2)** <u>injector. [2] The injector had 40 individual</u> spray elements, all printed as a single component rather than **(3)** <u>manufactured</u>. [3] The entire injector was created from just two **(4)** <u>parts, had</u> they used traditional manufacturing methods, engineers would have needed to make and then assemble 163 individual parts. [4] The 3-D printing technology saved time and money, and it allowed engineers to build parts that enhance rocket engine performance **(5)** <u>and</u> are less prone to failure. [5] The injector was similar in size to injectors that power small rocket engines and similar in design to injectors for large engines, such as the engine that will power NASA's Space Launch System (SLS) rocket, the heavy-lift, exploration class rocket under development to take humans beyond Earth orbit and to Mars. {6}

1. A) NO CHANGE
   B) have successfully tested
   C) has been successfully testing
   D) is successfully testing

2. A) NO CHANGE
   B) injector with 40 individual
   C) injector, which having been constructed, had 40 individual
   D) injector of

3. A) NO CHANGE
   B) manufactured and produced as separate components
   C) manufactured individually
   D) manufactured individually as separate components

4. A) NO CHANGE
   B) parts had
   C) parts. Had
   D) parts, however, had

5. A) NO CHANGE
   B) or
   C) but
   D) yet

6. Which of the following sentences most effectively functions as the topic sentence of the paragraph?

   A) Sentence 1
   B) Sentence 3
   C) Sentence 4
   D) Sentence 5

"We wanted to go a step beyond just testing an injector and demonstrate how 3-D printing could revolutionize rocket designs for increased system performance," said Chris Singer, director of Marshall's Engineering Directorate. "The parts performed exceptionally well during the tests."

(7) Additive manufacturing is more complicated than traditional manufacturing, yet it speeds up the entire design process. Using Marshall's in-house capability to design and produce small 3-D printed parts quickly, the propulsion and materials laboratories can work together to apply quick modifications to the test stand or the rocket component. "Having an in-house additive manufacturing capability allows us (8) to look at test data, to modify parts or the test stand based on the data, (9) materialize changes quickly, and get back to testing," said Nicholas Case, a propulsion engineer leading the testing. "This speeds up the whole design, development, and testing (10) process, allowing us to try innovative designs with less risk and cost to projects."

7. Which of the following sentences would provide the best transition between the fifth and sixth paragraphs?

A) NO CHANGE
B) Additive manufacturing may have limited practicality now, but Marshall's engineers hope to expand its uses in the near future.
C) Additive manufacturing not only helps engineers create better rocket parts, but also enables them to test faster and more intelligently.
D) Additive manufacturing allows several teams to work together as part of the design process.

8. A) NO CHANGE
B) look at the test data, and to modify
C) to look at the test data, modifying
D) to look at test data, modify

9. Which of the following is the most precise replacement for the underlined word?

A) NO CHANGE
B) implement
C) actualize
D) make good on

10. A) NO CHANGE
B) process allowing
C) process; allowing
D) process: allowing

Marshall engineers have tested increasingly complex injectors, rocket nozzles and other components with the goal of reducing the time and cost of building and assembling future engines. {11}

11. Which of the following, if added, would provide the best conclusion for the passage?

A) Additive manufacturing is a key technology for advancing this goal, and may one day enable missions into deep space.
B) Additive manufacturing is a key technology for enhancing industrial productivity.
C) Who knows what additive manufacturing will let us accomplish in the future?
D) Additive manufacturing may eventually have an impact on NASA's development process.

Practice Passage 9

The Modesty in Women's Clothing in the 1910s.

Modesty, as the word is commonly understood, is a distinctly human invention. While **(1)** you're understanding of the word may involve innocence, or inexperience, or even humility, these are not the case. It means **(2)** to be aware of your appearance and its appropriateness in the presence of the opposite gender.

{3} It is one of the innumerable proofs of our peculiar psychic power to attach emotions to objects without a faintest shadow of real connection. The different levels of modesty vary most strongly not by a person's class or wealth, but by his or her gender.

Men's clothing–hats, shirts, shoes–**(4)** are most modified by physical conditions. On the other hand, the clothing that women wear is most modified by psychic conditions. As **(5)** there usually restricted to a very limited field of activity, and as **(6)** they're personal comfort was of no importance to most people, it was possible to maintain in their dress the influence of primitive conditions long considered inconsequential to men.

Over time, men have grown their scope and responsibilities in our society. We see at once why the dress of men has developed along the line of practical efficiency and general human distinction. As women are given **(7)** fewer roles, and the dress of women is still most modified by the separation of gender. Women's dresses are exactly that: labels for women to wear to seem more feminine.

1. A) NO CHANGE
   B) you are
   C) your
   D) yours

2. A) NO CHANGE
   B) being
   C) you are being
   D) you ought to be

3. Which of the following transitions, if inserted here, would most closely match the author's style and tone?

   A) A most variable thing is this modesty.
   B) Modesty a concept that many people have different opinions on.
   C) Most people agree that a woman should cover her legs when out in public.
   D) Clearly there are cultural differences that determine the suitability of dress.

4. A) NO CHANGE
   B) must be
   C) they are
   D) is

5. A) NO CHANGE
   B) theirs
   C) their
   D) they're

6. A) NO CHANGE
   B) there
   C) their
   D) they are

7. A) NO CHANGE
   B) fewer roles, the
   C) fewer roles, therefore the
   D) fewer roles, this is the reason that the

A man may run in a city's streets in scant clothes—a lack of clothes, even—women would be called grossly immodest wearing the same. He may bathe, publicly, and in company with women, so nearly bare as to shock even himself; while the women beside him are covered far more fully than in evening dress. {8}

Why should it be "modest" for a woman to exhibit her neck, arms, shoulders, and back, but "immodest" to go bathing without stockings? It is because we have attached sentiments of modesty to certain parts of the human frame, and not to **(9)** others—that is all.

These certain parts vary. In certain African tribes, women are forbidden to reveal even part of their faces. The British peasant woman is forced cover her hair, for to show **(10)** it's an indecency.

We need not look for a reason where there never was one. These distinctions sprang from emotion or mere caprice, and vary with them. But whatever our notions of modesty in dress may be, we apply them to women for the most part and not to men. {11}

8. Which of the following facts would contradict the claims made in the previous paragraph?

    A) The rules of public decency have been applied in an unfair way since the beginning of the 20th century.
    B) A woman was arrested for public exposure when she left her house wearing a shirt which exposed her shoulders.
    C) The women's liberation movement has made great strides in achieving equality for women.
    D) A man was arrested for public exposure when he was picnicking with his family and removed his shirt.

9. A) NO CHANGE
    B) other
    C) other's
    D) others'

10. A) NO CHANGE
    B) it is
    C) its'
    D) it

11. Does the final sentence of this preceding paragraph effectively conclude the passage?

    A) No, because it does not address the main question of the passage, the inequalities between men and women.
    B) No, because it is does not address the specific issue discussed in the paragraph.
    C) Yes, because it summarizes the arguments made in the passage.
    D) Yes, because it defines what the rules of modesty should be.

Practice Passage 10

The Measle Resurgence

Today, more than 1 in 20 children nationwide enter kindergarten without the recommended vaccines. The risks of going without vaccinations **(1)** <u>are not isolated to unvaccinated children</u>; as the number of unvaccinated children grows, the potential for disease outbreaks increases dramatically. **(2)** <u>This is proven by facts.</u> In 2000, it appeared that the U.S. had nearly eliminated the measles. Since then, we have experienced numerous troubling outbreaks. In 2008, **(3)** <u>nearly 250 measles cases were confirmed</u> in the U.S., the largest outbreak since 1997. That record was **(4)** <u>beat in 2009 and again in 2010</u>. In 2014, **(5)** <u>more than 800 confirmed measles cases were reported</u>, the highest number in more than 20 years. According to the CDC, the spread of these outbreaks was attributable to "pockets of persons unvaccinated because of philosophical or religious beliefs."

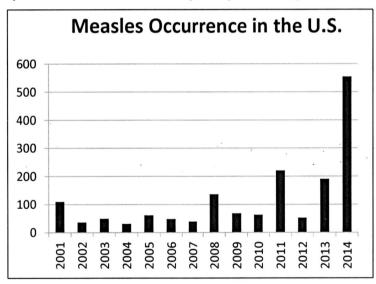

Measles Occurrence in the U.S.

1. A) NO CHANGE
   B) is not isolated to unvaccinated children
   C) are not isolated, to unvaccinated children
   D) were not isolated to unvaccinated children

2. Which of the following best fits the style and tone of the passage?

   A) NO CHANGE
   B) Don't believe it? Check this out.
   C) This is far from mere conjecture.
   D) Recent measles rates have been through the roof.

3. Which choice best completes the sentence with accurate data based on the graph provided?

   A) NO CHANGE
   B) nearly 550 measles cases were confirmed
   C) nearly 140 measles cases were confirmed
   D) nearly 80 measles cases were confirmed

4. Which of the following best fits the data provided on the graph?

   A) NO CHANGE
   B) beat in 2011 and again in 2013
   C) beat in 2010 and again in 2012
   D) beat in 2009 and again in 2013

5. Which choice best completes the sentence with accurate data based on the graph provided?

   A) NO CHANGE
   B) more than 1000 confirmed measles cases were reported
   C) more than 260 confirmed measles cases were reported
   D) more than 550 confirmed measles cases were reported

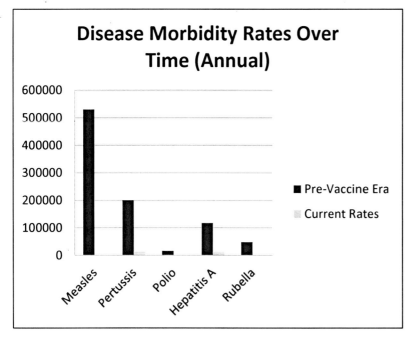

Disease Morbidity Rates Over Time (Annual)

In the decades since vaccines were introduced, millions of lives have been saved. Vaccines are responsible for the elimination of several deadly diseases, including polio. While many other vaccine-preventable diseases have not yet been eliminated, morbidity rates have dropped drastically since the introduction of vaccines. Measles, despite recent outbreaks, **(6)** is a far lesser threat than it once was. Prior to the widespread use of the measles vaccine, **(7)** nearly one hundred thousand people were infected each year. Today, even the most alarming outbreak seems minor by comparison. Pertussis (or whooping cough), another all-but-eliminated disease that has been making a slow resurgence as a result of the anti-vaccine movement, **(8)** once affected more than 700,000 Americans each year. Today that number is just 13,500, a 93% decrease. **(9)**

6. A) NO CHANGE
    B) are a far lesser threat
    C) is far less than a threat
    D) is less than a threat than

7. Which choice best completes the sentence with accurate data based on the graph provided?

    A) NO CHANGE
    B) over one million
    C) more than half a million
    D) almost two hundred thousand

8. Which choice best completes the sentence with accurate data based on the graph provided?

    A) NO CHANGE
    B) once affected approximately 13,500 Americans each year.
    C) once affected 200,000 Americans every year.
    D) once affected more than 550,000 Americans every year.

9. Which of the following, if added to this paragraph, would add additional accurate data to the passage?

    A) Measles has been a greater threat than other diseases such as pertussis.
    B) This has not been the case for other diseases, such as rubella and hepatitis A.
    C) Vaccines have helped reduce measles as well as other diseases.
    D) Other diseases, such as hepatitis A and rubella, have seen similar declines thanks to vaccines.

If vaccines are so important for public health, why are so many parents choosing not to vaccinate their children?

The modern anti-vaccine movement stems, in large part, from a **(10)** paper which was deceitful and improperly vetted, by Andrew Wakefield in 1998. The paper claimed to have found that Measles-Mumps-Rubella (MMR) vaccines contributed to a spike in autism cases between 1988 and 1993. The media seized the story, inciting public fear of the MMR and of vaccines in general. In 2010, the paper was fully retracted after reviews by the CDC, the Institute of Medicine, the UK National Health Service, and others found absolutely no link between vaccines and autism, but by then, the damage had been done.

All efforts to negate the misconception about the link between vaccines and autism have proved ineffective. If public education is **(11)** deficient to address the growing problem of unvaccinated children, perhaps the only alternative is through public policy. In some states, opting out of vaccination requires little more than a onetime signature on a form. Tightening these policies may be considerably more helpful than trying to win the hearts and minds of skeptical parents.

10. A) NO CHANGE
    B) paper from 1998, written by Andrew Wakefield, who was deceitful and improperly vetted
    C) deceitful, improperly vetted paper written by Andrew Wakefield in 1998
    D) paper which was written by Andrew Wakefield, deceptive and improperly vetted, in 1998

11. Which of the following is the most precise replacement for the underlined word?

    A) NO CHANGE
    B) inefficient
    C) defiant
    D) insufficient

Practice Passage 11

The Vietnam War: A Retrospective

Of all America's wars, the conflict in Vietnam **(1)** <u>was</u> perhaps the most controversial. Many protested America's involvement in Southeast Asia, questioning both motive and tactics. **(2)** <u>Whether</u> many dismissed the protestors in the early years of the war, their concerns seem quite prescient when viewed through the lens of retrospection. After all, the Vietnam War ultimately became one of America's deadliest wars **(3)**. The impact of the Vietnam War was so great that, nearly half a century later, historians still debate whether American involvement in Vietnam was justified.

American involvement in Vietnam began with the assassination of South Vietnam's dictator **(4)** <u>Ngo Dinh Diem</u> in 1963. Anarchy swept the country, and John Kennedy's administration sent advisers in an attempt to restore order. North Vietnam, a Communist country under the leadership of dictator Ho Chi Minh, began training southern insurgents, infiltrating the South Vietnamese government, and **(5)** <u>perpetuated propaganda</u> against the U.S. The situation quickly escalated, and Kennedy's successor, Lyndon B. Johnson, reacted by scheduling bombings and committing troops to the conflict. In a speech to the American people, Johnson **(6)** <u>declared</u> that "around the globe, from Berlin to Thailand, are people whose well-being rests, in part, on the belief that they can count on us if they are attacked. To leave Vietnam to **(7)** <u>its</u> fate would shake the confidence of all these people in the value of America's commitment, the value of America's word."

1. A) NO CHANGE
   B) will have been
   C) were
   D) had been

2. A) NO CHANGE
   B) Also,
   C) In addition,
   D) Though

3. Which of the following, if added to the end of the sentence, would best support the sentence's main idea?

   A) , with American soldiers killing almost 1,100,000 North Vietnamese soldiers
   B) , much more deadly than the Korean War
   C) , third only to the American Civil War and World War II in casualties.
   D) , leaving many homeless and disabled veterans at the end of the war

4. A) NO CHANGE
   B) – Ngo Dinh Diem –
   C) (Ngo Dinh Diem)
   D) , Ngo Dinh Diem,

5. A) NO CHANGE
   B) had perpetuated propaganda
   C) perpetuating propaganda
   D) began perpetuating propaganda

6. Within the context of the passage, which of the following is the best replacement for the underlined word?

   A) NO CHANGE.
   B) swore
   C) implied
   D) suggested

7. A) NO CHANGE
   B) it's
   C) their
   D) your

[1] Supporters of the Vietnam War argued that allowing South Vietnam to fall to communist forces would have led to a 'domino effect' in which more and more nations might fall under the yoke of communism. [2] After World War II, they argued, the United States was a moral force in the world, protecting countries that could not protect themselves against the larger menace of communism. [3] Johnson's speech says much to this regard. {8}

{9} Over 47,000 American soldiers died in the conflict, often as a result of being ill-trained to fight in the sweltering jungles of Vietnam against the guerilla tactics of the North Vietnamese. The financial costs were great, as well. {10} Had the United States stayed out of this conflict and allowed South Vietnam to surrender to the North Vietnamese, this could have been a minor passing incident in Southeast Asia's history. After all, once American troops withdrew from Vietnam in 1973, the North soon took over South Vietnam, rendering the conflict pointless. In the end, America can't act as the world's police – often it **(11)** butts in where it is not wanted, and besides, America has problems of its own to address before it starts sending young men five thousand miles away from home to die for an idea.

8. Which of the following sentences should be eliminated in order to improve the focus of the paragraph?

A) Sentence 1
B) Sentence 2
C) Sentence 3
D) NONE OF THE ABOVE

9. Which choice most effectively establishes the main topic of the paragraph?

A) Was this a war that was worth fighting?
B) Others argued that the war was not worth the effort and expense.
C) The expense of the war, both financially and in terms of human life, proved that the conflict was not worth fighting.
D) If you want to see whether the war was worth fighting, look at the expense.

10. Which of the following facts, if added, would best support the previous sentence?

A) The war was enormously unpopular at home.
B) The war cost approximately $111 billion, which by modern standards calculates to $700 billion.
C) None of the soldiers knew what they were getting into.
D) The war was continued by Richard Nixon.

11. A) NO CHANGE
B) interferes
C) goes places
D) pries

Practice Passage 12

The Paradoxes of Zeno of Elea

In the fifth century B.C.E., Zeno of Elea **(1)** had offered arguments that led to conclusions contradicting what we all know from our physical experience – that runners run, that arrows fly, and that there are many different things in the world. These arguments were paradoxes for the ancient Greek philosophers. Since most of the arguments turn crucially on the notion that space and time are infinitely divisible —for example, that for any distance there is such a thing as half that distance, and so on — Zeno was the first person in history to show that the concept of infinity is problematic.

{2} [1] In **(3)** his Achilles Paradox, Achilles races to catch a slower runner – for example, a tortoise that is crawling away from him. [2] Achilles was a mythical Greek hero who was one of the leaders of the Greek forces that invaded the city of Troy. [3] The tortoise has a head start, so if Achilles hopes to overtake it, he must run at least to the place where the tortoise presently is, but by the time he arrives there, it will have crawled to a new place, so then Achilles must run to this new place, but the tortoise meanwhile will have crawled on, and so forth. [4] Because of this, Achilles will never catch the tortoise, says Zeno. [5] Therefore, good reasoning shows that fast runners never can catch slow ones. [6] Zeno argued that this **(4)** invalidated the claim that motion really occurs. {5}

1. A) NO CHANGE
   B) has offered
   C) offered
   D) offers

2. Which choice most effectively establishes the main topic of the paragraph?

   A) According to Zeno, the Achilles Paradox proves that motion does not exist.
   B) Achilles will never catch the tortoise.
   C) Using good reasoning can lead to false conclusions.
   D) Achilles must run to at least to the place where the tortoise is before he can catch up to it.

3. A) NO CHANGE
   B) the
   C) Zenos'
   D) Zeno's

4. Which of the following is the most precise replacement for the underlined word?

   A) NO CHANGE
   B) disproved
   C) neutralized
   D) disqualified

5. Which of the following sentences should be eliminated in order to improve the focus of the passage?

   A) Sentence 1
   B) Sentence 2
   C) Sentence 3
   D) Sentence 4

Although no modern scholar would agree with Zeno's conclusion, one cannot escape the paradox by jumping up from **(6)** your seat and chasing down a tortoise, nor by saying Achilles should run to some other target place ahead of where the tortoise is at the moment. {7}

[1] Although many of Zeno's ideas may seem outlandish, he has had a marked influence on Western thinking. [2] Let's begin with his influence on the ancient Greeks. [3] Zeno also drew new attention to the idea that the way the world appears to us is not how it is in reality. [4] Before Zeno, philosophers expressed their philosophy in **(8)** poetry, and he was the first philosopher to use prose arguments. [5] This new method of presentation **(9)** destined to shape almost all later philosophy, mathematics, and science. [6] Awareness of Zeno's paradoxes made Western intellectuals more aware that **(10)** illusions can be made when thinking about infinity, continuity, and the structure of space and time, and it made them wary of any claim that a continuous magnitude could be made of discrete parts. {11}

6. A) NO CHANGE
   B) our
   C) its
   D) one's

7. Which of the following sentences would provide the best transition into the next paragraph?

   A) Logical paradoxes cannot be addressed so easily because they require irrefutable reasoning to be solved.
   B) Having suitably demonstrated the fallacies in the paradox, Zeno's influence in modernity has greatly diminished.
   C) In the same manner, one cannot deny that simply because his paradoxes have been solved does not mean that Zeno has lacked for influence.
   D) After all, a paradox is by definition unsolvable.

8. A) NO CHANGE
   B) poetry; and
   C) poetry,
   D) poetry and

9. A) NO CHANGE
   B) has been destined
   C) had been destined
   D) was destined

10. Which of the following is the most precise replacement for the underlined word?

    A) NO CHANGE
    B) delusions
    C) corrections
    D) mistakes

11. For the sake of the coherence of this paragraph, sentence 3 should be placed

    A) where it is now.
    B) before sentence 2.
    C) after sentence 5.
    D) after sentence 6.

THIS PAGE IS LEFT INTENTIONALLY BLANK

Writing Practice – Answer Key

Explanations can be found online at http://www.tpgenius.com/

Practice Passage 1	Practice Passage 2	Practice Passage 3	Practice Passage 4	Practice Passage 5	Practice Passage 6
1. C	1. C	1. D	1. B	1. C	1. C
2. A	2. D	2. A	2. D	2. D	2. A
3. C	3. B	3. B	3. B	3. B	3. B
4. C	4. A	4. A	4. C	4. A	4. A
5. B	5. C	5. D	5. D	5. D	5. B
6. B	6. C	6. B	6. A	6. A	6. D
7. A	7. B	7. C	7. A	7. D	7. C
8. A	8. D	8. A	8. D	8. A	8. D
9. D	9. D	9. D	9. B	9. B	9. D
10. C	10. C	10. D	10. C	10. C	10. A
11. D	11. A	11. C	11. A	11. C	11. C

Practice Passage 7	Practice Passage 8	Practice Passage 9	Practice Passage 10	Practice Passage 11	Practice Passage 12
1. C	1. B	1. C	1. A	1. A	1. C
2. A	2. B	2. B	2. C	2. D	2. A
3. B	3. C	3. A	3. C	3. C	3. D
4. A	4. C	4. D	4. B	4. D	4. B
5. D	5. A	5. D	5. D	5. C	5. B
6. C	6. C	6. C	6. A	6. A	6. D
7. D	7. C	7. B	7. C	7. A	7. C
8. B	8. D	8. D	8. C	8. C	8. A
9. B	9. B	9. A	9. D	9. C	9. D
10. D	10. A	10. B	10. C	10. B	10. D
11. C	11. A	11. C	11. D	11. B	11. C

Explanations can be found online at http://www.tpgenius.com/

Section 4
Math

Pre-Algebra Review
Concept & Strategy Lesson

The following reminders, tips, and tricks review many of the topics covered in Pre-Algebra. Carefully read each topic and then try the problems on the next pages for extra practice.

Operations on Integers
- Instead of subtracting two numbers, change the subtraction sign to an addition sign and then change the sign of the second number: $3 - -5 = 3 + +5 = 8$.
- When multiplying or dividing two numbers with the same signs, you will get a positive answer: $-3 \times -2 = 6$.
- When multiplying or dividing two numbers with different signs, you will get a negative answer: $-3 \times 5 = -15$.

Fractions
- To add/subtract fractions, you must have a common denominator. $\frac{2}{3} + -\frac{1}{2} = \frac{4}{6} - \frac{3}{6} = \frac{1}{6}$
- You do not need a common denominator to multiply fractions. $\frac{7}{8} \times -\frac{5}{14} = -\frac{5}{16}$
- To divide one fraction by another, change the division sign to a multiplication sign and then take the reciprocal of the second number: $\frac{3}{4} \div -\frac{2}{3} = \frac{3}{4} \times -\frac{3}{2} = -\frac{9}{8}$.

Decimals
- To change a decimal to a percentage, move the decimal point two places to the left (or multiply it by 100 and add a percent sign): $0.23 = 23\%$.
- To change a percentage to a decimal, move the decimal point two places to the right (or divide it by 100 and remove the percent sign): $372\% = 3.72$.
- To change a fraction into a decimal, divide the denominator into the numerator. $\frac{3}{4} = 0.75$

Percentages
- $\frac{\text{part}}{\text{whole}} \times 100 = \%$
- $\frac{\text{final} - \text{initial}}{\text{initial}} \times 100\% =$ percent increase (positive answer) or percent decrease (negative answer)

Exponents and Radicals
- An exponent is like a repeated multiplication: $g^5 = g \times g \times g \times g \times g$.
- When multiplying exponents, add the powers: $a^2 \times a^3 = a^5$.
- When dividing exponents, subtract the powers: $\frac{b^8}{b^6} = b^2$.
- When raising an exponent to a power, multiply the powers: $(c^5)^7 = c^{35}$.
- $x^1 = x$
- $x^0 = 1$
- $d^{-1} = \frac{1}{d}$

- $\sqrt[5]{x^3} = x^{\left(\frac{3}{5}\right)}$
- $j^m k^m = (jk)^m$

Order of Operations
- **PEMDAS**
  Parentheses
  Exponents
  Multiply / **D**ivide (From left to right)
  Add / **S**ubtract (From left to right)

Absolute Value
- Treat absolute value bars as parentheses for the purpose of PEMDAS
- After performing all of the operations inside the absolute value bars, change the final answer to a positive number. $|5 - 8| = |-3| = 3$

Coordinate Geometry
- The **midpoint** between two points, (x_1, y_1) and (x_2, y_2), can be found by using the midpoint formula: $\left(\frac{x_1 + x_2}{2}, \frac{y_1 + y_2}{2}\right)$.
- The **distance** between two points, (x_1, y_1) and (x_2, y_2), can be found by using the distance formula: $d = \sqrt{(x_2 - x_1)^2 + (y_2 - y_1)^2}$.

Reference Formulas and Information

The following formulas and information will be given to you on the SAT. While you don't necessarily have to memorize this, the more of it you know by heart, the better you will do:

1. The use of a calculator [is / is not] permitted.
2. All variables and expressions used represent real numbers unless otherwise indicated.
3. Figures provided in this test are drawn to scale unless otherwise indicated.
4. All figures lie in a plane unless otherwise indicated.
5. Unless otherwise indicated, the domain of a given function f is the set of real numbers x for which $f(x)$ is a real number.

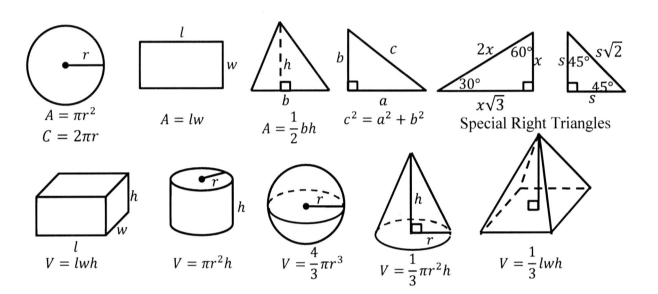

$$A = \pi r^2$$
$$C = 2\pi r$$

$$A = lw$$

$$A = \frac{1}{2}bh$$

$$c^2 = a^2 + b^2$$

Special Right Triangles

$$V = lwh$$

$$V = \pi r^2 h$$

$$V = \frac{4}{3}\pi r^3$$

$$V = \frac{1}{3}\pi r^2 h$$

$$V = \frac{1}{3}lwh$$

The number of degrees of arc in a circle is 360.

The number of radians of arc in a circle is 2π.

The sum of the measures in degrees of the angles of a triangle is 180.

Pre-Algebra Review
Practice Problems

1. The temperature in Lincoln, Nebraska, is currently $-19°F$. If the temperature decreases by another $8°F$ tonight, what will be the temperature be tomorrow?

   A) $-27°F$
   B) $-11\ °F$
   C) $11°F$
   D) $27°F$

2. A grocery store takes a loss of 25 cents every time it sells a gallon of milk. If the grocery store currently is projected to make \$1054.50 before accounting for milk sales, what will its profit be after selling 340 gallons of milk?

   A) $-\$969.50$
   B) $-\$85.00$
   C) \$969.50
   D) \$1139.50

3. Which of the following numbers is closest to $\frac{16}{25}$?

   A) 0.60
   B) 0.65
   C) 0.70
   D) 0.75

4. Before driving to work, Marcel completely filled his 20-gallon fuel tank. On his way to work, Marcel used $\frac{1}{4}$ of his gasoline. On his way home, Marcel used $\frac{1}{3}$ of the remainder of his fuel, then used 2 gallons of gasoline to go to his friend's place and back home. How many gallons of gasoline will Marcel need to buy to re-fuel his tank after returning home?

   A) 7
   B) 8
   C) 10
   D) 12

5. Which of the following numbers is not equal to the other three?

   A) 0.03
   B) $\frac{3}{100}$
   C) 0.03%
   D) 3%

6. After a chemical reaction, the amount of sulfur dioxide in a beaker decreased from 24.6 mg to 12.3 mg. What was the percent decrease in mass of sulfur dioxide in the beaker?

   A) 50%
   B) 100%
   C) 150%
   D) 200%

7. Jonathan wants to leave a 20% tip on the post-tax price of his family's meal. If the meal cost him $80.00 and the sales tax is 8%, how much did Jonathan pay for the meal in all?

   A) $69.12
   B) $88.32
   C) $102.40
   D) $103.68

8. A jacket in a retail clothing store is on sale for 30% off. Because of a coupon, an additional 10% is taken off the sales price of the jacket at the register. If the jacket normally costs j, what is the price of the jacket, in dollars, after both the sale and the coupon are taken into account?

   A) $0.4j$
   B) $0.6j$
   C) $0.63j$
   D) $0.67j$

9. 36.4% of 12.8 is equivalent to 1.28% of

   A) 0.364
   B) 3.64
   C) 36.4
   D) 364

10. The price of a house increases from $125,000 to $150,000. By what percentage did the price of the house increase?

    A) $16\frac{2}{3}\%$
    B) 20%
    C) 25%
    D) $83\frac{1}{3}\%$

11. $(3 \times 10^2)(6 \times 10^3) =$

    A) 1.8×10^5
    B) 1.8×10^6
    C) 18×10^6
    D) 180,000

12. $\frac{(-xy)^5}{x^5 y^5} =$

    A) -1
    B) 0
    C) 1
    D) xy

13. The population of kangaroos in a wildlife preserve is currently 124, and the population increases by 3% each year. Which of the following expressions shows the number of kangaroos after 5 years?

    A) $124(3)^5$
    B) $124(1.3)^5$
    C) $124(1.03)^5$
    D) $124(0.03)^5$

14. The population of kangaroos in another wildlife preserve is currently 86, and the population decreases by 3% each year. Which of the following expressions shows the number of kangaroos after 5 years?

    A) $86(-3)^5$
    B) $86(0.97)^5$
    C) $86(-0.03)^5$
    D) $86(0.7)^5$

15. $3 - \dfrac{6+12 \div 3}{5} - \dfrac{2(3+5)}{4} =$

    A) $-\dfrac{139}{20}$

    B) $-\dfrac{31}{5}$

    C) -3

    D) 1

16. $\left(\dfrac{9}{|2^2-5|}\right)^{(3-6 \div 2)} =$

    A) -27

    B) 0

    C) $\dfrac{1}{27}$

    D) 1

17. $\left(\dfrac{5}{4}\right)^{(3-4)} =$

    A) $-\dfrac{5}{4}$

    B) $-\dfrac{4}{5}$

    C) $\dfrac{4}{5}$

    D) $\dfrac{5}{4}$

18. $\left(\dfrac{3}{4}\right)^{2}\left(\dfrac{4}{5}\right)^{3}\left(\dfrac{5}{3}\right)^{4} =$

    A) $\dfrac{9}{20}$

    B) $\dfrac{12}{25}$

    C) $\dfrac{25}{12}$

    D) $\dfrac{20}{9}$

19. The endpoints of the diameter of a circle are located at $(-3,\ 4)$ and $(0,0)$. At what point is the center of the circle located?

    A) $(-1.5, 2)$

    B) $(3, -4)$

    C) $(-6, 8)$

    D) $(0.5, 2)$

20. The endpoints of the diameter of a circle are located at $(-3,\ 4)$ and $(0,0)$. What is the length of the diameter of the circle?

    A) 0.5

    B) 1.5

    C) 2.5

    D) 5

*Challenge Problem *

21. A line segment has endpoints of $(-12, -5)$ and (a, b) and a length of 13. Which of the following points could be (a, b)?

    A) $(0, 10)$

    B) $(0, -10)$

    C) $(-7, 10)$

    D) $(-7, -10)$

Linear Equations and Inequalities
Concept & Strategy Lesson

Students will be expected to create, solve, and interpret linear expressions in one variable.

Solving Linear Equations
- To solve an equation, you must isolate the variable.
- First, simplify both sides of the equation by using the distributive property, eliminating fractions, combining like terms, and whatever else is necessary.
- To solve a one-variable equation, add or subtract all of your variable terms to one side of the equation and all of your constant terms to the other side.
- When solving an equation, whatever you do to one side of the equation you must do to the other as well.

Solving Linear Inequalities
- Linear inequalities can be solved just like linear equations.
- Whenever you multiply or divide both sides of the inequality by a negative number, you MUST flip the inequality sign (so $<$ becomes $>$, or $\geq$ becomes $\leq$).

Example 1:

$$\frac{3(y-2)+7}{5} = \frac{2-(2-y)}{7}$$

In the equation above, what is the value of y?

A) $-\frac{35}{26}$

B) $-\frac{7}{16}$

C) $\frac{3}{20}$

D) $\frac{7}{16}$

$$\frac{3(y-2)+7}{5} = \frac{2-(2-y)}{7}$$

First, let's use the distributive property to simplify the numerator of each side of our expression.

$$\frac{3y-6+7}{5} = \frac{2-2+y}{7}$$

Next, let's combine like terms.

$$\frac{3y+1}{5} = \frac{y}{7}$$

Next, we'll cross-multiply.

$$7(3y+1) = 5y$$

Now we can simplify and solve.

$$21y+7 = 5y$$

Page 154

$$16y = -7$$
$$y = -\frac{7}{16}$$

The answer is B.

Creating and Interpreting Equations and Inequalities
- Word problems on the Redesigned SAT will focus primarily on real-world situations.
- The SAT will usually tell you which quantity you are solving for and assign it a variable.
- Occasionally, the SAT will ask you to interpret the meaning of part of an equation.
- Always be aware of keywords for addition, subtraction, multiplication, division, equality, and each of the inequality signs.

Algebraic Term	Key Words
+	more than, increased by, greater than, additional, exceeds, sum
−	less than, decreased by, fewer than, difference
×	of, each, product
÷	per, ratio of, for every
=	is, equals, is equivalent to
<	less than, fewer than
>	more than, greater than
≤	at most, no more than, no greater than
≥	at least, no less than, no fewer than

Example 2:

A sheep farmer needs to make at least $115,000 per year to remain profitable. Currently, each of his 2,500 sheep produces enough wool to make him $40 per year. Which of the following inequalities can be solved to find the number of sheep, s, that the sheep farmer needs to acquire to make his farm profitable?

A) $40(2500 - s) \geq 115000$
B) $40(2500 + s) \geq 115000$
C) $40(2500 - s) \leq 115000$
D) $40(2500 + s) \leq 115000$

We know that the farmer must make at least $115,000 this year, so our variable portion of the equation must be greater than or equal to $115,000. We know that he currently has 2,500 sheep and needs to acquire, or increase his amount by, s more. We also know that each of his $(2500 + s)$ sheep makes $40 of wool, so we should multiply these two terms.

$$40(2500 + s) \geq 115000$$

So, our answer is B.

Linear Equations and Inequalities
Practice Problems

$$\frac{3(2-y)+3}{5} = \frac{2(y-3)+2}{3}$$

1. In the equation above, what is the value of y?

   A) $\frac{32}{19}$

   B) $\frac{23}{11}$

   C) $\frac{47}{19}$

   D) $\frac{47}{13}$

$$\frac{1}{2}(5x-2) = \frac{1}{4}(10x-15)$$

2. In the equation above, what is the value of x?

   A) $-\frac{11}{20}$

   B) 0

   C) All real numbers.

   D) No real solution exists.

$$0.85(a-3) - 0.75 = 3.25a$$

3. In the equation above, what is the value of a?

   A) -1.5625

   B) -1.375

   C) -0.9375

   D) 0.9375

$$s = 117 + 2t$$

4. The equation above is used to model the relationship between the number of surfboards, s, rented per day at a beach and the average daily temperature, t, in degrees Fahrenheit. According to the model, what is the meaning of the 2 in the equation?

   A) For every increase of 1°F, two more surfboards will be rented.

   B) For every decrease of 1°F, two more surfboards will be rented.

   C) For every increase of 2°F, one more surfboard will be rented.

   D) For every decrease of 2°F, one more surfboard will be rented.

$$5m - 8(-7m-1) = 8$$

5. In the equation above, what is the value of m?

6. If $3t - 1 > \frac{16}{7}$, then

   A) $t > \frac{3}{7}$

   B) $t > \frac{5}{7}$

   C) $t > \frac{17}{21}$

   D) $t > \frac{23}{21}$

$$\frac{3}{4}u - \frac{1}{2} \geq \frac{1}{3}u$$

7. In the inequality above, which of the following is a possible value of u?

   A) $\frac{1}{2}$
   B) 1
   C) $\frac{11}{10}$
   D) $\frac{3}{2}$

8. If $-5x + 15 \leq -3x - 5$, then

   A) $x \geq -10$
   B) $x \leq -10$
   C) $x \geq 10$
   D) $x \leq 10$

9. If $-3 < 4h + 5 \leq -1$, which of the following is not a possible value of h?

   A) -2.0
   B) -1.9
   C) -1.7
   D) -1.5

10. If $j \geq 3$ and $k \leq -4$, which of the following is a possible value of jk?

   A) -10.5
   B) -11.0
   C) -11.5
   D) -12.0

11. The recommended daily iron intake for a pregnant woman is 27 milligrams (mg). One serving of beef liver contains 5 mg of iron and one serving of white beans contains 8 mg of iron. Which of the following inequalities represents the possible number of servings of beef liver b and servings of white beans w a pregnant woman could eat in a day to meet or exceed the recommended daily iron intake from these foods alone?

   A) $\frac{5}{b} + \frac{8}{w} \geq 27$
   B) $\frac{5}{b} + \frac{8}{w} > 27$
   C) $5b + 8w \geq 27$
   D) $5b + 8w > 27$

12. A hotel owner estimated that the cost C, in dollars, of renting out n rooms for one night is $C = 65n + 750$. The company rents each room for $90 a night. The company makes a profit when total income from renting out rooms is greater than the total cost of renting out the rooms. Which of the following inequalities gives all possible values of n for which the hotel owner estimates that the hotel will make a profit?

   A) $n < 12$
   B) $n < 30$
   C) $n > 12$
   D) $n > 30$

13. A restaurant buffet charges a fee of $1.95 plus 95 cents per pound of food for to-go orders. On top of the cost of the fee and food, a sales tax of 10% is added. Which of the following equations gives the cost, C, of n pounds of food taken to go at the buffet after tax?

A) $C = 0.1(1.95 + 0.95n)$
B) $C = 0.1(1.95 + 95n)$
C) $C = 1.1(1.95 + 0.95n)$
D) $C = 1.1(1.95 + 95n)$

Questions 14 and 15 refer to the following information.

A group of researches predicted that the population of a local group of hedgehogs will increase linearly at a rate of 50 hedgehogs per 10 years. The population at the beginning of 2015 was estimated to be 2,000 hedgehogs.

14. If P represents the population n years after 2015, then which of the following equations represents the researchers' model of the population over time?

A) $P = 2000 + 50\left(\frac{10}{n}\right)$
B) $P = 2000 + 50\left(\frac{n}{10}\right)$
C) $P = 2000 + 50(10n)$
D) $P = 2000 \times \frac{50n}{10}$

15. How many hedgehogs would the group of researchers expect there to be at the beginning of 2030?

A) 2,033
B) 2,075
C) 9,500
D) 150,000

16. The temperature of a freezer, T, must be kept between 26.5°F and 29.5°F, inclusive. Which of the following equations represents all of the possible temperatures of the freezer?

A) $1.5 \geq |28 - T|$
B) $28 \geq |T - 1.5|$
C) $28 \leq |T - 1.5|$
D) $1.5 \leq |28 - T|$

17. To landscape a lawn, Kenji charges a fee of $25 for his equipment and $9.50 per hour spent landscaping. Seth charges a few of $20 for his equipment and $9.75 per hour spent landscaping. If x represents the number of hours spent landscaping, what are all the values of x for which Seth's total charge is greater than Kenji's total charge?

A) $x > 20$
B) $17.5 \leq x \leq 20$
C) $15 \leq x \leq 17.5$
D) $x < 15$

18. The formula $C = \frac{5}{9}(F - 32)$ can be used to convert a temperature from Celsius (C) to Fahrenheit (F). If the Celsius temperature in a chemical reaction increases from $-40°$ to $100°$, how much did the Fahrenheit temperature increase by?

19. Bob works as a carpenter and makes $19 per hour he works. In a typical workday, Bob can build 2 tables per hour. At the end of each week of work, Bob needs to work for 3 hours to do administrative work. If Bob builds 74 tables in one week, how much will he get paid?

20. Monique is visiting Atlanta for the first time and needs to choose between two hotels. The first hotel costs $79.95 per night and charges a one-time untaxed fee of $15.00 on the entire length of the stay. The second hotel costs $85.95 per night and charges a one-time untaxed fee of $35.00. However, Monique has a coupon that gives her 10% off the entire untaxed charge for the second hotel. If Monique needs to say in Atlanta for 4 nights, and chooses the cheaper hotel, how much will she pay before taxes are calculated?

A) $301.32
B) $334.80
C) $355.32
D) $394.80

*Challenge Problem *

21. Monique from the previous problem wants to figure out the number of nights at the hotel, x, for which the untaxed cost of the first hotel in problem 20 is more expensive than the untaxed cost of the second hotel. Which of the following inequalities can be used to model the situation?

A) $15 + 79.95x > 35 + 0.9(85.95x)$
B) $1.10(15 + 79.95x) > 35 + 85.95x$
C) $15 + 79.95x > 0.9(35 + 85.95x)$
D) $15 + 79.95x > 0.1(35 + 85.95x)$

Systems of Linear Equations and Inequalities
Concept & Strategy Lesson

Students will be expected to create, solve, and interpret systems of linear expressions in two variables.

Solving Systems of Linear Equations and Inequalities

- There are three common ways to solve a system of equations: Substitution, Elimination, and Graphing.
- Substitution requires you to solve one of the two equations for a variable, then to plug that variable's value into the second equation. You will use substitution most often.

$$\begin{matrix} 3x - y = 2 \\ y - x = 12 \end{matrix} \rightarrow \begin{matrix} 3x - y = 2 \\ y = x + 12 \end{matrix} \rightarrow 3x - (x + 12) = 2 \rightarrow 2x - 12 = 2 \rightarrow x = 7$$

$$y - (7) = 12 \rightarrow y = 19 \rightarrow \textbf{Solution: } (\textbf{7}, \textbf{19})$$

- Elimination requires you to multiply one of the two equations by a constant (if necessary), then to add the two equations together to eliminate a variable. Elimination is the fastest method when variables are easily eliminated.

$$\begin{matrix} 3x - y = 2 \\ y - x = 12 \end{matrix} \rightarrow 3x - x = 14 \rightarrow x = 7$$

$$3(7) - y = 2 \rightarrow y = 19 \rightarrow \textbf{Solution: } (\textbf{7}, \textbf{19})$$

- Graphing requires you to graph each of the two equations then find the point of intersection of the two lines. Graphing is the most time consuming of the three methods, especially if you do not get to use a calculator, and you should avoid using it if at all possible.

- Sometimes, two equations never intersect. In this situation, the system has no solution. These systems of equations occur when the two lines are parallel, as shown below:

$$3x - 2y = 16$$
$$6x = 4y - 8$$

- Sometimes, two equations overlap each other. In this situation, the system has an infinite number of solutions. These systems of equations occur when both lines are the same line, as shown below:

$$5x - y = 3$$
$$0 = 3y - 15x + 9$$

Example 1:

$$\frac{3}{5}x - uy = 12$$
$$6x - 120 = 10y$$

In the system of linear equations above, u is a constant. If the system has an infinite number of real solutions, what is the value of u?

    A) −10
    B) −1
    C) 1
    D) 10

Since the system of equations has an infinite number of solutions, the two lines must lie on top of each other, or be identical. Line up the terms first:

$$\frac{3}{5}x - uy = 12$$
$$6x - 10y = 120$$

It appears that each term in the bottom equation is 10 times greater than each term in the top equation. So, u must be 1. The answer is C.

Example 2:

A parking lot can admit no more than 300 vehicles each day. The parking lot charges $3.50 for each car it admits and $1.50 for each motorcycle it admits. If the parking lot needs to make at least $900 today, which of the following systems of inequalities can be used to yield the number of cars, c, and motorcycles, m, that can be let in today?

    A) $c + m \geq 300$
         $3.50c + 1.50m \geq 900$
    B) $c + m \leq 300$
         $3.50c + 1.50m \geq 900$
    C) $c + m \geq 900$
         $3.50c + 1.50m \leq 300$
    D) $c + m \leq 900$
         $3.50c + 1.50m \leq 300$

We know that the sum of the number of cars admitted and the number of motorcycles admitted must be less than or equal to 300, while the total charge of each car and motorcycle admitted must be greater than or equal to $900. Our answer must be B.

Page 161

Systems of Linear Equations and Inequalities
Practice Problems

$$x - y = 19$$
$$x - 3y = 12y + 5$$

1. Based on the system of equations above, what is the value of the quotient $\frac{x}{y}$?

A) -20

B) $-\frac{1}{20}$

C) $\frac{1}{20}$

D) 20

$$3x - 6y = -12$$
$$28 - 3y = fx$$

2. In the system of equations above, f is a constant. If the system has no real solutions, what is the value of f?

A) $-\frac{7}{3}$

B) $-\frac{3}{2}$

C) $\frac{3}{2}$

D) $\frac{7}{3}$

$$b > 2a - 4$$
$$a = 3a - 12$$

3. Based on the equation and inequality above, what is a possible value of b?

A) 6

B) 7

C) 8

D) 9

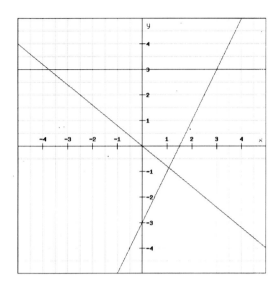

4. A system of three equations and their graphs in the xy-plane are shown above. How many solutions does the system have?

A) 0

B) 1

C) 2

D) 3

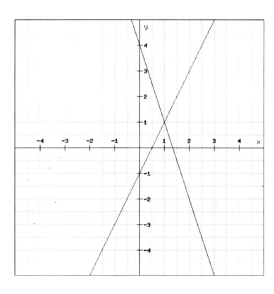

5. Which of the following points is a solution to the system of equations shown above?

   A) $(-1, -1)$
   B) $(-1, 1)$
   C) $(1, -1)$
   D) $(1, 1)$

6. A company sells two different types of math textbooks. The cost, C, of producing n copies of its Algebra book is $C = 12n + 3500$, while the cost of producing n copies of its Chemistry book is $C = 10n + 4000$. If the company wants to split costs evenly between the two books, how many copies of each book should it produce?

   A) 125
   B) 250
   C) 375
   D) 500

7. A local aquarium has two enclosures of otters. One enclosure has 36 members. Every year, one of the members dies, while two are born. The other enclosure has 24 members. Every year, two of the members die, while four are born. After how many years will the two enclosures have the same number of otters?

   A) 6
   B) 12
   C) 18
   D) 48

$$3x - y = 2y - 9$$
$$y - 3 = 2x - 7$$

8. Based on the system of equations above, what is the value of the sum of x and y?

   A) -3
   B) 7
   C) 10
   D) 17

9. If $\frac{1}{2}x + \frac{1}{2}y = 12$ and $2x + 2y = 48$, then $x + y =$

   A) 6
   B) 24
   C) 36
   D) It is impossible to determine.

Questions 10 and 11 refer to the following information.

The toll rates for a new highway are $2.50 for a truck and 75 cents for a car. During a three-hour period, a total of 212 trucks and cars crossed the tollbooth, and the total amount of money collected in tolls was $334.

10. Solving which of the following systems of equations yields the number of cars, c, and the number of trucks, t, that crossed the bridge during the three hours?

    A) $c + t = 334$
       $2.5t + 0.75c = 212$
    B) $c + t = 212$
       $2.5t + 75c = 334$
    C) $c + t = 212$
       $2.5t + 0.75c = 334 \times 2$
    D) $c + t = 212$
       $2.5t + 0.75c = 334$

11. Which of the following ordered pairs, (c, t) is a solution to the correct system of equations in the proceeding problem?

    A) $(22, 312)$
    B) $(100, 112)$
    C) $(112, 100)$
    D) $(312, 22)$

$$\frac{1}{3}x + 9 = -\frac{2}{3}y$$
$$4y = b - 2x$$

12. In the system of linear equations above, b is a constant. If the system has an infinite number of solutions, what is the value of b?

    A) -54
    B) -27
    C) 27
    D) 54

Questions 13 and 14 refer to the following information.

The path of a runner can be modeled by the equation $d = 23t$, where d is his distance traveled, in km, and t is the number of hours he's been running. Another runner, whose path can be modeled by the equation $d = 18t + 3$, begins running at the same time.

13. After how many minutes have the two runners traveled the same distance?

    A) $\frac{3}{5}$
    B) 20
    C) 24
    D) 36

14. How many kilometers did each runner travel after that time?

    A) 6.9
    B) 13.8
    C) 651
    D) 828

15. Jared hires two types of workers in his company; some of those workers get paid $120 per day, while the other workers get paid $160 per day. If Jared has 64 workers on staff today, and he pays out a total of $8840, how many workers did he pay $120 each?

A) 29
B) 32
C) 35
D) 64

16. The price of admission for a concert is $12 for adults and $10 for children. The concert needs to sell more than $1400 worth of tickets to make a profit. If 130 people bought tickets to the concert, which of the following numbers of adult tickets, a, and child tickets, c, could have met the concert's goals?

A) $a = 25, c = 105$
B) $a = 48, c = 82$
C) $a = 50, c = 80$
D) $a = 52, c = 78$

Questions 17 and 18 refer to the following information.

The population, P, of a seal colony can be represented by the equation $P = 12.3t + 340$, where t represents the number of years that have passed since 1990. The population of a neighboring seal colony, P, can be represented by the equation $P = 8.9t + 1360$.

17. In what year will the two colonies have the same population?

A) 300
B) 2290
C) 4030
D) 6020

18. What will be the combined population of the two colonies in that year?

A) 4030
B) 6020
C) 8060
D) 12040

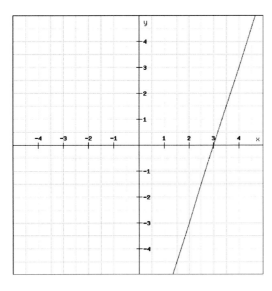

19. A line is graphed in the xy-plane above. At which of the following points, (x, y) does the line above intersect the line $2x = -3y$?

A) $\left(-\frac{27}{11}, -\frac{18}{11}\right)$

B) $\left(\frac{27}{11}, -\frac{18}{11}\right)$

C) $\left(-\frac{27}{11}, \frac{18}{11}\right)$

D) $\left(\frac{27}{11}, \frac{18}{11}\right)$

20. Which of the following lines intersects the line $\frac{3}{5}y - \frac{2}{3}x = 35$ at $(37.5, 100)$?

A) $2x - 2y = 125$

B) $2y = -125 - 2x$

C) $2x = 125 - 2y$

D) $2y - 2x = 125$

Challenge Problem

21. Every day, the temperature in a greenhouse is at its low temperature, 70°F, at 2 a.m. and at its high temperature, 84°F, at 2 p.m. Its temperature increases linearly between 2 a.m. and 2 p.m., and decreases linearly from 2 p.m. to 2 a.m. The outside temperature follows the same linear patterns, but has a low temperature of 60°F at 2 a.m. and a high temperature of 78°F at 2 p.m. At which of the following times will the temperature inside and outside the greenhouse be the same?

A) 8:00 a.m.

B) 12:00 noon

C) 4:00 p.m.

D) The two temperatures will never be the same.

Ratios and Percentages
Concept & Strategy Lesson

Students will use proportional relationships between variables to determine rates and percentages and solve problems.

Solving Ratios, Proportions, Rates, and Scale Drawing Problems

- A ratio is a relationship between two or more values and can generally be written as a fraction:

$$3 \text{ boys for every 5 girls} = 3 \text{ boys} : 5 \text{ girls} = \frac{3 \text{ boys}}{5 \text{ girls}}$$

- Proportions occur when ratios are set equal to each other and can be solved by cross multiplying:

$$\frac{3}{5} = \frac{2}{x} \rightarrow 3x = 10 \rightarrow x = \frac{10}{3}$$

- The most basic rate questions involve the equation below:

$$\text{distance} = \text{rate} \times \text{time}$$

- Rates are used to show a "distance" that happens over a period of time, for example, miles per hour. Note, however, that the distance does not have to be a physical distance. A pay rate, such as dollars per hour, is another common rate.

Example 1:

While Aqucer is working his paper route, he can deliver 48 newspapers per half hour. As he delivers papers, he travels at a rate of 3 miles per hour. If Aqucer starts his day with 720 newspapers, how many miles will he travel to deliver all of them?

A) 22.5
B) 25
C) 45
D) 50

We know that Aqucer starts with 720 papers and delivers 48 every half hour. Let's set up a $d = rt$ equation and solve for time:

$$720 = \left(\frac{48}{0.5}\right)t$$
$$t = 7.5 \text{ hours}$$

Now, we must figure out how many miles he travels in 7.5 hours:

$$d = 3 \times 7.5$$
$$d = 22.5 \text{ miles}$$

The answer is A.

Solving Percentage Problems

- We covered basic percentage rules in Chapter 1 –review them as necessary.
- The most common types of percentage problems on the Redesigned SAT will be word problems.
- **Tax** is a percentage added to the cost of a purchase. To calculate the cost of an item with, for example, a 5% tax, multiply the cost of the purchase by 1.05 – turn the percentage into a decimal, then add it to 1.
- **Commission** is a percentage used in calculating how much money certain salespeople make. For example, a 10% commission means that 10% of a salesperson's sales will be added on to his or her salary.
- If an item is on sale for 20% off, turn 20% into a decimal – 0.20, then subtract that from 1. Then take the difference, 0.80, and multiply it by the price of the item.

Example 2:

Cameron is going to a go-kart track that charges $1.25 per lap plus tax to drive the go-kart. The state's sales tax is 10%, and an additional fee of $6.95 is charged by the track for insurance before tax is applied. Which of the following represents the total charge, in dollars, if Cameron takes c laps around the track?

A) $(1.25 + 0.10c) + 6.95$
B) $1.10(1.25c + 6.95)$
C) $1.10(1.25c) + 6.95$
D) $1.10(6.95 + 1.25)c$

Since we know that Cameron will take c laps around the track and that he is charged $1.25 per lap, his per-lap fee is the product of those two numbers, or $1.25c$. Before tax is added on, we must add the additional fee of $6.95. Then, we can take that entire sum, $1.25c + 6.95$, and multiply it by 1.10 to add on the tax. Our answer is B.

Ratios and Percentages

Practice Problems

1. In 1998, the price of a two-bedroom condominium in Charlotte, North Carolina, was $125,000. In 2008, the price of the condominium was $150,000. In 2013, the price of the condominium decreased by the same percentage that it increased between 1998 and 2008. What was the price of the condominium in 2013?

   A) $120,000
   B) $125,000
   C) $140,000
   D) $180,000

2. In a molecule of sucrose, the atoms carbon, hydrogen, and oxygen appear in the ratio of 12:22:11, respectively, and no other atoms are present. If a lab technician prepares an amount of sucrose that contains 3,600 total atoms, how many hydrogen atoms does it contain?

   A) 880
   B) 960
   C) 1,760
   D) 1,840

3. At Central High School, there are currently 23 teachers and 414 students. The school's principal knows that 180 new students will be added next semester because of a merger with another school and that no students are currently expected to leave the school. How many teachers should the principal hire to keep the student to teacher ratio consistent?

   A) 5
   B) 10
   C) 18
   D) 23

Questions 4 and 5 refer to the following information.

A 10,000 gallon swimming pool is currently one-fourth full. Two hosepipes are being used to fill it: one hosepipe fills the pool at a rate of 6 gallons per minute, while the other fills the pool at a rate of 4 gallons per minute.

4. How long will it take to fill the pool completely?

   A) 4 hours and 10 minutes
   B) 8 hours and 20 minutes
   C) 12 hours and 30 minutes
   D) 16 hours and 40 minutes

5. After some time, the pool develops a leak that causes water to pour out of the pool at a rate of 1 gallon per minute. Approximately how long will it take to fill the pool completely if it currently is half full?

    A) 6 hours and 15 minutes
    B) 7 hours and 30 minutes
    C) 9 hours and 15 minutes
    D) 11 hours

6. A map of a subway system is set up so that every mile of the subway's route is equivalent to 8 inches on the map. Which of the following equations could be used to find the length of a route in miles, x, that is 15 inches long on the map?

    A) $\frac{1}{8} = \frac{15}{x}$
    B) $\frac{8}{1} = \frac{x}{15}$
    C) $8 = 15x$
    D) $\frac{1}{8} = \frac{x}{15}$

7. A 30-ounce solution of water and vinegar is currently 10% vinegar. How many ounces of vinegar need to be added to the solution so that is becomes 20% vinegar?

    A) 3
    B) 3.25
    C) 3.5
    D) 3.75

8. Two students, Jon and Rob, are working together to finish a science project. If Jon can finish the project alone in j hours and Rob can finish the project alone in r hours, how long will it take them to finish the project working together, in terms of r and j?

    A) $\frac{1}{r+j}$
    B) $r + j$
    C) $\frac{r+j}{rj}$
    D) $\frac{rj}{r+j}$

9. A furniture factory has recently developed a process that lets the factory improve the rate at which it can produce couches. Previously, the factory could produce 300 couches per hour; however, the new process improves that rate by 12%. How many more couches can the factory produce in a 12-hour shift at the new rate as opposed to the old rate?

    A) 96
    B) 336
    C) 432
    D) 4032

10. A barbeque restaurant charges $12.25 per pound for its smoked beef and 25 cents each for buns. The state's food sales tax is 6%. Which of the following represents the total charge, in dollars, to order y pounds of smoked beef and z buns?

    A) $1.06(12.25y + 25z)$
    B) $1.06(12.25y + 0.25z)$
    C) $1.06(12.25y) + 0.25z$
    D) $1.06(12.25y) + 25z$

11. Kerrie's gross monthly income is $1,600. If 14% is withheld for income taxes, 8% is withheld for Social Security, and 3% is withheld for her health insurance, what is her net monthly income after deducting these expenses?

A) $400
B) $800
C) $1,200
D) $2,000

12. Siwon invests $35,000 in a savings account that pays 2.5% annual interest. How much money will he have in his account after two years?

A) $36,750.00
B) $36,771.88
C) $175,000.00
D) $218,750.00

13. Rei is building a model ship on the scale ratio of 1:27. The real life ship is 162 feet long. After building his model, Rei decided to build another model on the scale ratio of 1:18. How much longer is his second ship than his first one?

A) 3 feet
B) 6 feet
C) 9 feet
D) 156 feet

14. Whitney bought 100 television sets from a wholesale dealer for $125 each, and she wishes to resell them in her furniture store. She wishes to sell each television set for 10% more than she paid for it, pocketing the difference as profit. Unfortunately, one of her employees dropped 10 of the televisions, rendering them unsellable. If Whitney wants to sell the remaining television sets at a price that will make her at least the same amount of profit she would have originally gotten, what should the price of each television set be?

A) $123.75
B) $137.50
C) $138.89
D) $152.78

15. Which of the following numbers is not equivalent to the other three?

A) The ratio of 3 to 800
B) 0.375%
C) $\frac{0.3}{8}$
D) 0.00375

16. While Anna is working as a chef, she can prepare 16 first-class meals per hour while working alone. The number of first-class meals that she can prepare per hour increases by 4 for every assistant she has helping her. If Anna works for 5 hours with one assistant and the last 3 hours with two more assistants, how many first-class meals can she prepare?

A) 148
B) 160
C) 172
D) 184

Questions 17 and 18 refer to the following information.

$$\text{Percent Yield} = \frac{\text{Actual Yield}}{\text{Theoretical Yield}} \times 100\%$$

17. The percent yield of a chemical reaction can be calculated using the formula above. If the percent yield of a reaction is 88%, and 76 grams of the product were actually produced, how many grams of product were expected to be produced?

A) 66.88
B) 86.37
C) 88
D) 115.79

18. A new laboratory technique increases the actual yield of a chemical reaction from 68 to 83 grams. If the original theoretical yield was 90 grams, by how many percentage points did the percent yield increase?

A) 6%
B) 15%
C) 16.67%
D) 30.32%

Questions 19 and 20 refer to the following information.

Ben charges $36.00 per hour for his tutoring service. He only takes customers in whole-number hour increments. In addition, if a customer purchases more than 40 hours, all of the hours after 40 are 25% cheaper.

19. If a customer purchases $h > 40$ hours of tutoring, which of the following represents the total cost to the customer in terms of h?

A) $0.75(36)(40) + 0.75(36)(h - 40)$
B) $36(40) + 0.75(36)(h)$
C) $36(40) + 0.75(36)(h - 40)$
D) $0.75(36)(h)$

20. A customer purchases 50 hours of tutoring, and also has a coupon for 10% off the entire cost. How much will this customer pay for 50 hours of tutoring?

A) $1215
B) $1539
C) $1900
D) $2511

Challenge Problem

21. A merchant normally tickets an item at x dollars, but the store always offers a 20% discount on the ticketed price of each item. Today, there is a sale that offers another 20% off that price. What percent of the ticketed price is today's price of the item?

   A) 36%
   B) 40%
   C) 60%
   D) 64%

Unit Conversions
Concept & Strategy Lesson

Students will use unit rates and unit conversions to solve multistep problems; students will calculate density and use density to solve multistep problems.

Unit Conversion Problems

- The easiest way to convert one unit to another unit is to use a table like the one below.

- Put your initial term in the top left corner. Then place unit conversions in subsequent columns in such a way that units cross out. Look at the example below:

Example 1:

A 30,000 gallon pool is being drained at a rate of 12 gallons per minute. However, due to city sewage ordinances, pools can only be drained for 4 hours per day. How much water will be left in the pool after 1 week of draining?

A) 2,880 gallons
B) 9,840 gallons
C) 20,160 gallons
D) 27,120 gallons

We'll start off by setting up our chart. We're starting at a rate of 12 gallons per minute, so put that in the left-hand column.

$$\frac{12 \text{ gallons}}{1 \text{ minute}}$$

We know that there are 60 minutes in an hour, 4 hours of draining available per day, and 7 days in a week.

At this point, minutes, hours, and days all cancel out, and we're left with a unit of gallons per week. Multiply across the top, then divide by each number on the bottom, and we'll have our rate. After 1 week, 20,160 gallons of water are drained. Since we're asked how much water will be left in the pool after 1 week, we must subtract this number from 30,000 gallons. Our answer is B.

Density Problems

- The density of a substance is its mass per unit volume.
- The formula to find density, ρ, is $\rho = \frac{m}{V}$.
- Density problems can most easily be solved using a combination of the formula and the table above.

Unit Conversions
Practice Problems

1. The density of an iron ingot is 7.87 grams per cubic centimeter. What is the mass, in kg, of an iron ingot with a volume of 3 cubic meters?

   A) 2.361
   B) 23.61
   C) 2,361
   D) 23,610

2. The ideal gas law, $PV = nRT$, relates the pressure (P in atm), volume, (V in L), amount of substance (n in moles), and temperature (T in Kelvin) of a substance. R is a constant. In order for the units of both sides of the ideal gas law equation to balance, what must be units of R?

   A) $atm \cdot L \cdot K \cdot mol$
   B) $\dfrac{atm \cdot L}{K \cdot mol}$
   C) $\dfrac{K \cdot mol}{atm \cdot L}$
   D) $\dfrac{1}{atm \cdot L \cdot K \cdot mol}$

3. The acceleration of an object can be found by dividing the change in velocity of an object by the time it takes for that change to occur. The velocity of an object increases from 32 m/s to 45 m/s over the course of 26 seconds. What is the acceleration of that object to the nearest hundredth of a km/min²?

   A) 0.03
   B) 0.3
   C) 0.5
   D) 1.8

$$V_{Au} = \frac{M_j \times \frac{kt}{24}}{19.32}$$

4. To find the volume of pure gold in a piece of gold jewelry, jewelers use the above formula, where V_{Au} is the volume of gold present, in mL, M_j is the total mass of the piece of jewelry in grams, and kt is the carat purity of the jewelry. To the nearest hundredth of a mL, what is the volume of pure gold present in a 22-carat golden ring that weighs 3.8 grams?

   A) 0.18
   B) 7.19
   C) 67.30
   D) 80.09

5. The gas mileage for Eugene's snowmobile is 32 miles per gallon when the snowmobile travels an average speed of 40 miles per hour. The snowmobile's gas tank has 15 gallons of gas at the beginning of the trip. If Eugene's snowmobile travels at an average speed of 40 miles per hour, which of the following functions f models the number of gallons of gas remaining in the tank t hours after the trip begins?

   A) $15 - \dfrac{4}{5t}$
   B) $15 - \dfrac{5t}{4}$
   C) $\dfrac{15 - 32t}{40}$
   D) $\dfrac{15 - 40t}{32}$

6. A typical photograph taken of a comet is 6.8 gigabits in size. A satellite near Earth can receive the data from the photograph at a data rate of 2.5 megabits per second for a maximum of 16 hours each day. If 1 gigabit equals 1,024 megabits, what is the maximum number of typical images that the tracking station could receive from the camera each day?

A) 1
B) 2
C) 20
D) 21

7. An online flooring company sells wood flooring by the box. Each box holds 34.69 square feet of flooring, and each box costs $155.11. If Jan and Kim need to refinish their 20 × 18 square foot living room with wood flooring, how much will they pay?

A) $80.51
B) $1494.66
C) $1609.67
D) $1706.21

8. The battery life of a popular cell phone decreases from 100% to 45% in 165 minutes of use. If the phone's battery drains at that rate over the course of a day, how long will it take the battery to go from 100% to 0%, to the nearest second?

A) 300 s
B) 5,445 s
C) 15,231 s
D) 18,000 s

9. The length of a marathon is approximately 26.2 miles. Rachelle wishes to run a marathon; however, she knows her pace for the first half of the length of the marathon will be slightly faster than her pace for the second half. If her pace for the first half of the marathon is 8 minutes per mile, and her pace for the second half is 20% slower than that, how long will it take her to finish the marathon, to the nearest minute?

A) 3 hours and 9 minutes
B) 3 hours and 30 minutes
C) 3 hours and 51 minutes
D) 4 hours and 3 minutes

10. The acceleration due to gravity on Earth is approximately 32.2 feet per second squared. The acceleration due to gravity on the moon is approximately one-sixth of that value. What is the acceleration due to gravity on the moon, to the nearest hundredth, in miles per minute squared? (There are 5280 feet in 1 mile.)

A) 3.66
B) 5.37
C) 131.73
D) 283.36

11. Mark and Ashley are building a 30 foot by 60 foot garden in their back yard. They set off 40 square yards of their garden's area for each different crop they are growing. How many different crops can they grow in their garden?

    A) 5
    B) 15
    C) 45
    D) 50

12. Mark and Ashley from the previous problem decide to put a border that is 1-foot wide around their garden. What is the area of this border, in square yards?

    A) $20\frac{4}{9}$
    B) $61\frac{1}{3}$
    C) $62\frac{2}{3}$
    D) $661\frac{1}{3}$

13. A 600-gallon septic tank is being drained at a rate of 2 gallons per minute by a septic tank service company. However, after every hour of work, the draining pump needs to be turned off for 10 minutes so that it can cool. If the company charges $50 per hour for service (including cool-off times), and always rounds up to the nearest hour, how much money will it cost to drain the septic tank?

    A) $200
    B) $250
    C) $300
    D) $350

14. The gas mileage for Jorge's van is 18 miles per gallon when the van travels an average speed of 45 miles per hour. The van's gas tank holds 20 gallons of gas and is half full at the beginning of the trip. If Jorge's van travels at an average speed of 45 miles per hour, how long will it take Jorge to run out of gas, to the nearest hour?

    A) 2
    B) 4
    C) 6
    D) 8

15. An item will generally float in a liquid if the item's density is less than the liquid's density. Which of the following items will float in ethanol (Density = 789 kg/m³)?

    A) A block of wood with mass of 155 grams and volume of 170 cm³
    B) A block of wood with mass of 55 grams and volume of 60 cm³
    C) A block of wood with mass of 85 grams and volume of 110 cm³
    D) A block of wood with mass of 65 grams and volume of 80 cm³

16. The running track around a school's football field is one-fourth of a mile long. Marcellus is practicing for a 5 km race and wants to figure out how many laps he needs to run. If 1 mile is equivalent to approximately 1.61 km, which of the following is closest to the number of laps that he needs to run?

A) 11.5
B) 12
C) 12.5
D) 13

17. If Marcellus from the previous problem can run one half of a mile in 126 seconds and wants to keep that pace through the entire 5 km run, approximately how long will the run take him?

A) 12.5 minutes
B) 13 minutes
C) 13.5 minutes
D) 14 minutes

18. When downloading files, Johnson can obtain data at a speed of 32.4 MB per second, while his upload speed is only 9.9 MB per second. If there are 1024 MB in a GB, how much longer will it take Johnson to upload a 3.2 GB file than it takes for him to download it?

A) 101.1 seconds
B) 145.6 seconds
C) 229.9 seconds
D) 331 seconds

19. Johnson signs up for a new Internet provider that has download speeds that are 50% faster than his previous provider's. How big of a file can he download in the same time that it took him to download the 3.2 GB file before?

A) 2.13 GB
B) 4.8 GB
C) 21.6 GB
D) 48.6 GB

20. A propane barbeque grill has a 6-gallon tank and uses propane at a rate of 4 ounces per minute. If it takes 45 minutes to cook 6 steaks and 25 minutes to cook 10 hamburgers, how much propane will be left after cooking 12 steaks and 30 hamburgers? (Note: there are 128 ounces in 1 gallon.)

A) 28
B) 48
C) 68
D) 108

Challenge Problem

A cellphone service provider offers the following monthly service plan:

$50 for the first GB of data
2.5 cents for each 16 MB between the first GB and the second GB
4.5 cents for each 8 MB after the second GB

21. If there are 1024 MB in a GB, how much will it cost to use 2.5 GB of data in one month?

    A) $51.14
    B) $54.48
    C) $94.80
    D) $498.00

Graphs of Equations
Concept & Strategy Lesson

Students must be able to make connections between the graphical representation of a relationship and properties of that graph, use a graph to identify a value or set of values, and determine what type of model best fits the connection between two variables.

Graphing Linear Equations

- The **slope**, m, of an equation represents the rate at which the y-values of the equation change as the x-values change.

- Given two points, (x_1, y_1) and (x_2, y_2), of a linear equation, the slope, or change in rise divided by change in run, of the equation can be found by the equation $m = \frac{\text{rise}}{\text{run}} = \frac{y_2 - y_1}{x_2 - x_1}$.

- The **y-intercept**, b, of an equation represents the initial point of the equation: the value of y when x equals 0.

- You can obtain the equation of a linear graph when you have either two of the points that lie on that line, or one of the points and the line's y-intercept.

- Use the equation $y = mx + b$, where m is the slope of the linear equation and b is its y-intercept, when you are given both the slope and the y-intercept of the line.

- Use the equation $y - y_1 = m(x - x_1)$ when you are given both the slope and a single point on the line.

Example 1:

If k is a positive constant different from 1, which of the following could be the graph of $x - y = \frac{x-y}{k}$ in the xy-plane?

A)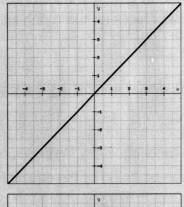

B)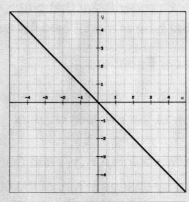

C)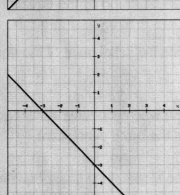

D)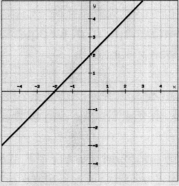

To solve this problem, we should first simplify the equation given:

$$x - y = \frac{x - y}{k}$$
$$k(x - y) = x - y$$
$$kx - ky = x - y$$
$$kx - x = ky - y$$
$$x(k - 1) = y(k - 1)$$
$$x = y$$

Since the $k - 1$ terms cancel out, we're left with $y = x$. The slope of the equation is 1 and its y-intercept is 0. Thus, our answer must be A.

Graphing Quadratic and Exponential Equations

- The highest term of a quadratic equation is x^2. The graphs of these functions are symmetric – thus, they increase and then decrease, or decrease and then increase, as shown below:

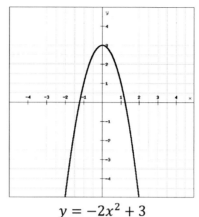

$$y = -2x^2 + 3$$

- The most common scenario modeled by a quadratic equation is projectile motion.
- Exponential equations are of the form $a \cdot b^x$, where a and b are both nonzero numbers. As a rule, exponential equations increase or decrease across their entire ranges. The rate of increase (or decrease) starts slowly at the beginning, then gets gradually larger over time.

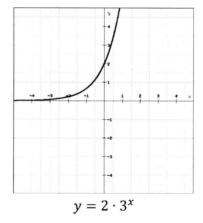

$$y = 2 \cdot 3^x$$

- Exponential equations usually model situations that involve continuous increases or decreases over time, such as a changing population or the amount of money in a bank account that is accruing interest.

Example 2:

An object is launched at a velocity of 7.9 m/s from a height of 2.4 m above the surface. The height of the object, $f(t)$, at time t can best be modeled by which of the following types of equations?

A) Linear
B) Quadratic
C) Exponential
D) None of the above

Since the situation deals with an object being launched, we know it must go up, then back down due to the effects of gravity. Projectile motion is best modeled by a quadratic equation, so our answer is B.

Graphs of Equations
Practice Problems

1. Line l is graphed in the xy-plane below.

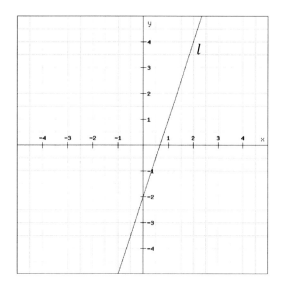

If line l is translated up 3 units and left 4 units, then what is the slope of the new line?

A) -3
B) -2
C) $\frac{6}{5}$
D) 3

Questions 2 and 3 refer to the following information.

The mean number of students per faculty member, y, at a university can be estimated using the equation $y = 0.13x + 13.6$, where x represents the number of years since 2005 and $0 \le x \le 10$.

2. Which of the following statements is the best interpretation of the number 0.13 in the context of this problem?

A) The estimated mean number of students per faculty member in 2005
B) The estimated mean number of students per faculty member in 2015
C) The estimated yearly decrease in the mean number of students per faculty member
D) The estimated yearly increase in the mean number of students per faculty member

3. Which of the following statements is the best interpretation of the number 13.6 in the context of this problem?

A) The estimated mean number of students per faculty member in 2005
B) The estimated mean number of students per faculty member in 2015
C) The estimated yearly decrease in the mean number of students per faculty member
D) The estimated yearly increase in the mean number of students per faculty member

4. Which of the following is the graph of $\frac{1}{2}x - \frac{1}{3}y = -\frac{1}{4}$ in the xy-coordinate plane?

A)

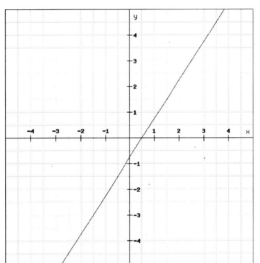

B)

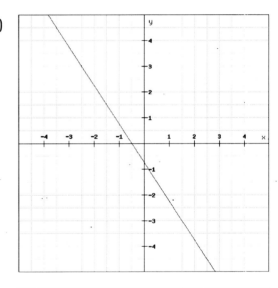

C)

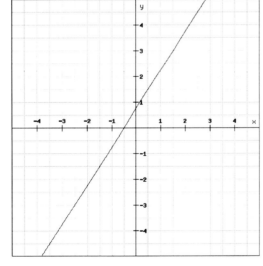

D)

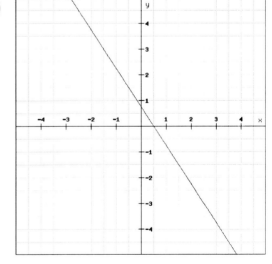

5. The population of an Asian nation doubles every 34 years, starting in 1900. The population of the nation, $p(t)$, t years after 1900, can best be modeled by which of the following types of equations?

A) Linear
B) Quadratic
C) Exponential
D) None of the above

6. Line l has the equation $3x - 2y = -12$ in the xy-plane. If line l is translated down 1 units and right 2 units, then what is the y-intercept of the new line?

A) 2
B) 3
C) 4
D) 5

7. Which of the following lines has the same slope, when graphed in the xy-plane, as the graph of $\frac{3-x}{2} = -\frac{1}{3}y$?

A) $y = -\frac{3}{2}x - 9$
B) $y = \frac{3}{2}x - 9$
C) $y = -\frac{2}{3}x - 9$
D) $y = \frac{2}{3}x - 9$

8. The graph of which of the following equations does not have a line of symmetry?

A) $y = 3x + 2$
B) $y = 3x^2 + 2$
C) $y = -3x^2 - 2$
D) $y = 3^x + 2$

9. If k is a positive constant greater than 1, which of the following could be the graph of $y + x = k(x - y)$ in the xy-plane?

A)

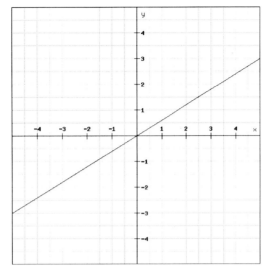

B)

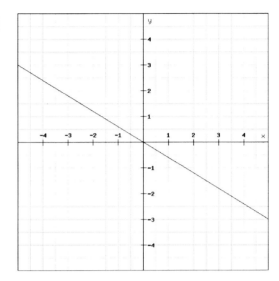

C)

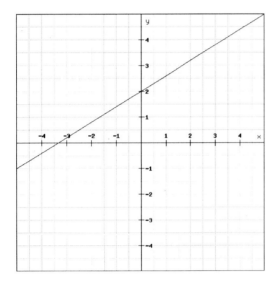

D)

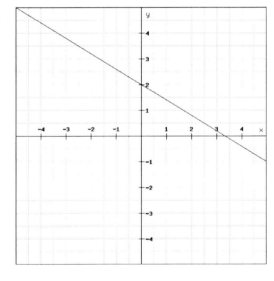

10. Which of the following lines contains the points $(-3, 2)$ and $(-5, 6)$?

A) $y = 3x + 11$
B) $y = -4x - 14$
C) $y = -3x - 7$
D) $y = -2x - 4$

11. A deep-sea diver is exploring the sunken ruins of an ocean liner. When he dives to a depth of 350 feet below the surface, the pressure is 170.2 psi. As the diver descends, the pressure increases linearly. At a depth of 500 feet, the pressure is 236.9 psi. If the pressure increases at a constant rate as the scientist's depth below the surface increases, which of the following linear models best describes the pressure p in psi at a depth of d feet below the surface?

A) $p = 0.44d + 0.92$
B) $p = 0.44d + 16.2$
C) $p = 2.2d - 1.1$
D) $p = 2.2d - 600$

Questions 12 and 13 refer to the following information.

The mean age of the population of India, y, can be estimated using the equation $y = 0.03x + 27.6$, where x represents the number of years since 1990 and $x > 0$.

12. What would be the estimated mean age of the population of India in 1980?

A) 27.3
B) 27.6
C) 27.9
D) It is unable to be determined

13. Which of the following statements is the best interpretation of the number 27.6 in the context of this problem?

A) The estimated mean age of the population of India in 1990
B) The estimated mean age of the population of India after 1990
C) The estimated yearly decrease in the mean age of the population of India
D) The estimated yearly increase in the mean age of the population of India

14. A newborn calf weighs 65 pounds when it is born and gains 72 pounds per month until it reaches 9 months of age. After that point, the rate of linear growth of the mass of the calf slows to 34 pounds per month. Which of the following sets of equations can be used to model the calf's mass, m, for the time n months after its birth?

A) $m = \begin{cases} 72 + 65n & \text{if } 1 \leq n \leq 9 \\ 657 + 34n & \text{if } n > 9 \end{cases}$

B) $m = \begin{cases} 72 + 65n & \text{if } 0 \leq n \leq 9 \\ 657 + 34n & \text{if } n > 9 \end{cases}$

C) $m = \begin{cases} 65 + 72n & \text{if } 1 \leq n \leq 9 \\ 713 + 34n & \text{if } n > 9 \end{cases}$

D) $m = \begin{cases} 65 + 72n & \text{if } 0 \leq n \leq 9 \\ 713 + 34n & \text{if } n > 9 \end{cases}$

15. Which of the following lines does not intersect the line $-\frac{2}{3}y = -\frac{3}{4}x + 16$?

A) $y = -\frac{8}{9}x + 8$
B) $y = -\frac{9}{8}x - 12$
C) $y = \frac{8}{9}x + 9$
D) $y = \frac{9}{8}x + 7$

16. For all values of $k \neq 0$, which of the following lines is perpendicular to $ky = -x - 3$?

A) $y = -\frac{1}{k}x + \frac{1}{3}$

B) $y = \frac{1}{k}x - \frac{1}{3}$

C) $y = -kx - \frac{1}{3}$

D) $y = kx + \frac{1}{3}$

Questions 17 and 18 refer to the following information.

A mountain climber is climbing Mt. Everest. When she is 10,000 feet up the mountain, the pressure is 69.7 kPa. As the climber ascends, the pressure decreases linearly. As she approaches the summit, the pressure is 37.6 kPa at 25,000 feet.

17. If the pressure decreases at a constant rate as the scientist's height above the surface increases, which of the following linear models best describes the pressure p in kPa at a height of h feet above the surface?

A) $p = -467.29h + 7429.9$

B) $p = -467.29h + 22570.1$

C) $p = -0.00214h - 15.9$

D) $p = -0.00214h + 91.1$

18. The height of Mt. Everest is approximately 29,000 feet. What is the approximate pressure at this height?

A) 19 kPa

B) 29 kPa

C) 79 kPa

D) 99 kPa

Questions 19 and 20 refer to the graph of line *l* below.

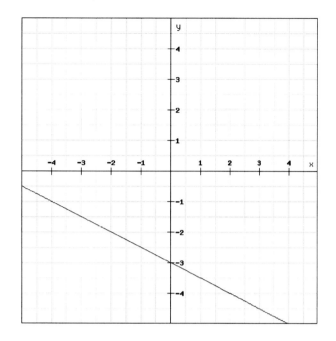

19. What is the sum of the x- and y-intercepts of the graph of the linear function above?

    A) -18
    B) -9
    C) 3
    D) 9

20. Line k is perpendicular to line l and intersects it at the point $(-2, -2)$. Which of the following is the equation of line k?

    A) $y = 2x - 2$
    B) $y = 2x + 2$
    C) $y = -2x + 6$
    D) $y = -2x - 6$

Challenge Problem

21. The pressure, in psi, below the surface of the ocean increases linearly as the depth, in meters, increases. If the pressure at 1000 m below the surface is $1.16 \frac{\text{kg}}{\text{cm}^2}$, which of the following equations could model the pressure, p, in terms of the depth, d?

    A) $p = 0.44d + 16.2$
    B) $p = 0.00014d + 1.02$
    C) $p = -0.44d + 441.16$
    D) $p = -0.00014d + 1.3$

Scatterplots
Concept & Strategy Lesson

Students will be given scatterplots and be asked to select the equation of the line or curve of best fit, interpret the line in the context of the situation, and use the line or curve to make predictions.

Scatterplots

- A scatterplot shows the relationship between two sets of value. Look at the example below:

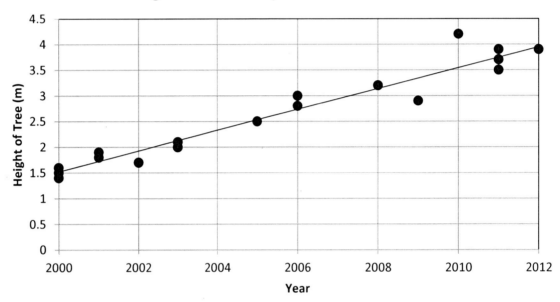

Height of Randomly Selected Pine Trees

- The x-axis shows the year, while the y-axis shows the height of a randomly selected pine tree.
- Always check the title of each axis for the units that it measures.
- The line of best fit shown above shows the general trend of how the height of a random pine tree changes with respect to the year.
- Most of the lines of best fit on the Redesigned SAT will be linear, though you will see the occasional quadratic or exponential line of best fit as well.
- Some scatterplot questions will ask you to match the equation of the line of best fit to one of four choices.
- To find the equation of a linear line of best fit, find the slope of the line first by selecting two points on the line and using the slope formula, $m = \frac{y_2 - y_1}{x_2 - x_1}$. Then plug the slope and one of those two points into the point-slope formula, $y - y_1 = m(x - x_1)$.
- For non-linear lines of best fit, it is easier to plug points from the line into the four equations given until you get one that works. You generally will not have time to find the equation by any other means.

- To predict another data point that is not given, you should expand the line of best fit to points beyond those given. If the line of best fit is linear, plug the point (x or y) into the line of best fit that you have found.

Example 1:

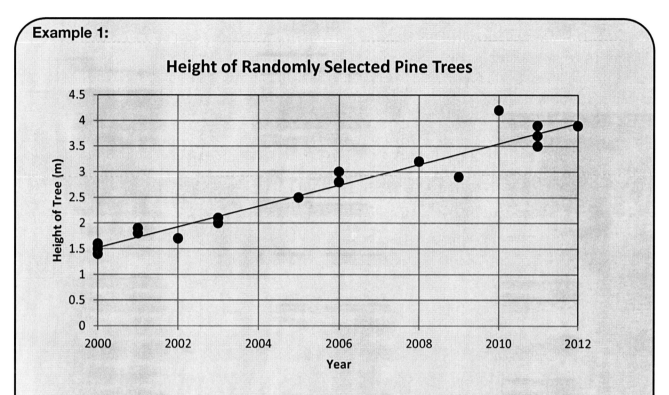

The scatterplot above shows heights of randomly selected pine trees from a commercial pine tree farm in Georgia. Based on the line of best fit to the data shown, which of the following values is closest to the average yearly increase in the height of a randomly selected pine tree from this farm?

A) 0.15 feet
B) 0.30 feet
C) 0.60 feet
D) 1.20 feet

To solve this question, we need to understand what "average yearly increase in the height of a randomly selected pine tree from this farm" means. We need to use the line of best fit to figure out how much the height increases per year. In this case, the numbers seem easy to estimate: In 2000, the height seems to be approximately 1.6 feet; in 2002, the height is approximately 1.9. So, we have an increase in 0.3 feet over the span of 2 years. Thus, our yearly increase is 0.15 feet; the answer is A.

Scatterplots
Practice Problems

Questions 1 – 3 refer to the following information.

Armspan is the physical measurement of the length from one of an individual's arms (measured at the fingertips) to the other end when raised parallel to the ground at shoulder height. The scatterplot below shows the relationship between the height and armspan of 9 people. The line of best fit is also shown.

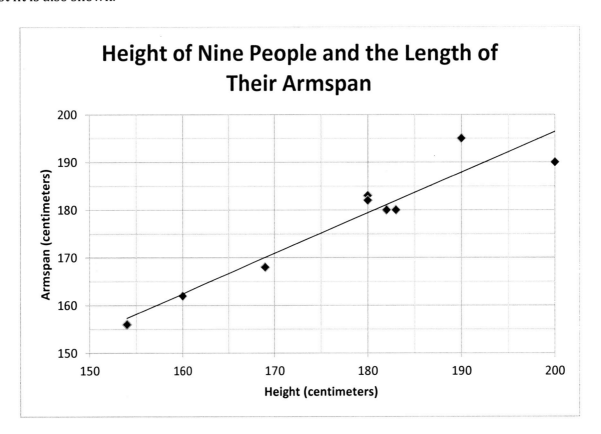

1. How many of the nine people have an actual height that differs by more than 5 centimeters from the height predicted by the line of best fit?

   A) 0
   B) 1
   C) 2
   D) 3

2. Which of the following is the best interpretation of the slope of the line of best fit in the context of this problem?

   A) The predicted length of armspan increase in centimeters for every centimeter increase in height.
   B) The predicted height increase in centimeters for every centimeter increase in length of armspan.
   C) The predicted height in centimeters of a person with a length of armspan of 0 centimeters.
   D) The predicted length of armspan in centimeters of a person with a height of 0 centimeters.

3. Based on the line of best fit, what is the predicted length of armspan for someone with a height of 185 centimeters?

   A) 180 centimeters
   B) 183.5 centimeters
   C) 187 centimeters
   D) 192.5 centimeters

Questions 4 – 6 refer to the following information.

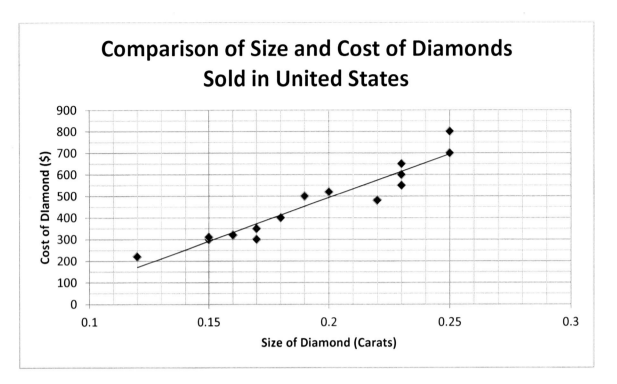

4. Which of the following equations is the line of best fit of the data shown above?

    A) $y = 4000x - 300$
    B) $y = 4000x + 50$
    C) $y = \frac{1}{4000}x - 300$
    D) $y = \frac{1}{4000}x + 50$

5. Based on the line of best fit, what is the predicted cost of a 0.1 carat diamond?

    A) $50
    B) $100
    C) $450
    D) $3700

6. Based on the line of best fit, a diamond that costs $1500 would be how many carats?

    A) 0.36
    B) 0.40
    C) 0.45
    D) 0.75

Questions 7 – 9 refer to the following information.

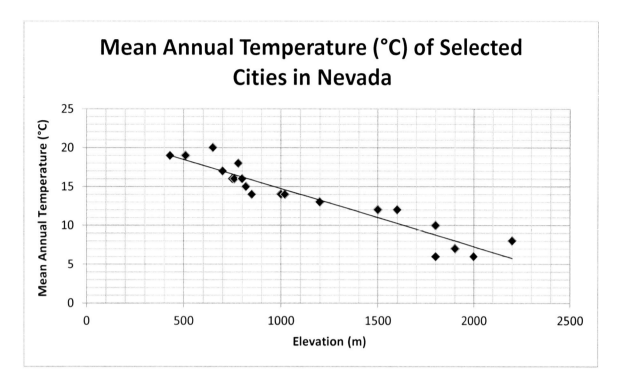

7. Based on the line of best fit to the data shown above, what type of correlation exists between the mean annual temperature of a city in Nevada and its elevation?

A) Positive
B) Negative
C) Exponential
D) No correlation exists

8. Which of the following is the best interpretation of the slope of the line of best fit in the context of this problem?

A) The predicted mean annual temperature decrease in degrees Celsius for one meter increase in elevation.
B) The predicted decrease in elevation in meters for one degree Celsisus mean annual temperature increase.
C) The predicted elevation of a Nevada city with a mean annual temperature of 0 degrees Celsius.
D) The predicted mean annual temperature of a city in Nevada at elevation 0 meters.

9. What would be the difference in expected mean annual temperature between a Nevada city at elevation 1000 m and one at 1500 m?

    A) 3.5°C
    B) 4.5°C
    C) 5.5°C
    D) 6.5°C

Questions 10 – 12 refer to the following information.

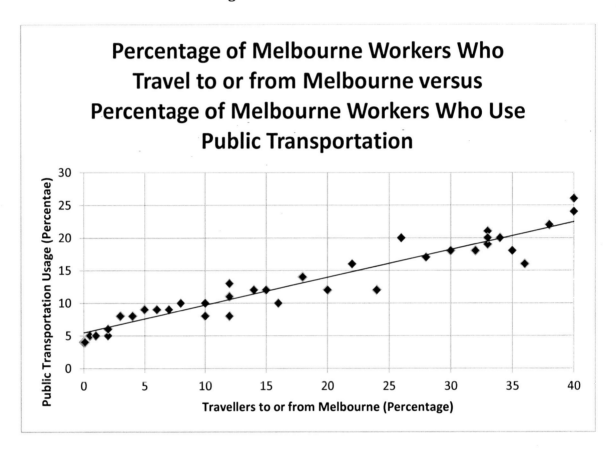

10. On a day in which 22.5% of Melbourne workers travel to or from Melbourne, what percentage of workers is expected to use public transportation?

    A) 10%
    B) 15%
    C) 22.5%
    D) 40%

11. Which of the following data points, if added to the scatterplot on the previous page, would create the largest positive change in the slope of the line of best fit to the data?

A) $(5, 20)$
B) $(15, 15)$
C) $(30, 20)$
D) $(35, 30)$

12. The slope of the line of best fit to the data above is approximately

A) 0.2
B) 0.4
C) 0.6
D) 0.8

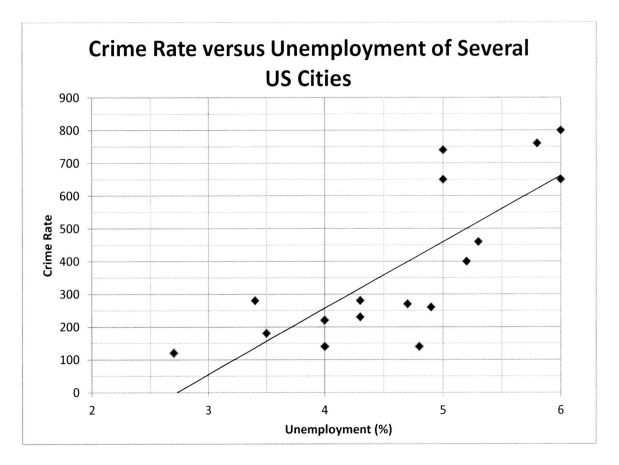

13. How many of the seventeen cities have a crime rate that differs by less than 50 from the crime rate predicted by the line of best fit?

    A) 4
    B) 8
    C) 9
    D) 13

14. Which of the following equations is the line of best fit of the data shown above?

    A) $y = -0.005x - 2.667$
    B) $y = 0.005x + 2.667$
    C) $y = 195x - 520$
    D) $y = -195x - 520$

15. If a city's unemployment rate drops by 2 percentage points, its crime rate is expected to

    A) decrease by approximately 400 points
    B) decrease by approximately 200 points
    C) increase by approximately 200 points
    D) increase by approximately 400 points

Questions 16 – 18 refer to the following information.

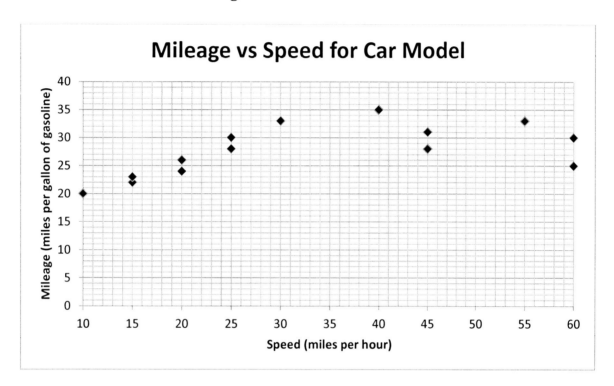

16. Which type of line of best fit best matches the data points in the scatterplot above?

    A) Constant
    B) Linear
    C) Quadratic
    D) Exponential

17. At a speed of 25 miles per hour, the expected mileage of the car model is

    A) 20 miles per gallon
    B) 30 miles per gallon
    C) 40 miles per gallon
    D) 50 miles per gallon

18. An increase in speed of 10 miles per hour equates to what change in mileage?

    A) −5 miles per gallon
    B) +5 miles per gallon
    C) +10 miles per gallon
    D) It is impossible to determine

Questions 19 – 21 refer to the following information.

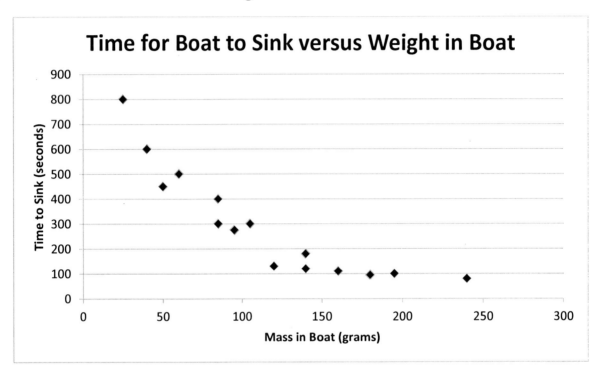

19. Which type of line of best fit best matches the data points in the scatterplot above?

    A) Constant
    B) Linear
    C) Quadratic
    D) Exponential

20. When the mass in the boat increases from 50 grams to 200 grams, the time it takes for the boat to sink

    A) decreases by 400 seconds.
    B) decreases by 100 seconds.
    C) increases by 100 seconds.
    D) increases by 400 seconds.

Challenge Problem

21. Which of the following lines of best fit matches the data in the scatterplot on the previous page?

   A) $y = 3x - 650$
   B) $y = -3x + 650$
   C) $y = 870(0.98^x)$
   D) $y = -870(0.98^x)$

Two-Way Tables
Concept & Strategy Lesson

Students will summarize categorical data and use that data to calculate relative frequencies, conditional probabilities, association of variables, and independence of events.

Two-Way Tables

- Two-way tables show data from one group that pertains to two distinct categories.
- Below is an example of a two-way table.

	VOTED YES	VOTED NO	DID NOT VOTE	TOTAL
18- to 39-year-olds	356	123	562	1,041
40- to 59-year-olds	562	453	203	1,218
People 60 years-old and over	392	476	135	1,003
Total	**1,310**	**1,052**	**900**	**3,262**

- Notice that each cell in the final row and final column is a total amount.
- The **relative frequency** of a value is the fraction or proportion of times the value occurs. So, the relative frequency of people 60 years-old and over in the survey above is $\frac{1003}{3262}$.
- **Conditional frequency** is the ratio of a subtotal to the value of a total. In the two-way table above, the conditional frequency of 18- to 39-year olds who voted no is $\frac{123}{1041}$. The conditional frequency of people who voted no who are 18 to 39 years-old, on the other hand, is $\frac{123}{1052}$.
- **Conditional probability** is the probability that an event occurs, given that another event has already occurred. The probability of a person voting no provided that he or she is 18 to 39 years-old is also $\frac{123}{1052}$.
- Two events are **independent** if the occurrence of one event does not affect the probability of the occurrence of the other event.

A survey was conducted among a randomly chosen sample of Wyoming residents about whether or not they voted for a proposition in a recent election. The table below displays a summary of the survey results.

	VOTED YES	VOTED NO	DID NOT VOTE	TOTAL
18- to 39-year-olds	356	123	562	1,041
40- to 59-year-olds	562	453	203	1,218
People 60 years-old and over	392	476	135	1,003
Total	1,310	1,052	900	3,262

Example 1:

According to the table, which of the following groups had the highest relative frequency?

A) 18- to 39-year-olds who did not vote
B) 18- to 39-year-olds who voted yes
C) 18- to 39-year-olds who voted no
D) 40- to 59-year-olds who voted no

Since we're looking for a relative frequency, simply divide each of the indicated entries by the total. A is the correct answer, as $\frac{562}{3262}$ is larger than all of the other frequencies.

Example 2:

Of the people 60 years-old and over who reported voting, 200 were selected at random to do a follow-up survey in which they were asked to choose from among 3 candidates for governor. The results of the follow-up survey are included below. Using the data from both the initial survey and the follow-up survey, which of the following is most likely to be an accurate statement?

	CANDIDATE A	CANDIDATE B	CANDIDATE C	NO PREFERENCE
# of Voters	86	53	46	15

A) About 225 people over the age of 60 in the initial survey would choose to support Candidate A.

B) About 375 people over the age of 60 in the initial survey would choose to support Candidate A.

C) About 375 people over the age of 60 in the initial survey would choose to support Candidate B.

D) About 275 people over the age of 60 in the initial survey would choose to support Candidate B.

We know that 868 of the people over the age of 60 in the initial survey voted. We know that $\frac{86}{200}$ people in the follow-up survey supported Candidate A. We can assume that that ratio holds true for everyone in the group, so multiply. $\frac{86}{200} \times 868 = 373.24$. So, our answer is B.

Two-Way Tables

Practice Problems

Questions 1 – 3 refer to the information below.

The table below classifies the number of visitors to several Caribbean islands in February based on their continent of origin.

	Grenada	Jamaica	Puerto Rico	Total
North America	82	156	180	418
South America	168	46	26	240
Europe	71	24	123	218
Total	321	226	329	876

1. What fraction of all visitors from South America went to either Jamaica or Puerto Rico?

2. Which of the following conditional probabilities is greatest?

   A) The probability that a visitor from Europe vacationed in Jamaica.
   B) The probability that a visitor from South America vacationed in Puerto Rico.
   C) The probability that a visitor from South America vacationed in Jamaica.
   D) The probability that a visitor from North America vacationed in Grenada.

3. Of the people who visited Grenada, 200 were surveyed and asked whether or not they would visit again. 45% of those surveyed answered yes, 40% answered no, and the remainder were unsure. Based on those results, approximately how many of the 321 people who visited Grenada would definitely visit Grenada again?

   A) 90
   B) 120
   C) 144
   D) 193

Questions 4 – 6 refer to the information below.

The table below classifies the reptiles of Turkey by their preferred habitat.

	Turtles	Lizards	Snakes	Total
Forest	4	23	42	69
Grassland	7	27	11	45
Chaparral	0	18	3	21
Total	11	68	56	135

4. What fraction of Turkish lizards prefer chaparral?

5. Lizards and snakes make up approximately what percentage of the reptiles of Turkey?

    A) 21%
    B) 46%
    C) 82%
    D) 92%

6. The chaparral is home to what fraction of Turkey's animal species?

    A) 0
    B) $\frac{7}{45}$
    C) $\frac{9}{34}$
    D) It is impossible to determine from the information provided.

Questions 7 through 9 use the information below.

The table below shows the destination airport, by season, of travelers (in thousands) at Missoula International Airport.

	Spring	Summer	Fall	Winter	Total
Seattle	16.3	31.2	17.0	2.9	67.4
Denver	16.3	18.9	14.7	23.2	73.1
Minneapolis	14.6	18.3	16.4	6.5	55.8
Total	47.2	68.4	48.1	32.6	196.3

7. What percentage of all of the travelers who went from Missoula to Seattle travelled during the winter?

    A) 4.3%
    B) 8.9%
    C) 16.6%
    D) 34.3%

8. Of the people who travelled to Minneapolis, 2000 were selected at random and asked whether or not they would use the same airline again. 640 of those surveyed answered yes, 1120 answered no, and the remainder were unsure. Based on those results, approximately how many of the people who visited Minneapolis would not use the same airline again?

A) 31
B) 31,248
C) 35,584
D) 43,136

9. Which of the following conditional probabilities is least?

A) The probability that a traveler to Seattle traveled in the spring.
B) The probability that a traveler to Denver traveled in the spring.
C) The probability that a spring traveler traveled to Seattle.
D) The probability that a spring traveler traveled to Denver.

Questions 10 – 12 refer to the information below.

A survey was conducted among a randomly chosen sample of Georgia residents about voter participation in the 2014 Senate election.

Reported Voting by Age (in hundreds)				
	Voted	**Did Not Vote**	**No Response**	**Total**
18- to 34-year-olds	595	3,658	346	4,599
35- to 54-year-olds	923	1,171	378	2,472
55- to 74-year-olds	796	1,278	200	2,274
People 75 years old and over	248	1,235	113	1,596
Total	2,562	7,342	1,037	10,941

10. According to the table, for which age group did the smallest percentage of people report that they had voted?

A) 18- to 34-year-olds
B) 35- to 54-year-olds
C) 55- to 74-year-olds
D) People 75 years old and over

11. Of the people 75 years old and over who reported voting, 350 were selected at random to do a follow-up survey in which they were asked which candidate they voted for. 150 people in this survey voted for Candidate A, 175 voted for Candidate B, and the rest voted for someone else. Using the data from both the follow-up survey and the initial survey, which of the following is most likely to be an accurate statement?

A) About 10,000 of the people 75 years old and over would report voting for Candidate A in the election.
B) About 68,400 of the people 75 years old and over would report voting for Candidate A in the election.
C) About 109,800 of the people 75 years old and over would report voting for Candidate A in the election.
D) About 468,900 of the people 75 years old and over would report voting for Candidate A in the election.

12. The initial survey was very thorough – nearly 10% of all of the people of voting age in Georgia were surveyed. Approximately how many people in the state of Georgia are 55 years old or over?

A) 1.25 million
B) 1.75 million
C) 2.25 million
D) 3.87 million

Questions 13 – 15 refer to the information below.

The table below classifies 1,037 animal species in the Nile River-Lake Victoria Basin by location.

	Amphibian	Fish	Reptile	Total
Nile River	137	249	18	404
Lake Victoria	76	343	13	432
Surrounding Wetlands	58	136	7	201
Total	271	728	38	1,037

13. What fraction of Reptile species in the Nile River-Lake Victoria Basin live in the Nile River?

14. What percentage of amphibians in the Nile River-Lake Victoria Basin live in the surrounding wetlands?

A) 21.40%
B) 28.86%
C) 33.91%
D) 50.55%

15. What percentage of the animal species listed on the previous page as being from Lake Victoria are either amphibians or reptiles?

A) 20.60%
B) 29.80%
C) 32.34%
D) 38.37%

Questions 16 – 18 refer to the information below.

The table below lists all four types of hits compiled by four members of a baseball team.

	Singles	Doubles	Triples	Home Runs	Total
Player A	110	43	4	18	175
Player B	88	34	2	29	153
Player C	116	27	0	10	153
Player D	115	26	3	11	155
Total	429	130	11	68	638

16. Which player has the greatest probability of one of his hits being a triple or a home run?

A) Player A
B) Player B
C) Player C
D) Player D

17. A player's Batting Average is calculated by taking his total hits and dividing that number by his number of At Bats. Each of the four player's At Bats is listed below. Which player has the highest Batting Average?

	At Bats		At Bats
Player A	607	**Player C**	582
Player B	566	**Player D**	573

A) Player A
B) Player B
C) Player C
D) Player D

18. Which player has the greatest ratio of Doubles to Home Runs?

A) Player A
B) Player B
C) Player C
D) Player D

Questions 19 – 21 refer to the information below.

A survey was conducted among a randomly chosen sample of U.S. residents about their income.

	Below $30,000	Between $30,000 and $100,000	Above $100,000	Total
Southeast	623	879	687	2,189
Northeast	486	1,171	952	2,609
Southwest	698	1,089	852	2,639
Northwest	532	599	423	1,554
Total	2,339	3,738	2,914	8,991

19. The proportion of people who earn below $30,000 is greatest among the people of which region?

A) Southeast
B) Northeast
C) Southwest
D) Northwest

20. The proportions of people surveyed from each area are indicative of their proportion of the adult U.S. population. If the population of U.S. adults is 242 million, approximately how many adults live in the Southwest?

A) 41 million
B) 59 million
C) 71 million
D) 78 million

Challenge Problem

21. The survey group is considering splitting the population of the Northeast into two groups: Atlantic and New England. New England contains 58% of the population of the Northeast. Furthermore, the breakdowns of these two groups, by percentage, are as follows:

	Below $30,000	Between $30,000 and $100,000	Above $100,000	Total
Atlantic	32%	46%	22%	100%
New England	28%	48%	24%	100%

Of the original people surveyed, how many from the Atlantic region would earn between $30,000 and $100,000, to the nearest person?

Measures of Center and Spread
Concept & Strategy Lesson

Students will calculate measures of center and spread, including mean, median, mode, and range, for a set of data. Students must use given statistics, including standard deviation, to compare two different sets of data.

Measures of Center

- The **mean** of a data set can be found by summing the value of each point in the data set, then dividing that sum by the number of points in the data set.
- Generally, the mean is the most commonly used measure of center.
- However, the mean is an inappropriate measure of center when outliers exist in the data set or when the data are heavily skewed in one direction.
- The **median** of a data set is the point in the middle.
- To find the median, first make sure all the data points are in ascending (increasing) order.
- If there is an even number of points in the data set, the median is the mean of the two middle points.
- The median is the most appropriate measure of center when the data set is skewed or contains outliers.
- The **mode** of a data set is the most frequent data point.
- If two or more data points are the most frequent, all of them are considered to be the mode.
- Note that for a data point to be the mode, there must be more than one instance of that point in the data set.
- The mode is the most appropriate measure of center when you are looking for the most popular response.

Measures of Range

- The **range** of a data set is the difference between the highest and lowest data points in the data set.
- You will never have to calculate the **standard deviation** of a data set, but you must know what it is used for.
- The more spread out the data points are from the mean of a set, the greater the standard deviation. The closer the data points are to the mean of a set, the smaller the standard deviation.
- If all of the data points in a data set are the same, its standard deviation is 0.

Softball Player Heights (inches)		Basketball Player Heights (inches)	
61	61	65	68
62	62	70	70
63	63	70	71
65	68	71	72
69	69	73	
69	70		
71	71		

The data above show the heights of Somerville High School's girls' softball and girls' basketball teams.

Example 1:

Based on the information in the data sets above, which of the following statements is true?

A) The mean height of the girls' softball team is larger than the mean height of the girls' basketball team.
B) The mean height of the girls' basketball team is larger than the mean height of the girls' softball team.
C) The median height of the girls' softball team is larger than the median height of the girls' basketball team.
D) The range of heights on the girls' basketball team is larger than the range of heights on the girls' softball team.

The correct answer is B. The mean height of the girls' basketball team is $70\frac{1}{3}$, while the mean height of the girls' softball team is 66.

Example 2:

The standard deviation of the heights of the girls' softball team is 3.903, while the standard deviation of the heights of the girls' basketball team is 2.345. Based on his information and the information in the data sets above, which of the following statements is true.

A) The player heights for the softball team are less spread apart than the player heights for the basketball team.
B) The average player height for the softball team is greater than the average player height for the basketball team.
C) The player heights for the basketball team are less spread apart than the player heights for the basketball team.
D) Every player on the basketball team is taller than every player on the softball team.

The answer is C. Standard deviation is a measure of how spread apart the data points are from the mean. Since the basketball team heights have a smaller standard deviation, its data points must be less spread apart.

Measures of Center and Spread
Practice Problems

1. At a retirement home, the mean age of all the men is 78 years old, and the mean age of all the women is 82 years old. Which of the following must be true about the mean age m of the combined group of men and women at the retirement home?

    A) $m = 80$
    B) $m > 80$
    C) $m < 80$
    D) $78 < m < 82$

15	16	16	18	20	22	23	23	23
24	24	25	28	30	32	32	35	36

2. Which of the following lists the mean, median, and mode of the above data set in ascending order?

    A) median, mode, mean
    B) mode, median, mean
    C) mean, mode, median
    D) mode, mean, median

Questions 3 – 5 refer to the following information.

College Football Player Weights (pounds)		High School Football Player Weights (pounds)	
256	261	165	268
150	196	170	136
180	162	136	182
178	182	156	209
210	196	136	212
223	146	182	200
276	187	156	199

The data above show the weights of randomly selected football players from one college team and one high school team.

3. Based on the information in the data sets above, which of the following statements is true?

    A) The mean weight of the high school football team is larger than the mean weight of the college football team.
    B) The mean weight of the college football team is larger than the mean weight of the high school football team.
    C) The median weight of the high school football team is larger than the median weight of the college football team.
    D) The range of weights on the college football team is larger than the range of weights of the high school football team.

4. In comparison to the median weight of the players selected from the high school football team, the median weight of the players selected from the college football team is

   A) approximately 20 pounds heavier.
   B) approximately 15 pounds heavier.
   C) approximately 15 pounds lighter.
   D) approximately 20 pounds lighter.

5. In comparison to the range of weights of the players selected from the high school football team, the range of weights of the players selected from the college football team is

   A) approximately 2 more
   B) approximately 16 more
   C) approximately 16 less
   D) approximately 2 less

Questions 6 and 7 refer to the following information.

Number of GB of Data Used per Month – Group A	Number of GB of Data Used per Month – Group B
11, 12, 8, 9, 7, 6, 12, 9, 8, 15, 14, 13, 13, 14, 15, 16, 12, 8, 9, 7, 6, 2, 8, 11	15, 12, 19, 11, 8, 9, 3, 5, 16, 15, 85, 3, 0, 11, 12, 15, 16, 18, 12, 11, 8

6. Which measure of center best represents the average number of GB of data used per month for the people in Group A?

   A) Mean
   B) Median
   C) Mode
   D) Range

7. Which measure of center best represents the average number of GB of data used per month for the people in Group B?

   A) Mean
   B) Median
   C) Mode
   D) Range

8. The values below give the heights, in inches, of the members of a basketball team.

$$71, 74, 74, 74, 75, 75, 77, 79, 79, 80, 81, 85$$

A new player of height 76 inches is added to the team. Which of the following measures does this effect?

A) Mean
B) Median
C) Mode
D) Range

Questions 9 – 12 refer to the following information.

The cost of a ferry at a local company is dependent on both the weather conditions and the number of passengers. Each **x** below represents one instance of that cost in the last 3 weeks.

Cost of Ferry									
			X		X				
			X	X	X				
	X	X	X	X	X	X	X		
X	X	X	X	X	X	X	X		X
$20	$22	$24	$26	$28	$30	$32	$34	$36	38

9. To the nearest integer, what is the mean ferry cost over the previous 3 weeks?

A) $26
B) $28
C) $29
D) $30

10. Adding which of the following data sets to the Cost of the Ferry data above will increase the median of the data set by the largest amount?

A) {26, 26, 28}
B) {28, 28, 30}
C) {30, 30, 32}
D) {26, 36, 36}

11. Which of the following statements about the data above is true?

A) The distribution of data points is symmetric.
B) The mean of the data set is greater than at least one of its modes.
C) The median of the data set is greater than its mean.
D) The ferry will never cost less than $20 or more than $36.

12. The standard deviation of the data above is 4.5. Adding which of the following data sets to the Cost of the Ferry data on the previous page will increase the standard deviation by the largest amount?

A) {26, 28}
B) {22, 34}
C) {22, 30}
D) {28, 34}

13. Which of the following datasets has the smallest standard deviation?

A) {2, 5, 7, 9}
B) {2, 8, 10, 12}
C) {4, 8, 11, 17}
D) {5, 5, 5, 5}

Questions 14 – 16 refer to the following information.

The number of patrons at a certain restaurant was counted at 1:00 PM on two different days, Friday and Saturday, during the school year. The data are shown below. Each **x** represents one patron.

Age of Restaurant Patrons – Friday Lunch							
			x				
			x	x			
		x	x	x			
		x	x	x	x		x
x		x	x	x	x	x	x
x	x	x	x	x	x	x	x
1-10 years	11-18 years	19-25 years	26-35 years	36-45 years	46-55 years	56-65 years	66 + years

Age of Restaurant Patrons – Saturday Lunch							
	x						
	x			x			
	x		x	x	x		
	x	x	x	x	x	x	
	x	x	x	x	x	x	x
x	x	x	x	x	x	x	x
1-10 years	11-18 years	19-25 years	26-35 years	36-45 years	46-55 years	56-65 years	66 + years

14. Which of the following statements about the above data is true?

   A) The median age of the restaurant's Friday Lunch patrons is less than that of the restaurant's Saturday Lunch patrons.
   B) The median age of the restaurant's Friday Lunch patrons is greater than that of the restaurant's Saturday Lunch patrons.
   C) The mode of the ages of the restaurant's Friday Lunch patrons is less than that of the restaurant's Saturday Lunch patrons.
   D) The range of the ages of the restaurant's Friday Lunch patrons is greater than that of the restaurant's Saturday Lunch patrons.

15. Which of the following is the most likely cause of the largest disparity in both days' data?

   A) The restaurant is much less popular among people in the 11-18 year old age bracket on Fridays because of the increased presence of people in the 36-45 year old age bracket.
   B) Far more people visit the restaurant on the weekend than during the week.
   C) The restaurant is very popular among people who are still in school, but those people are unable to visit the restaurant during the week.
   D) Far fewer people in the 66+ year old age bracket are able to leave their houses during the weekend.

16. Which of the following statements about the above data is true?

   A) The range of ages of the restaurant's Friday Lunch patrons is less than that of the restaurant's Saturday Lunch patrons.
   B) The range of ages of the restaurant's Friday Lunch patrons is greater than that of the restaurant's Saturday Lunch patrons.
   C) The range of ages of the restaurant's Friday Lunch patrons is equivalent to that of the restaurant's Saturday Lunch patrons.
   D) The range of ages of both datasets is unable to be determined.

Questions 17 and 18 refer to the following information.

The hourly salaries of employees, in dollars, of three different companies are listed below.

Company A
10, 10, 10, 10, 12, 12, 12, 12, 12, 12, 12, 15, 15, 30, 100
Company B
12, 12, 12, 12, 12, 12, 12, 12, 15, 15, 15, 15, 25, 30, 30
Company C
15, 15, 15, 15, 15, 15, 15, 15, 15, 15, 15, 15, 20, 20, 20

17. The hourly salaries of which company above has the highest standard deviation?

   A) Company A
   B) Company B
   C) Company C
   D) It is impossible to determine.

18. Which measure of center would best determine the average hourly salary of each of the companies on the previous page?

   A) Mean
   B) Median
   C) Mode
   D) The best method of determining average hourly salary is different for each company.

Questions 19 – 21 refer to the following information.

Two chemistry classes taught by the same teacher each took the same test. The grades of each student in each class are listed below.

Class A Grades		Class B Grades	
36	80	60	72
65	80	60	75
65	82	65	75
68	85	65	78
70	88	68	82
75	92	72	85
75	95	72	100

19. Which class performed better on the exam?

   A) Class A because it had a higher mean exam score.
   B) Class A because it had a higher median exam score.
   C) Class B because its extreme values are larger than Class A's extreme values.
   D) Class B because its range of exam scores is lower.

20. What is the difference in the median scores of the two classes above?

   A) 1.93
   B) 3.00
   C) 5.50
   D) 8.00

Challenge Problem

21. Halfway through grading Class B's exams, the teacher discovered the key had a mistake. Thus, half of the grades listed above for Class B are 5 points too low. What is the new mean exam score for Class B?

   A) 73.5
   B) 76
   C) 78.5
   D) It is impossible to determine.

Population Parameters and Data Collection
Concept & Strategy Lesson

Students must be able to estimate a population parameter given the results of a random sample of the population. Students must be able to understand and use, but not calculate, confidence intervals and measurement error. Students must be able to evaluate reports to make inferences and justify the appropriateness of data collection methods and be able to justify conclusions about those methods.

Population Parameters

- A **sample** is a smaller portion of a population that is selected to represent that population.
- In order to use statistics to learn information about a population, the sample should be selected at random.
- A **parameter** is a characteristic of a population. For example, if a randomly chosen sample of 1000 people from Coweta County has a mean age of 37, you can conclude that the average age of the people of Coweta County is also 37.
- A **confidence interval** is a range of likely values of a population parameter. It contains two parts, an interval of likely values and our confidence that the population parameter likes within that interval.
- For example, a 95% confidence interval states that the population mean of the weights of males in Volusia County, Florida is 181 ± 1.9 pounds. This means that we expect 95% of estimates of the weights of males of that county are between 179.1 and 182.9 pounds. The 1.9 pounds on either side of the mean is known as our **margin of error**.
- **Measurement error** is a form of bias due to improper research. Measurement error will increase the margin of error of a confidence interval and provide biased results.

Data Collection

- Data should be collected in as non-biased a way as possible. Ideally, all subgroups of a population should be equally represented within the sample.
- A **convenience sample** is a common way of creating bias within a sample. Convenience samples only poll members of the population who are easy to access, so certain members of the population are more likely to be polled.
- A **voluntary sample** is another common way of creating bias within a sample. Voluntary samples only poll members of the population who want to be polled, so generally only people with very strong opinions are represented in the sample.
- A **simple random sample** occurs when each member of a population is given a random number, and a certain number of random numbers are selected to poll.
- A **stratified random sample** occurs when members of a population are broken into groups based on certain characteristics, such as age or income. Then, random members are selected in proportion to how often those characteristics appear in the population at large. For example, the sample of a population in which 20% of the

population makes more than $100,000 a year and 80% makes less than $100,000 would attempt to retain that income ratio. So, stratified random sampling is more representative, but also more time-consuming.

A survey was conducted among a randomly chosen sample of 3,000 New York City football fans about their favorite football team. The table below displays a summary of the survey results.

	NEW YORK OGRES	NEW YORK COPTERS	BOSTON NATIONALISTS	OTHER TEAM	TOTAL
Poll Results	1,236	1,069	365	330	3,000

Example 1:

The population of New York City is 8.406 million people and approximately 50% of those residents have a favorite football team. Assuming that the data above are representative of the city as a whole, how many New York City residents cite the New York Copters as their favorite team?

A) 1.498 million
B) 1.732 million
C) 2.995 million
D) 3.463 million

Since we know that the information in the table above is representative of New York City football fans, we know that the approximate ratios must be the same as the population as a whole. As there are approximately 4.203 million football fans in New York City, let's set up a ratio to solve:

$$\frac{1069}{3000} = \frac{x}{4203000}$$

Our answer must be A.

Example 2:

The population of the United States as a whole is approximately 320 million people, and approximately 40% of those are football fans with a favorite team. How many Americans like a team besides the Ogres or the Copters?

A) 14.1 million
B) 29.6 million
C) 98.3 million
D) The answer cannot be obtained from the information given.

We need to figure out how many Americans like a team other than the Ogres or the Copters. However, there is a problem: We do not know that the information provided for New York City residents is representative of the nation as a whole. In fact, it makes sense that residents of other cities and states would display a preference for other teams that aren't even mentioned in the survey. Thus, our answer must be D.

Population Parameters and Data Collection
Practice Problems

1. A statistician randomly selected 100 employees from the list of all the salaried employees of a company. She asked each of the 100 employees, "How many hours do you typically work per week?" The mean number of working hours in the sample was 45.8 and the margin of error for this estimate was 2.4 hours. Another statistician intends to replicate the survey and will attempt to get a smaller margin of error. Which of the following samples will most likely result in a smaller margin of error for the estimated mean number of weekly working hours of employees in the company?

   A) 50 randomly selected salaried employees of the company
   B) 50 randomly selected employees of the company
   C) 500 randomly selected salaried employees of the company
   D) 500 randomly selected employees of the company

Questions 2 and 3 refer to the following information.

A researcher wants to know if there is an association between height and speed of long-distance runners in Canada. He obtained survey responses from a random sample of 3000 Canadian long-distance runners and found convincing evidence of a positive association between height and speed.

2. Which of the following conclusions is well supported by the data?

   A) There is a positive association between height and speed for long-distance runners in Canada.
   B) There is a positive association between height and speed for long-distance runners in the world.
   C) Using height and speed as defined by the study, an increase in height is caused by an increase in speed for long-distance runners in Canada.
   D) Using height and speed as defined by the study, an increase in speed is caused by an increase in height for long-distance runners in Canada.

3. Canadian long-distance runner Jay is 183 cm tall, while Canadian long-distance runner Kim is 172 cm tall. Based on the information above, you can tell that

   A) Kim definitely runs faster than Jay does.
   B) Kim most likely runs faster than Jay does.
   C) Jay most likely runs faster than Kim does.
   D) Jay definitely runs faster than Kim does.

4. Which of the following samples will most likely result in the largest margin of error for the estimated mean height of adult New York City residents?

A) Randomly selecting 100 New York City residents at a grocery store.
B) Randomly selecting 200 New York City residents at a movie theater.
C) Randomly selecting 200 New York City residents at a movie theater.
D) Randomly selecting 500 New York City residents at a grocery store.

5. A statistician set up a survey outside of a Detroit football stadium before a game and surveyed 100 volunteer respondents. He asked each of the 100 volunteers, "Who is your favorite football team?" 87% of the respondents answered Detroit, 10% answered the visiting team, Chicago, and 3% answered another team. The statistician concludes that approximately 87% of the country lists Detroit as its favorite football team. Is this conclusion logical?

A) Yes, because the sample size of the survey is large enough to be representative of the population of the country.
B) Yes, because the statistician used voluntary sampling to obtain his results.
C) No, because volunteers never give unbiased answers.
D) No, because the survey is biased towards Detroit fans.

6. Which of the following surveys is most likely to have the smallest amount of measurement error?

A) A survey of 500 students.
B) A survey of 1000 students.
C) A survey of 2500 students.
D) A survey of 5000 students.

7. At an aquarium, the mean age of male whale sharks is 35 years and the mean age of female whale sharks is 30 years. Which of the following must be true about the mean age m of the combined group of male and female whale sharks at the aquarium?

A) $m = 32.5$
B) $m > 32.5$
C) $m < 32.5$
D) $30 < m < 35$

Questions 8 and 9 refer to the following information.

A survey was conducted among a randomly chosen sample of 2,000 deli shoppers about their favorite lunch meat. The table below displays a summary of the survey results.

	Turkey	Salami	Pastrami	Corned Beef	TOTAL
Poll Results	682	645	135	538	2,000

8. The survey above was given to 5,000 deli shoppers in a different city, and the same approximate results ratios were obtained. Which of the following is the least likely result from that survey?

   A) 1361 people picked "Turkey"
   B) 1592 people picked "Salami"
   C) 340 people picked "Pastrami"
   D) 1340 people picked "Corned Beef"

9. The survey above did not contain an "other" selection, so shoppers were forced to choose between the four selections listed above. A second survey added the fifth "Other" category. 10% of the shoppers chose "Other", while the approximate ratios of the other four categories remained constant. Approximately how many of those responders chose either "Turkey" or "Salami"?

   A) 133
   B) 1194
   C) 1261
   D) 1460

Questions 10 and 11 refer to the following information.

A researcher wants to know if there is an association between height and wingspan of college men's basketball players. He obtained survey responses from a random sample of 1,000 college men's basketball players and found convincing evidence of a positive association between height and wingspan.

10. One of the players surveyed had a height of 192 cm and a wingspan of 191 cm. Another player had a height of 187 cm. His wingspan is most likely

    A) 185 cm
    B) 186 cm
    C) 187 cm
    D) It cannot be determined from the information provided.

11. Which of the following conclusions is well supported by the data?

    A) There is a positive association between height and wingspan for college basketball players.
    B) There is a positive association between height and wingspan for basketball players
    C) Using height and wingspan as defined by the study, a taller men's college basketball player will generally have a longer wingspan.
    D) Using height and wingspan as defined by the study, more wingspan equates to more height.

Questions 12 and 13 refer to the following information.

A survey was conducted among a randomly chosen sample of 2,485 students of a particular university in regards to what region of the country they are from. The results are shown below.

	Southeast	Northeast	Southwest	Northwest	TOTAL
Poll Results	896	536	790	623	2,845

12. The university has 23,596 enrolled students. Assuming the results of the survey are consistent with the university as a whole, approximately how many of the university's students are not from the Southwest?

    A) 7,501
    B) 8,508
    C) 15,088
    D) 16,095

13. The following year, the university is concerned that too many of its students are from the Southeast and wants to decrease the number of students from that region by 10%, assuming that an equal number of students from the other three regions will take their places. If the university wants to increase its enrollment to 25,000 people, how many people should it expect to have from the Northwest?

    A) 5,694
    B) 6,569
    C) 7,169
    D) 8,113

Questions 14 – 16 refer to the following information.

A 90% confidence interval states that the population mean of the weights of adult males in Fulton County, Georgia is 169 ± 4.3 pounds and the population mean of the weights of adult females in Fulton County, Georgia, is 130 ± 3.7.

14. Which of the following is the least likely mean weight of adult males in Fulton County, Georgia?

   A) 133.7 pounds
   B) 166.2 pounds
   C) 171.5 pounds
   D) It is unable to be determined from the given information.

15. Which of the following is the least likely mean weight of adult females in Fulton County, Georgia?

   A) 128.2 pounds
   B) 133.7 pounds
   C) 164.7 pounds
   D) It is unable to be determined from the given information.

16. Which of the following is the least likely mean weight of adults in Fulton County, Georgia?

   A) 133.7 pounds
   B) 149.5 pounds
   C) 171.5 pounds
   D) It is unable to be determined from the given information.

17. On a football team, the mean weight of special teams players is 196 pounds, the mean weight of offensive players is 256 pounds, and the mean weight of defensive players is 263 pounds. Which of the following must be true about the mean weight m of the entire football team?

   A) $m = 238.33$
   B) $238.33 < m < 263$
   C) $196 < m < 238.33$
   D) $196 < m < 263$

18. Which of the following methods should be used to obtain the most accurate data about the mean income of the population of a certain state?

    A) Use voluntary sampling; people in the state will self-select to provide the most accurate income information.
    B) Ask 100 random people from each county in the state to provide income information.
    C) Simple random sampling; ask 10,000 random people from a list of every person in the state as a whole to provide income information.
    D) Determine the population of each county in the state, then ask a number of random people from each county, in proportion with the population of that county, to provide income information.

Questions 19 – 21 refer to the following information.

A survey was conducted among a randomly chosen sample of nation-wide voters about their preferred presidential candidate. The table below displays a summary of the survey results.

	Candidate A	Candidate B	Candidate C	TOTAL
Poll Results	13,523	14,569	1,897	29,989

19. The surveyors have determined that each value is accurate to within 5%; that is, the number of voters for each candidate can be either 5% higher or 5% lower than the numbers shown above. Based on that information, which candidate is most likely to win the election?

    A) Candidate A
    B) Candidate B
    C) Candidate C
    D) It is impossible to determine.

20. In an election in which 100,000 people vote and the ratio above is maintained, approximately how many people will vote for Candidate B?

    A) 20,584
    B) 45,093
    C) 48,581
    D) 63,257

Challenge Problem

The voters who selected Candidate B above were asked to participate on another survey about their support for Resolution 192. The information obtained is provided below.

	Support	Oppose	No Opinion	TOTAL
Poll Results	5,244	6,993	2,332	14,569

21. Approximately what percentage of the voters who selected Candidate A would be expected to oppose Resolution 192?

    A) 16%
    B) 36%
    C) 48%
    D) It cannot be determined from the information provided.

Functions
Concept & Strategy Lesson

Students must be able to create and solve quadratic and exponential functions that model situations.

Functions

- A **function** is a relationship between a set of inputs and a set of outputs wherein each input is related to exactly one output.
- The inputs, or x-values of the function, are known as its **domain**. The outputs, or y-values of the function, are known as its **range**.
- The ordered pair (x, y) is a solution to the function $f(x)$.
- Roots, or zeros, of a function are the points where the function crosses the x-axis. These roots can usually be found by setting the function equal to 0 and solving or graphing the function.

Quadratic Functions

- Quadratic functions are typically of the form $f(x) = ax^2 + bx + c$.
- Every quadratic function has either a maximum (if a is negative) or a minimum (if a is positive).
- This maximum or minimum is always located at the vertex of the function. The x-coordinate of the vertex always has the value of $-\frac{b}{2a}$, while the y-coordinate of the vertex can be found by plugging this x-value into the function.
- A quadratic function will always have at most 2 real roots.

Example 1:

The function f is defined by $f(x) = 2x^2 - hx - 3$, where h is a constant. In the xy-plane, the graph of f intersects the x-axis at the two points $(-3, 0)$ and $(j, 0)$. What is the value of $h - j$?

A) -5.5
B) -4.5
C) 4.5
D) 5.5

Since we know that the function has a root at $(-3, 0)$, we can plug this point into the function and solve for h.

$$f(x) = 2x^2 - hx - 3$$
$$0 = 2(-3)^2 - h(-3) - 3$$
$$-15 = 3h$$
$$-5 = h$$

Now that we know the value of h, factor the quadratic (or graph it if you're allowed to use your calculator) to find the value of j.

$$0 = 2x^2 + 5x - 3$$
$$0 = (2x - 1)(x + 3)$$
$$0 = 2x - 1 \qquad 0 = x + 3$$
$$x = \frac{1}{2} \qquad x = -3$$

So, the value of j is $\frac{1}{2}$. Now, we can obtain our answer: $h - j = -5 - \frac{1}{2} = -5\frac{1}{2}$. Our answer is A.

Exponential Functions

- Exponential functions are typically of the form $f(x) = a \cdot b^x + c$, where b is a positive constant not equal to 1.
- Every exponential function has a vertical asymptote, which can be found at $y = c$. If $a > 0$, then every point on the function will be greater than this asymptote. If $a < 0$, then every point on the function will be less than this asymptote.
- An exponential function will have at most 1 real root.

Example 2:

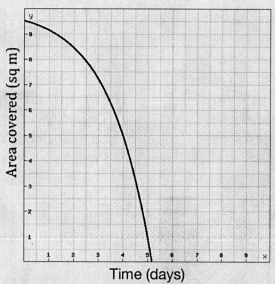

Time (days)

A researcher studies a large mat of moss that has been invaded by a particular fungus. After initially measuring the area that the moss covers, the research measures and records the area covered by living moss every 6 hours and records her results. The data for the moss were fit by a smooth curve, as shown above, where the curve represents the area of living moss as a function of time, in days. Which of the following is a correct statement about the data above?

A) After 2 hours, only 8.5 square meters of living moss remained.
B) At time $t = 2.5$ days, 25% of the initial mat of moss had already died.
C) At time $t = 4$ days, 50% of the initial mat of moss had already died.
D) The moss is dying at a greater initial rate for the first 2 days than the final 2 days.

The answer is C. After 4 days, approximately 4.75 of the initial 9.5 square m of moss remained. Note that answer choice A would be correct as well if the time were in days instead of hours.

Functions
Practice Problems

1. The surface area of the Aral Sea shrunk by approximately 3% each year from 1960 to 2004. Its surface area in 1960 was approximately 68,000 km². If $A(t)$ represents the area of the Aral Sea t years after 1960, then which of the following equations represents the model of the lake's surface area over time?

   A) $A(t) = 68000(-0.03)^t$
   B) $A(t) = 68000(0.03)^t$
   C) $A(t) = 68000(-0.97)^t$
   D) $A(t) = 68000(0.97)^t$

2. Every five years, the amount of money in a savings account increases by 12%. If F represents the current amount of money in the savings account and $f(t)$ represents the amount of money in the savings account t years later, then which of the following equations represents the model of the amount of money in the savings account over time?

   A) $f(t) = F(0.12)^{\frac{t}{5}}$
   B) $f(t) = F(0.12)^{\frac{t}{5}}$
   C) $f(t) = F(1.12)^{\frac{t}{5}}$
   D) $f(t) = F(1.12)^{5t}$

Questions 3 and 4 refer to the following information.

A cannonball is launched at 19.6 meters per second from a platform that is 2.3 meters tall. The equation for the cannonball's height s at time t seconds after launch is
$s(t) = -4.9t^2 + 19.6t + 2.3$.

3. At what time does the cannonball reach its maximum height?

   A) 1 s
   B) 2 s
   C) 3 s
   D) 4 s

4. What is the maximum height, $s(t)$, that the cannonball reaches?

   A) 2.3 m
   B) 17 m
   C) 19.6 m
   D) 21.9 m

5. The function f is defined by $f(x) = |ax - 3| - 2$, where a is a constant. In the xy-plane, the graph of f intersects the x-axis at the two points $(2.5, 0)$ and $(b, 0)$. What is a possible value of $a + b$?

   A) 0.4
   B) 2.4
   C) 2.5
   D) 4.5

6. A culture contains 60,000 bacteria. Every 3 hours, the population of the bacteria decreases by half. Which of the functions below represents the number of bacteria, $f(t)$, present in the culture after t hours?

A) $60{,}000 \times t^{\frac{1}{3}}$

B) $60{,}000 \times \left(\frac{1}{2}\right)^{3t}$

C) $60{,}000 \times \left(\frac{1}{2}\right)^{\frac{t}{3}}$

D) $60{,}000 \times (t)^{\frac{3}{2}}$

7. Approximately how many bacteria are left in the culture after one day?

A) 0
B) 15
C) 234
D) 7,500

8. Which of the following best describes the range of the function $f(x) = 3x^2 - 12x + 18$?

A) $(2, \infty)$
B) $(6, \infty)$
C) $(-\infty, 18)$
D) $(-\infty, \infty)$

9. The graph of $y = (3x - 3)(x - 3)$ is a parabola in the xy-plane. In which of the following equivalent equations do the x- and y-coordinates of the vertex of the parabola appear as constants or coefficients?

A) $y = 3x^2 - 12x + 9$
B) $y = 3(x - 2)^2 - 3$
C) $y = 3x(x - 4) + 9$
D) $y = (x - 1)(3x - 9)$

Questions 10 – 12 refer to the following information.

$$y = 3x^2$$
$$y = 2^x - 1$$

A business chooses to model its growth power, y, based on the number of months it's been in operation, x, with the two simple models shown above.

10. The business starts in January, 2014 ($x = 0$). After how many months will the growth power expected by the exponential growth model overtake the growth expected by the quadratic growth model?

A) 6
B) 8
C) 10
D) 12

11. In what month will the growth power predicted by the quadratic growth model exceed 50?

A) March, 2014
B) April, 2014
C) May, 2014
D) June, 2014

12. In January, 2015, the business discovered that its growth power was 450. Which model most accurately predicted the grow power?

A) The quadratic model
B) The exponential model
C) Both models worked equally well.
D) It is impossible to say which model worked better.

13. The function f is defined by
$f(x) = -5x^2 - 8x - k$, where k is a constant. In the xy-plane, the graph of f intersects the y-axis at one point, $(0, -3)$. What is the value of k^2?

A) -9
B) -3
C) 5
D) 9

Questions 14 and 15 refer to the following information.

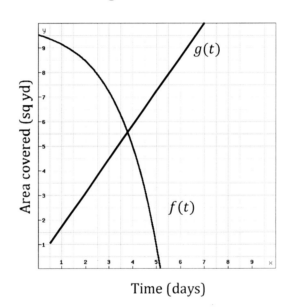

Time (days)

A researcher studies a large mat of moss that has been invaded by a particular fungus. After initially measuring the area that the moss covers, the research measures and records the area covered by living moss, represented by $f(t)$ above, every 6 hours and records her results. The data for the moss were fit by a smooth curve, as shown above, where the curve represents the area of living moss as a function of time, in days. The researcher also measures and records the area covered by the fungus, represented by $g(t)$ above, every 5 hours.

14. Which of the following is a correct statement about the data above?

A) After approximately 3.5 hours, the moss and fungus cover the same area.
B) After approximately 5 hours, the moss was completely killed off.
C) After approximately 3.5 days, the moss and fungus both covered approximately 36 square feet.
D) Initially, the fungus covered approximately 9 square feet.

15. Which of the following functions best describes $g(t)$?

    A) $g(t) = -1.5t - 0.4$
    B) $g(t) = -1.5t + 0.4$
    C) $g(t) = 1.5t - 0.4$
    D) $g(t) = 1.5t + 0.4$

Questions 16 – 18 refer to the following information.

A robotic diver leaps at a velocity of 9.8 meters per second from a platform that is 14.7 meters above the water. The equation for the diver's height s at time t seconds after launch is $s(t) = -4.9t^2 + 9.8t + 14.7$.

16. At what time does the diver hit the water?

    A) 1 s
    B) 2 s
    C) 3 s
    D) 4 s

17. What is the maximum height, $s(t)$, that the diver reaches?

    A) 4.9 m
    B) 9.8 m
    C) 19.6 m
    D) 29.4 m

18. Suppose that the robotic diver had been programmed to dive on the moon, where the force of gravity is only 1.6 m/s. If the diver's initial velocity and platform height are the same, approximately what maximum height will the diver reach now? The equation for the diver's height s at time t seconds after launch is $s(t) = -1.6t^2 + 9.8t + 14.7$.

    A) 4.9 m
    B) 9.8 m
    C) 19.6 m
    D) 29.7 m

Questions 19 and 20 refer to the function below.

$$f(x) = -3(2)^{x-2} + 6$$

19. What is the domain of the function above?

    A) $(-6, \infty)$
    B) $(6, \infty)$
    C) $(-\infty, 2)$
    D) $(-\infty, \infty)$

20. What is the range of the function above?

    A) $(-6, \infty)$
    B) $(6, \infty)$
    C) $(-\infty, 6)$
    D) $(-\infty, \infty)$

Challenge Problem

21. If $f(x) = \frac{3x-2}{x-2}$, what value does $f(x)$ approach as x gets infinitely larger?

    A) −2
    B) −1
    C) $\frac{3}{2}$
    D) 3

Operations on Polynomials
Concept & Strategy Lesson

Students must be able to add, subtract, multiply, and simplify the results of polynomial expressions.

Operations on Polynomials

- Expressions with **like terms** have the same exact variables raised to the same powers.
- You can only add or subtract like terms. Thus, $3xy^2 + 9xy^2 = 12xy^2$, but $6ab^2 + 7a^2b$ cannot be combined.
- To multiply terms, follow the rules we showed in **Chapter 1**. However, you should only add the exponents of like variables. Thus, $(3x^2y^6)(-6xy^{-1}) = -18x^3y^5$.

Distributive Property

- $3x(x - 5) = 3x(x) + 3x(-5) = 3x^2 - 15x$

FOILing

- When multiplying two binomials, remember the mnemonic device **FOIL**: **F**irst, **O**uter, **I**nner, **L**ast.
- To multiply $(2x - 5)(4x - 9)$, first multiply the first terms, then the outer terms, then the inner terms, then the last terms. Finally, simplify by combining like terms:

$$2x(4x) + 2x(-9) + -5(4x) + -5(-9) = 8x^2 - 38x + 45$$

Example 1:

$$3x(2x - y) + (x^2 - y)(x + 3)$$

Which of the following expressions is equivalent to the expression above?

A) $x^3 + 7x^2 - 4xy + 3$
B) $x^3 + 9x^2 - 4xy - 3$
C) $x^3 + 7x^2 - 4xy - 3y$
D) $x^3 + 9x^2 - 4xy - 3y$

Let's use the distributive property to multiply the terms on the left side, then FOIL on the right side:

$$3x(2x - y) + (x^2 - y)(x + 3)$$
$$6x^2 - 3xy + x^3 + 3x^2 - xy - 3y$$

Now combine like terms:

$$6x^2 - 3xy + x^3 + 3x^2 - xy - 3y$$
$$9x^2 - 4xy + x^3 - 3y$$

Since the order of addition doesn't matter, our answer must be D.

Operations on Polynomials
Practice Problems

1. If $a = 3c^2 + c - 8$ and $b = 3c^3 - 4c^2 + 8$, what is $b - a$ in terms of c?

   A) $3c^3 - 7c^2 - c$
   B) $3c^3 - c^2 - c + 16$
   C) $3c^3 - 7c^2 - c + 16$
   D) $3c^3 + 7c^2 - c - 16$

2. Which of the following expressions is equivalent to $3x^3 - 12x^2 + 9x$?

   A) $3x(x - 3)(x - 1)$
   B) $(3x + 3)(x - 3)$
   C) $3x(x + 3)(x - 1)$
   D) $3(x^2 - 3)(x - 1)$

3. If $f = 3g + 3$ and $h = g + 1$, what is $-\frac{h}{f}$ in terms of g?

   A) -3
   B) $-\frac{1}{3}$
   C) 3
   D) $\frac{1}{3}$

4. $(3g + 4h)^3$ is equivalent to which of the following expressions?

   A) $64g^3 + 144g^2h + 108gh^2 + 27h^3$
   B) $27g^2 + 108g^2h + 144gh^2 + 64h^2$
   C) $27g^3 + 108g^2h + 144gh^2 + 64h^3$
   D) $27g^3 + 144g^2h + 108gh^2 + 64h^3$

5. $(3st - 4rst + 5sr) - (4st - sr + 2srt) =$

   A) $-st - 2rst + 4sr$
   B) $-st - 2rst + 6sr$
   C) $-st - 6rst + 4sr$
   D) $-st - 6rst + 6sr$

6. If $(x - y) = A$ and $(x + y) = B$, then $-AB =$

   A) $x^2 - y^2$
   B) $y^2 - x^2$
   C) $x^2 + y^2$
   D) $-y^2 - x^2$

7. If $(g - 3)(g + 5) = 49$, then $(g - 4)(g + 6) =$

   A) 40
   B) 48
   C) 50
   D) 58

8. $(a - b - c)(a + b + c) + (a^2 + b^2 + c^2) =$

   A) $2(a^2 + b^2 + c^2)$
   B) $2(bc - a^2)$
   C) $2(a^2 - bc)$
   D) $2(a^2 - b^2 - c^2)$

9. If $X = a^2 - 4$ and $Y = a + 2$, what is $\frac{Y}{X}$ in terms of a?

   A) $a - 2$
   B) $-a - 2$
   C) $\frac{1}{a-2}$
   D) $\frac{-1}{a-2}$

Questions 10 – 12 refer to the following information:

$$A = 19 - 3x$$
$$B = 11 + 2x$$
$$C = 3 - 5x$$

10. $Ax + Bx + Cx =$

   A) $33x$
   B) $33 - 6x^2$
   C) $33x - 6x^2$
   D) $627x - 60x^2$

11. $ABC =$

   A) $30x^3 - 43x^2 - 1030x + 627$
   B) $30x^3 - 7x^2 + 1030x + 627$
   C) $30x^3 + 7x^2 - 1060x + 627$
   D) $30x^3 - 43x^2 - 1060x + 627$

12. $Ax^2 - Bx - C =$

   A) $-3x^3 + 17x^2 - 6x - 3$
   B) $-3x^3 + 21x^2 - 6x - 3$
   C) $-3x^3 + 17x^2 - 16x - 3$
   D) $-3x^3 + 21x^2 - 16x - 3$

13. If $f(x) = 3ab + 2a^2b^3$ and $g(x) = 5ab^2 - ba$, then $\frac{f(x)}{g(x)} =$

   A) $\frac{3+2ab}{5b-1}$
   B) $\frac{3+2ab^2}{5b}$
   C) $\frac{3+2ab}{5b}$
   D) $\frac{3+2ab^2}{5b-1}$

14. $x^{16} - 256$ is equivalent to

   A) $(x^2 - 4)(x^2 + 4)(x^4 + 16)$
   B) $(x^4 + 4)^2(x^8 + 16)$
   C) $(x^2 - 2)(x^2 + 2)(x^4 + 4)(x^8 + 16)$
   D) $(x^2 + 2)^2(x^4 + 4)(x^8 + 16)$

15. $3(abc - ab - a) - 2(a - ab - abc) =$

   A) $abc - ab - 5a$
   B) $5abc - ab - 5a$
   C) $abc + ab - 5a$
   D) $5abc + ab - 5a$

16. $(x + y)(3x - 2) - 2x(y - x) =$

   A) $5x^2 - 2x - 2y - xy$
   B) $5x^2 - 2x - 2y + xy$
   C) $x^2 - 2x - 2y + xy$
   D) $x^2 - 2x - 2y - xy$

Questions 17 – 19 refer to the following information:

$$A = xy^2 - xyz$$
$$B = xz + xyz^2$$
$$C = x - xy - xyz$$

17. What is the greatest common factor of A, B, and C?

   A) 1
   B) x
   C) xz
   D) xy

18. The value of $B - A$ is equivalent to

A) $xz + xyz^2 - xy^2 + xyz$
B) $xz + xyz^2 - xy^2 - xyz$
C) $xz + xyz^2 + xy^2 + xyz$
D) $xz + xyz^2 + xy^2 - xyz$

19. If $x = 3, y = 2$, and $z = -3$, what is the value of $A - C$?

20. If $(h + 8)(h + 2) = 100$, then $(h + 4)(h + 6) =$

Challenge Problem

21. The length and width of a bookshelf must both be 3 inches less than half its height, h. Which of the following expressions can be used to find the volume of the bookshelf, in inches?

A) $h\left(\frac{1}{2}h - 3\right)^2$
B) $h\left(\frac{1}{2}h + 3\right)^2$
C) $h(2h - 3)^2$
D) $h(2h + 3)^2$

Radicals and Exponents
Concept & Strategy Lesson

Students must be able to solve and create equivalent expressions involving radicals and rational exponents, including those with extraneous solutions.

Radicals and Exponents

- We covered many of the rules for simplifying terms with radicals and exponents in **Chapter 1**. Review them carefully.
- Sometimes, you will have to solve an equation that contains radicals or exponents. As with solving any other equation, always do the opposite of what is being done to the variable.
- So, if you need to get rid of an exponent, for example $x^2 = 9$, take the square root of both sides.
- If you need to get rid of a radical, raise both sides to that power. So, when solving the equation $\sqrt[3]{x} = \frac{2}{3}$, your first step would be to cube both sides.
- Whenever you obtain a final solution for an equation featuring radicals or exponents, always plug your answer back into the initial expression to make sure it works. If it does not check out, it is an **extraneous solution**.

Example 1:

$$\sqrt{(x + 2)^3} = 8$$

Which of the following is a solution to the equation above?

A) -2
B) 0
C) 2
D) No solution exists.

First, let's get rid of the square root symbol by squaring both sides:

$$\sqrt{(x + 2)^3} = 8$$
$$\left(\sqrt{(x + 2)^3}\right)^2 = 8^2$$
$$(x + 2)^3 = 64$$

Next, cube root both sides to get rid of the exponent:

$$(x + 2)^3 = 64$$

$$\sqrt[3]{(x+2)^3} = \sqrt[3]{64}$$
$$x + 2 = 4$$

So, $x = 2$. Plug the answer into the equation to see if it works.

$$\sqrt{(2+2)^3} = 8$$
$$\sqrt{4^3} = 8$$
$$\sqrt{64} = 8$$
$$8 = 8$$

The answer must be C.

Example 2:

$$T = 2\pi\sqrt{\frac{L}{g}}$$

The formula above is used to solve for the length of the swing of a pendulum, T, given L, the length of the pendulum, in meters, and g, the acceleration of gravity, in $\frac{m}{s^2}$. Which of the following expressions relates the length of the pendulum in terms of g and T?

A) $L = \frac{T^2 g}{4\pi^2}$

B) $L = \frac{T^2 g^2}{4\pi^2}$

C) $L = \frac{T^2 g}{4\pi}$

D) $L = \frac{T^2 g^2}{4\pi}$

Relating the length of the pendulum in terms of g and T means that we're solving for L. First, we'll divide both sides of the equation by 2π.

$$T = 2\pi\sqrt{\frac{L}{g}} \rightarrow \frac{T}{2\pi} = \sqrt{\frac{L}{g}}$$

Next square both sides and simplify.

$$\left(\frac{T}{2\pi}\right)^2 = \left(\sqrt{\frac{L}{g}}\right)^2$$
$$\frac{T^2}{4\pi^2} = \frac{L}{g}$$
$$\frac{T^2 g}{4\pi^2} = L$$

Our answer is A.

Radicals and Exponents
Practice Problems

1. Which of the following is the set of all real solutions to the equation $(3x - 2)(2x - 1)^2 = 0$?

   A) $x = -\frac{3}{2}, -2$

   B) $x = -\frac{1}{2}, -\frac{2}{3}$

   C) $x = \frac{3}{2}, 2$

   D) $x = \frac{1}{2}, \frac{2}{3}$

2. The equation $KE = \frac{1}{2}mv^2$ relates the kinetic energy, KE, of an object to its mass, m, and velocity, v. Which of the following expressions relates the velocity of an object in terms of its mass and kinetic energy?

   A) $v = \pm\sqrt{\frac{2KE}{m}}$

   B) $v = \pm\sqrt{\frac{KE}{2m}}$

   C) $v = \pm 2\sqrt{\frac{KE}{m}}$

   D) $v = \pm\frac{1}{2}\sqrt{\frac{KE}{m}}$

3. Which of the following is a solution to the equation $3 = \sqrt[3]{\dfrac{3}{x}}$?

   A) $-\frac{1}{3}$

   B) $-\frac{1}{9}$

   C) $\frac{1}{9}$

   D) $\frac{1}{3}$

$$v = \sqrt{\frac{F}{m/L}}$$

4. Which of the following contains all of the excluded values of the equation above?

   A) $m \le 0$

   B) $L \le 0$

   C) $m \le 0, L \le 0, F < 0$

   D) $m \le 0, L \le 0, F \le 0$

$$I = \frac{P}{4\pi r^2}$$

5. Given the expression above, $\dfrac{1}{r^2} =$

   A) $\frac{P}{4\pi I}$

   B) $\sqrt{\frac{P}{4\pi I}}$

   C) $\frac{4\pi I}{P}$

   D) $\sqrt{\frac{4\pi I}{P}}$

$$\sqrt{\frac{x}{5}} = -3$$

6. Which of the following is a solution to the equation above?

   A) -45

   B) 0

   C) 45

   D) No solution exists.

7. If $f(x) = \sqrt[3]{x^2 + 5}$, what is the value of $\dfrac{1}{f(\sqrt{3})}$?

A) -2

B) $-\dfrac{1}{2}$

C) $\dfrac{1}{2}$

D) 2

x	-5	-4	-3	-2	-1
$f(x)$	2.714	2.224	1.587	-1	-1.587

8. Which function best models the data above?

A) $f(x) = \sqrt[3]{x^2 - 5}$

B) $f(x) = \sqrt[3]{x^2 + 5}$

C) $f(x) = \sqrt{x^3 - 5}$

D) $f(x) = \sqrt{x^3 + 5}$

9. If $\sqrt[3]{-x - 8} = -4$, then $x =$

A) -72

B) -56

C) 56

D) 72

$$T = 2\pi\sqrt{\dfrac{L}{g}}$$

10. The formula above is used to solve for the length of the swing of a pendulum, T, given L, the length of the pendulum, in meters, and g, the acceleration of gravity, in $\dfrac{m}{s^2}$. Which of the following expressions relates the acceleration of gravity in terms of L and T?

A) $g = \dfrac{T^2 L}{4\pi^2}$

B) $g = \dfrac{4\pi^2 L}{T^2}$

C) $g = \dfrac{T^2 4\pi}{L}$

D) $g = \dfrac{4\pi L^2}{T^2}$

11. The equation $x^4 - x^2 = 0$ has how many distinct, real solutions?

A) 1

B) 2

C) 3

D) 4

12. If $x^{\frac{1}{2}} - 3 = x$, then $x + x^2 - 2x^{\frac{3}{2}} =$

A) -9

B) $-\sqrt{3}$

C) $\sqrt{3}$

D) 9

13. Which of the following is the set of all real solutions to the equation $(3x - 6)^2(x - 2) = 0$?

A) $x = -2$

B) $x = -2, 2$

C) $x = 0$

D) $x = 2$

x	0	1	2	3	4
$f(x)$	2	1	0	1	2

14. Which function best models the data above?

   A) $f(x) = \sqrt{(x+2)^2}$
   B) $f(x) = \sqrt{(x-2)^2}$
   C) $f(x) = -\sqrt{(2-x)^2}$
   D) $f(x) = \sqrt{(-x-2)^2}$

15. If $x^{-2} = -\frac{1}{25}$, then $x^4 =$

   A) -625
   B) $\frac{1}{625}$
   C) 25
   D) 625

16. If $\sqrt{x} + 5 = 4$, then $x =$

   A) -1
   B) 0
   C) 1
   D) There is no real answer for x.

Questions 17 and 18 refer to the following information.

$$f(x) = -\left(\sqrt{1-x} + 2\right)^3$$

17. What is the domain of $f(x)$?

   A) $[-1, \infty)$
   B) $[1, \infty)$
   C) $(-\infty, 1]$
   D) $(-\infty, \infty)$

18. What is the range of $f(x)$?

   A) $[-8, \infty)$
   B) $[8, \infty)$
   C) $(-\infty, -8]$
   D) $(-\infty, \infty)$

19. If $\sqrt{2x^2 - 7} = 3 - x$, then $x =$

   A) $-8, 2$
   B) $-2, 8$
   C) $-8, -2$
   D) $2, 8$

20. If $\sqrt{x-3} - \sqrt{x} = 3$, then $\sqrt{x} =$

   A) -4
   B) -2
   C) 2
   D) There is no real solution.

Challenge Problem

21. If $\sqrt{x-3} + \sqrt{x} = 3$, then $\sqrt{x} =$

   A) -4
   B) -2
   C) 2
   D) 4

Isolating and Identifying Terms
Concept & Strategy Lesson

Students must be able to use structure to isolate or identify a quantity of interest in an expression or equation.

Isolating and Identifying Terms

- Often times, the SAT will ask you to solve for a quantity such as $x + 2$ or $3x$ instead of simply solving for x.
- Many times, the easiest way to solve these is to simply solve for x, then plug your value of x into the indicated expression. Remember that the SAT will usually include the value of x in the answer choices to try to trick you.
- Other times, it'll be impossible to solve for a single term. In these cases, it'll be easier to adjust the initial expression in some way (add 2 to both sides, factor it out, multiply it by some number) to obtain the term that you're looking for.
- Only practice will allow you to figure out which way is best for a particular problem.

Example 1:

If $\frac{3}{4}c - \frac{2}{3}d = -12$, what is the value of $8d - 9c$?

Since we have two variables but only one equation, we are not able to solve for c or d. Thus, we must try to manipulate the equation to obtain the expression that we're looking for. But how do we turn $\frac{3}{4}c - \frac{2}{3}d$ into $8d - 9c$? Multiply both sides of the equation by -12.

$$-12\left(\frac{3}{4}c - \frac{2}{3}d\right) = -12(-12)$$
$$-9c + 8d = 144$$

So, our answer is 144.

Example 2:

$$3x - 6y = 178.5$$
$$5y - 2x = 161.5$$

For the system of equations above, what is the value of $x - y$?

While we could spend a lot of time solving this equation, it would be fairly tedious without a calculator. However, look what happens when you add the two equations together:

$$3x - 6y + 5y - 2x = 178.5 + 161.5$$
$$x - y = 340$$

Isolating and Identifying Terms
Practice Problems

1. If $\frac{3}{1-c} = -\frac{9}{d}$ where $c \neq 1$ and $d \neq 0$, what is d in terms of c?

   A) $d = 3c - 3$

   B) $d = 3 - 3c$

   C) $d = \frac{1}{3}c - 3$

   D) $d = 3 - \frac{1}{3}c$

2. If $x^{-\frac{1}{4}} = y$, where $y > 0$ and $x > 0$, which of the following equations gives x in terms of y?

   A) $x = \frac{1}{\sqrt[4]{y}}$

   B) $x = \frac{1}{y^4}$

   C) $x = \sqrt[4]{y}$

   D) $x = -x^4$

3. If $F = \frac{1}{4\pi\epsilon_0}\frac{q_1 q_2}{r^2}$, $F \neq 0, r \neq 0$, and $\epsilon_0 \neq 0$, then $r^2 =$

   A) $\frac{1}{4\pi\epsilon_0}\frac{q_1 q_2}{\sqrt{F}}$

   B) $\frac{1}{4\pi\epsilon_0}\frac{q_1 q_2}{F}$

   C) $4\pi\epsilon_0\frac{F}{q_1 q_2}$

   D) $4\pi\epsilon_0\frac{\sqrt{F}}{q_1 q_2}$

$$3x = -5y$$
$$-y - x = \frac{7}{4}$$

4. For the system of equations above, what is the value of $2x + 4y$?

   A) $-\frac{7}{4}$

   B) $-\frac{4}{7}$

   C) $\frac{4}{7}$

   D) $\frac{7}{4}$

$$v = v_0 + at$$
$$x = x_0 + v_0 t + \frac{1}{2}at^2$$

5. Given the two equations above, what is the value of x_0 in terms of $x, v, a,$ and t?

   A) $x - vt + \frac{1}{2}at^2$

   B) $x - vt - \frac{1}{2}at^2$

   C) $x + vt - \frac{1}{2}at^2$

   D) $x + vt + \frac{1}{2}at^2$

6. A rectangle has perimeter P, length l, and width w. Which of the following represents w in terms of P and l?

   A) $w = P - l$

   B) $w = \frac{P - 2l}{2}$

   C) $w = \frac{2P - l}{2}$

   D) $w = 2P - 2l$

$$5(x - y) = y$$

7. If (x, y) is a solution to the equation above and $y \neq 0$, what is the ratio of $\frac{x}{y}$?

   A) $-\frac{6}{5}$

   B) $-\frac{4}{5}$

   C) $\frac{4}{5}$

   D) $\frac{6}{5}$

8. If $w \neq 0$, what is the value of $\frac{18(2w)^3}{(4w)^3}$?

9. If $3 < \sqrt{j} < 4$, then which of the following is a possible value of j^2?

   A) 12

   B) 81

   C) 100

   D) 256

10. In the xy-plane, if the parabola with the equation $y = ax^2 + bx + c$, where a, b, and c are constants, passes through the point $(-1, -1)$. Which of the following must be true?

    A) $a - b = c - 1$

    B) $a + c = -b - 1$

    C) $a - b = c + 1$

    D) $b - a = c + 1$

11. In right triangle ABC, where C is a right triangle, a, b, and c are all side lengths of the triangle, with c being its hypotenuse. Which of the following represents b in terms of a and c?

    A) $b = a - c$

    B) $b = c - a$

    C) $b = \sqrt{a^2 - c^2}$

    D) $b = \sqrt{c^2 - a^2}$

12. If $\sin^2 x + \cos^2 x = 1$, then $\sin x =$

    A) $\sqrt{\cos^2 x - 1}$

    B) $\sqrt{1 - \cos^2 x}$

    C) $\sqrt{\cos^2 x + 1}$

    D) $\sqrt{1 + \cos^2 x}$

$$8\left(\frac{x^2}{y}\right) = y$$

13. If (x, y) is a solution to the equation above and $x \neq 0, y \neq 0$, what is the ratio of $\frac{y}{x}$?

    A) 2

    B) $2\sqrt{2}$

    C) 4

    D) 64

14. If $\frac{5}{6}h - \frac{2}{9}j = -7$, what is the value of $4j + 15h$?

    A) −126

    B) 42

    C) 126

    D) It is unable to determined.

15. A trapezoid has area A, height h, and base lengths l_1 and l_2. Which of the following represents l_1 in terms of A, l_2, and w?

A) $l_1 = A - \frac{h}{2} - l_2$

B) $l_1 = \frac{2A - hl_2}{h}$

C) $l_1 = \frac{hl_2 - 2A}{h}$

D) $l_1 = \frac{2A - h}{l_2}$

16. If $\frac{1+x}{1-x} = \frac{1+x}{x-1}$ where $x \neq 1$, what is the value of x?

A) -1

B) 0

C) 1

D) 2

17. If $(ab)^3 = c$, which of the following equations gives b in terms of a and c?

A) $b = \sqrt[3]{\frac{c}{a}}$

B) $b = \frac{c^3}{a}$

C) $b = \sqrt[3]{\frac{c}{a^3}}$

D) $b = \frac{a^3}{c}$

18. The volume of a cone can be found by using the formula $V = \frac{\pi r^2 h}{3}$. If the height of a cone is twice the length of its radius, what is the height of the cone in terms of its volume?

A) $h = \sqrt[3]{\frac{12\pi}{V}}$

B) $h = \sqrt[3]{\frac{\pi V}{12}}$

C) $h = \sqrt[3]{\frac{12V}{\pi}}$

D) $h = \sqrt[3]{\frac{\pi}{12V}}$

Questions 19 – 21 refer to the following information.

$$f = \frac{\omega}{2\pi} \qquad T = \frac{1}{f} \qquad \omega = \omega_0 + \alpha t$$

19. Which of the following represents ω_0 in terms of f, a, and t?

A) $\omega_0 = \frac{2\pi f}{at}$

B) $\omega_0 = \frac{at}{2\pi f}$

C) $\omega_0 = 2\pi f - at$

D) $\omega_0 = 2\pi f + at$

20. Which of the following represents ω in terms of T?

A) $\omega = \frac{2\pi}{T}$

B) $\omega = 2\pi T$

C) $\omega = 2\pi - T$

D) $\omega = \frac{T}{2\pi}$

Challenge Problem

21. Which of the following represents ω_0 in terms of t, a, and T?

A) $\omega_0 = \frac{2\pi - atT}{T}$

B) $\omega_0 = \frac{atT - 2\pi}{T}$

C) $\omega_0 = \frac{2\pi T - at}{T}$

D) $\omega_0 = \frac{at - 2\pi T}{T}$

Lines, Angles, Triangles
Concept & Strategy Lesson

Students must be able to use concepts and theorems about congruence and similarity to solve problems above lines, angles, and triangles.

Lines and Angles

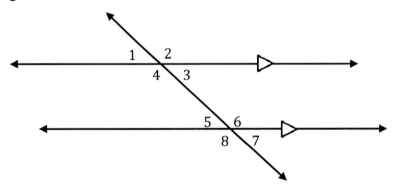

- Given two parallel lines cut by a transversal, certain angles formed are always **congruent** (have equal angle measures), and certain pairs of angles are always **supplementary** (their angle measures add up to 180°).
- In the image above, each odd-numbered angle is congruent to each other odd-numbered angle, and each even-numbered angle is congruent to each other even-numbered angle.
- Likewise, each odd-numbered angle is supplementary to each even-numbered angle, and each even-numbered angle is supplementary to each odd-numbered angle.
- Two angles that are across from each other, such as Angles 1 and 3, are **vertical angles**. Vertical angles are always congruent.

Triangles

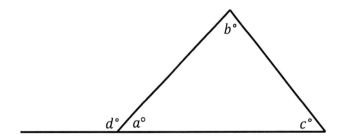

- The measures of the interior angles of a triangle sum to 180° ($a + b + c = 180$).
- The measure of an exterior angle of a triangle is equal to the sum of the two interior angles of the triangle that are not adjacent to that exterior angle ($d = b + c$).

- The longest side of a triangle is always opposite the largest interior angle of the triangle. Likewise, the shortest side of a triangle is always opposite the smallest interior angle of the triangle.
- If two of the interior angles of a triangle have equal measures, then the sides opposite those two angles have equal lengths.
- The lengths of any two sides of a triangle must add up to more than the third side of the triangle.
- A triangle with two equal sides and two equal angles is called an **isosceles triangle**.
- A triangle with three equal sides and three equal angles is called an **equilateral triangle**.
- If two triangles have at least two equal angles, then they are similar (their side lengths are proportional).
- Two triangles are congruent if they have exactly the same 3 side lengths and the same 3 angle measures. The following are enough to prove that two triangles are congruent:
  - SSS – Two triangles with all three side lengths equal
  - SAS – Two triangles with two side lengths and the angle between those side lengths equal
  - ASA – Two triangles with two angles and the side between those angles equal
  - AAS – Two triangles with two angles and a side adjacent to, but not between, those angles equal
  - HL – Two right triangles that have an equal pair of hypotenuses and an equal pair of legs

Example 1:

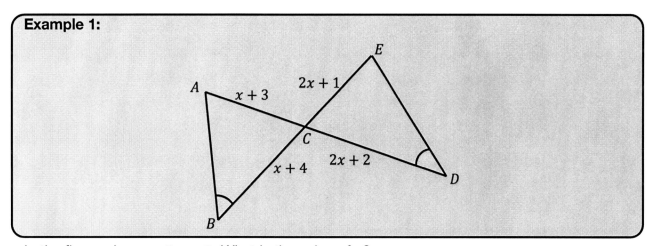

In the figure above, $\angle B \cong \angle D$. What is the value of x?

Since angles ACB and ECD are vertical angles, they must be congruent. Now that we have two triangles that have two congruent angles, we know they must be similar. Thus, their corresponding parts are proportional. Let's set up an equation:

$$\frac{x+3}{x+4} = \frac{2x+1}{2x+2}$$

Now we can cross multiply and solve for x:

$$(x + 3)(2x + 2) = (x + 4)(2x + 1)$$
$$2x^2 + 8x + 6 = 2x^2 + 9x + 4$$
$$x = 2$$

Lines, Angles, Triangles
Practice Problems

Questions 1 and 2 refer to the following information.

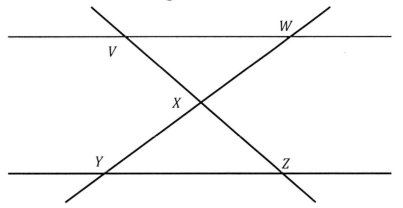

Note: Figure not drawn to scale.

In the figure above, $\triangle VWX \sim \triangle ZYX$.

1. Which of the following must be true?

   A) $\overline{VZ} \perp \overline{WY}$
   B) $\overline{VW} \perp \overline{ZY}$
   C) $\overline{VZ} \parallel \overline{WY}$
   D) $\overline{VW} \parallel \overline{ZY}$

2. If $m\angle XZY$ is 50° and $m\angle VXW$ is 45°, what is $m\angle VWX$?

   A) 75°
   B) 85°
   C) 95°
   D) 105°

3. Which of the following could not be the set of lengths of the sides of a triangle?

   A) 6, 7, 8
   B) 10, 12, 22
   C) 15, 16, 30
   D) 1, 98, 98

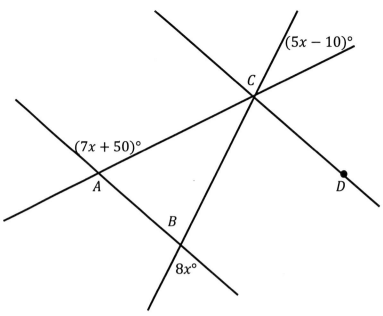

4. In the figure above, $\overline{AB} \parallel \overline{CD}$. What is the value of x?

A) 5
B) 7
C) 10
D) 12

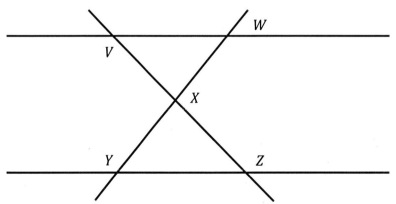

Note: Figure not drawn to scale.

5. In the figure above, $\overline{VW} \parallel \overline{YZ}$. Which of the following pieces of information is enough to prove that $\Delta VXW \cong \Delta ZXY$?

A) $\overline{VX} \cong \overline{XY}$
B) $\overline{WX} \cong \overline{XY}$
C) $\overline{VW} \cong \overline{XY}$
D) $\overline{VX} \cong \overline{YZ}$

Questions 6 – 8 refer to the following information.

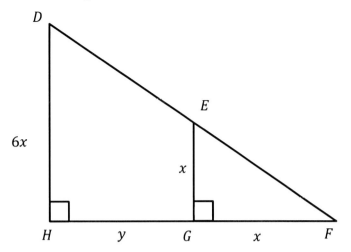

6. In the figure above, $y =$

    A) $4x$
    B) $5x$
    C) $6x$
    D) $8x$

7. What is the approximate angle measure of $\angle DEG$?

    A) $135°$
    B) $142°$
    C) $154°$
    D) It is unable to be determined.

8. What is the area of trapezoid $DEGH$ in terms of x?

    A) $\dfrac{7x^2}{2}$
    B) $15x^2$
    C) $\dfrac{35x^2}{2}$
    D) $21x^2$

Questions 9 and 10 refer to the following information.

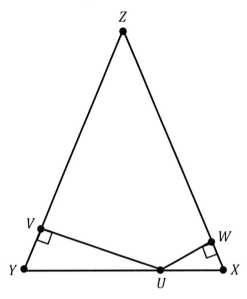

Note: Figure not drawn to scale.

9. Triangle XYZ above is isosceles with $YZ = XZ$ and $YX = 52$. The ratio of UW to UV is $4 : 9$. What is the length of UY?

   A) 13
   B) 14
   C) 26
   D) 36

10. What of the following is equivalent to $\frac{\angle VUY}{\angle WUX}$?

   A) $\frac{4}{9}$
   B) 1
   C) $\frac{13}{9}$
   D) $\frac{9}{4}$

Questions 11 and 12 refer to the following information.

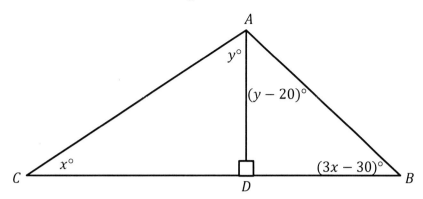

Note: Figure not drawn to scale.

11. What is the value of $y - x$?

    A) 15
    B) 25
    C) 40
    D) 65

12. What is the measure of $\angle BAC$?

    A) 25°
    B) 45°
    C) 90°
    D) 110°

13. The length of a triangle's base is three less than twice its height. If its area is 52 square meters, what is the length of its base?

    A) 5.9 m
    B) 8 m
    C) 8.8 m
    D) 13 m

14. Which of the following is not enough information to prove that $\Delta ABC \sim \Delta DEF$?

    A) $\angle ABC \cong \angle DEF, \ \angle BCA \cong \angle EFD$
    B) $\frac{DE}{AB} = \frac{EF}{BC}, \frac{AB}{AC} = \frac{DE}{DF}$
    C) $BC = 3, AC = 4, EF = 12, DF = 16, \ \angle BCA \cong \angle EFD$
    D) $AC = 5, AB = 7, DF = 15, EF = 21, \ \angle BAC \cong \angle EFD$

15. A triangle has side lengths of 12 and 15. Which of the following could be the length of the third side of the triangle?

    A) 3
    B) 4
    C) 27
    D) 28

16. A triangle has side lengths of $x - 2$, $x + 6$, and $3x - 1$. Which of the following gives the range of all possible values of x?

    A) $2 < x < 3$
    B) $2 \leq x \leq 3$
    C) $3 < x < 5$
    D) $3 \leq x \leq 5$

Questions 17 – 19 refer to the following information.

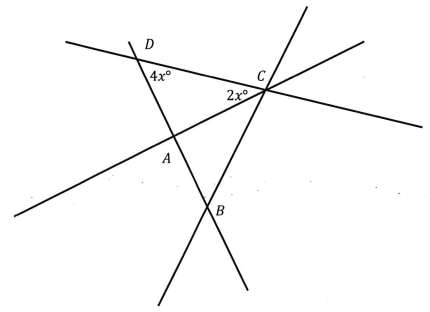

Note: Figure not drawn to scale.

17. If CA bisects both DB and $\angle BCD$ and $CB = DC$, what is the measure of $\angle BCD$?

    A) 20°
    B) 40°
    C) 60°
    D) 80°

18. Based on the information obtained in Question 17, what is the measure of $\angle DAC$?

   A) 30°
   B) 60°
   C) 90°
   D) 120°

19. Which of the following side lengths is longest?

   A) AB
   B) BC
   C) AC
   D) It is impossible to determine.

20. A triangle has a perimeter of 24 and an area of 36. What is the length of its longest side?

   A) 6
   B) 8
   C) 12
   D) It is impossible to determine.

Challenge Problem

21. A triangle is made from the vertex and zeroes of the parabola $y = -x^2 + 4x + 5$. What is the area of that triangle?

Right Triangles
Concept & Strategy Lesson

Students must understand and be able to use the relationship between similarity, right triangles, and trigonometric ratios. Students must be able to use the relationship between sine and cosine of complementary angles.

Similarity

- If two figures are similar, then they have the same shape, but not necessarily the same size. So, the ratio of the lengths of their corresponding sides is equal.
- Solving problems involving similar figures generally involves setting up a cross proportion for two sets of corresponding sides, then cross multiplying.

Pythagorean Theorem

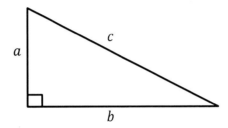

- For a right triangle with leg lengths a and b and hypotenuse of length c, the relation $a^2 + b^2 = c^2$ must hold true.
- The most common right triangle lengths on the Redesigned SAT are in the ratio of $3 : 4 : 5$. The ratio $5 : 12 : 13$ is also common, as is the ratio $8 : 15 : 17$.

Trigonometric Ratios

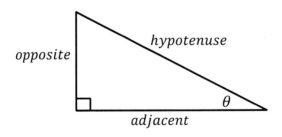

- Use trigonometric ratios to find missing side lengths or angle measurements of right triangles.
- **SOH CAH TOA:** $\sin \theta = \dfrac{opposite}{hypotenuse}$ $\qquad \cos \theta = \dfrac{adjacent}{hypotenuse}$ $\qquad \tan \theta = \dfrac{opposite}{adjacent}$
- $\sin \theta = \cos(90 - \theta)$ and $\cos \theta = \sin(90 - \theta)$
- $\dfrac{\sin \theta}{\cos \theta} = \tan \theta$

Example 1:

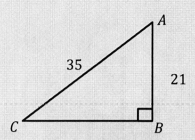

Given triangle ABC above, what is the value of $\cos C$?

A) $\frac{3}{5}$

B) $\frac{3}{4}$

C) $\frac{4}{5}$

D) $\frac{4}{3}$

We know that the cosine of Angle C is equivalent to the length of its adjacent side, CB, divided by the length of its hypotenuse, 35. Since we don't have the length of $\overline{CB}$, we must use the Pythagorean Theorem to find it:

$$a^2 + b^2 = c^2$$
$$21^2 + b^2 = 35^2$$
$$b = 28$$

So, we know that $\cos C = \frac{28}{35} = \frac{4}{5}$. Our answer is C.

Example 2:

Joe is looking up to the top of an 85-foot vertical cliff with an angle of elevation, from the ground, of 45°. If he walks towards the cliff until his angle of elevation to the top of the cliff is 60°, how far, to the nearest tenth of a foot, did he walk?

You should always start out any geometry or trigonometry word problem by drawing a picture. We'll do this on the next page:

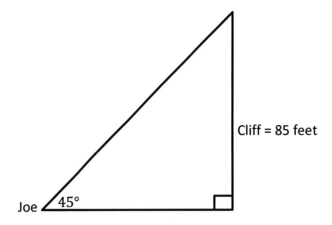

Next, fill in any information that you can figure out:

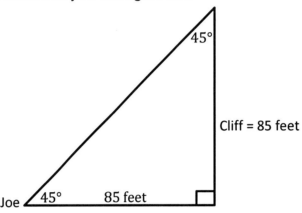

Joe is going to walk forward until his angle of elevation is 60°.

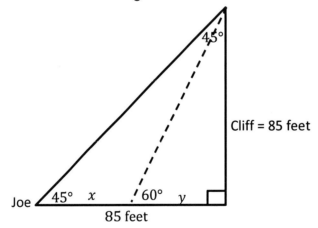

To solve for x, we need to first find the distance between Joe's current spot and the cliff, y, then subtract that from 85. We can use tan to figure out the length of y.

$$\tan 60 = \frac{85}{y}$$

The length of $y = 49.1$ feet, so $x = 35.9$. Joe walked forward 35.9 feet.

Right Triangles
Practice Problems

Questions 1 – 4 refer to the following information.

An architect drew the sketch below while designing a house roof. The dimensions shown are for the interior of the triangle.

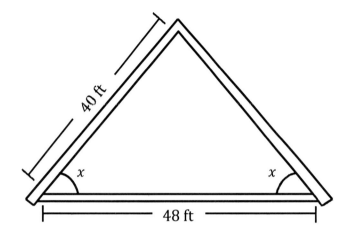

1. What is the value of $\cos x$?

2. What is the value of $\sin x$?

3. What is the value of $\tan x$?

4. What is the height of the roof above, to the nearest foot?

5. Which of the following is equal to $\cos(85°)$?

   A) $-\sin(5°)$
   B) $-\cos(5°)$
   C) $\sin(5°)$
   D) $\sin(85°)$

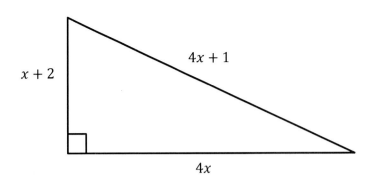

6. In the figure above, $x =$

    A) -1 only
    B) 1 only
    C) 3 only
    D) 1 or 3

Questions 7 and 8 refer to the following information.

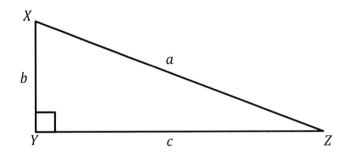

7. Given the right triangle XYZ above, which of the following is equal to $\frac{b}{a}$?

    A) $\cos X$
    B) $\cos Z$
    C) $\tan X$
    D) $\tan Z$

8. Given the right triangle XYZ above, $\sin X =$

    A) $\cos X$
    B) $\cos Z$
    C) $\sin Z$
    D) $\tan X$

9. It is given that $\cos k = j$, where k is the radius measure of an angle and $\pi < k < \frac{3\pi}{2}$. If $\cos h = -j$, which of the following could be the value of h?

A) $3\pi - k$
B) $k - 2\pi$
C) $k + 2\pi$
D) $k + 3\pi$

10. A right triangle has legs of length x and $x\sqrt{3}$. What is the angle measure of the smallest angle of the right triangle?

A) $15°$
B) $30°$
C) $45°$
D) It is unable to be determined.

11. The lengths of the three legs of a right triangle exist in the ratio of $x : x + 7 : x + 8$. What is the area of the triangle?

A) 30
B) 32.5
C) 60
D) 65

12. The diagonal of a rectangle measures 20 inches. If the length of the rectangle is 4 inches longer than its width, what is the area, in square feet, of the rectangle?

A) $\frac{2}{3}$
B) $1\frac{1}{3}$
C) 96
D) 192

13. A square with side length 10 inches is inscribed inside of a circle. What is the area of the circle?

A) $25\sqrt{2}\pi$
B) 50π
C) $50\sqrt{2}\pi$
D) 100π

Questions 14 – 16 refer to the following information.

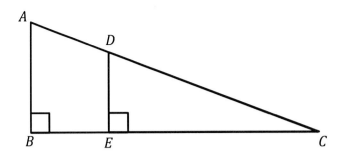

14. $\frac{AB}{CB}$ is equivalent to

   A) $\sin \angle DCE$
   B) $\sin \angle CDE$
   C) $\tan \angle DCE$
   D) $\tan \angle CDE$

15. $m\angle A > m\angle C$. Based on this information, which of the following pieces of information is true?

   A) $DC > BC$
   B) $EC > AB$
   C) $AB > BE$
   D) $CE > ED$

16. $\sin \angle A =$

   A) $\frac{EC}{DC}$
   B) $\frac{ED}{DC}$
   C) $\frac{EC}{ED}$
   D) $\frac{ED}{EC}$

17. $\tan \pi =$

   A) $\sin \pi$
   B) $\cos \pi$
   C) $-\cos \pi$
   D) $\tan 2\pi$

Questions 18 and 19 refer to the following information.

Samir is facing a 200-foot tower and stands 150 feet away from the base of it.

18. To the nearest degree, what is Samir's angle of elevation when he looks at the top of the tower?

    A) 31°
    B) 37°
    C) 51°
    D) 53°

19. Samir turns around 180° and, using the same angle of elevation, views the top of a 300-foot tower. To the nearest foot, how far away is he from the tower?

    A) 136 feet
    B) 226 feet
    C) 239 feet
    D) 398 feet

20. The side lengths of four triangles are given below. Which is not a right triangle?

    A) 6, 8, 10
    B) 4, $4\sqrt{2}$, $4\sqrt{2}$
    C) 6, $6\sqrt{3}$, 12
    D) 8, 15, 17

Challenge Problem

21. The angle of elevation, from an observer at ground level to the top of a 450-foot tower, is 30°. If the observer walks forward 500 feet, what is the approximate angle of elevation to the top of the tower?

    A) 17°
    B) 32°
    C) 58°
    D) 73°

Math Practice Answer Keys

Pre-Algebra Review	Linear Equations and Inequalities	Systems of Linear Equations and Inequalities	Ratios and Percentages	Unit Conversions
1. A	1. C	1. D	1. A	1. D
2. C	2. D	2. B	2. C	2. B
3. B	3. B	3. D	3. B	3. D
4. D	4. A	4. A	4. C	4. A
5. C	5. $m = 0$	5. D	5. C	5. B
6. A	6. D	6. B	6. D	6. C
7. D	7. D	7. B	7. D	7. D
8. C	8. C	8. D	8. D	8. D
9. D	9. A	9. B	9. C	9. C
10. B	10. D	10. D	10. B	10. A
11. B	11. C	11. C	11. C	11. A
12. A	12. D	12. A	12. B	12. A
13. C	13. C	13. D	13. A	13. C
14. B	14. B	14. B	14. C	14. B
15. C	15. B	15. C	15. C	15. C
16. D	16. A	16. C	16. D	16. C
17. C	17. A	17. B	17. B	17. B
18. D	18. 252°F	18. C	18. C	18. C
19. A	19. $760	19. B	19. C	19. B
20. D	20. B	20. D	20. B	20. D
21. B	21. C	21. D	21. D	21. B

Graphs of Equations	Scatterplots	Two-Way Tables	Measures of Center and Spread	Population Parameters and Data Collection
1. D	1. C	1. 3/10	1. D	1. C
2. D	2. A	2. D	2. B	2. A
3. A	3. B	3. C	3. B	3. C
4. C	4. A	4. 9/34	4. B	4. A
5. C	5. B	5. D	5. D	5. D
6. A	6. C	6. D	6. A	6. D
7. B	7. B	7. A	7. B	7. D
8. D	8. A	8. B	8. A	8. A
9. A	9. A	9. B	9. B	9. B
10. D	10. B	10. A	10. C	10. D
11. B	11. D	11. B	11. B	11. C
12. D	12. B	12. D	12. B	12. D
13. A	13. A	13. 9/19	13. D	13. B
14. D	14. C	14. A	14. B	14. A
15. D	15. A	15. A	15. C	15. C
16. D	16. C	16. B	16. D	16. D
17. D	17. B	17. A	17. A	17. D
18. B	18. D	18. C	18. B	18. D
19. B	19. D	19. D	19. B	19. D
20. B	20. A	20. C	20. C	20. C
21. B	21. C	21. 504	21. B	21. D

Explanations can be found online at http://www.tpgenius.com/

Functions	Operations on Polynomials	Radicals and Exponents	Isolating and Identifying Terms	Lines, Angles, Triangles
1. D	1. C	1. D	1. A	1. D
2. C	2. A	2. A	2. B	2. B
3. B	3. B	3. C	3. B	3. B
4. D	4. C	4. C	4. D	4. C
5. D	5. D	5. C	5. A	5. B
6. C	6. B	6. C	6. B	6. B
7. C	7. A	7. C	7. D	7. A
8. B	8. C	8. A	8. 9/4	8. C
9. B	9. C	9. C	9. C	9. D
10. B	10. C	10. B	10. D	10. B
11. C	11. A	11. C	11. D	11. C
12. A	12. A	12. D	12. B	12. D
13. D	13. D	13. D	13. B	13. D
14. D	14. C	14. B	14. D	14. D
15. D	15. B	15. D	15. B	15. B
16. B	16. B	16. D	16. A	16. C
17. C	17. B	17. C	17. C	17. C
18. D	18. A	18. C	18. C	18. C
19. D	19. 15	19. A	19. C	19. B
20. C	20. 108	20. D	20. A	20. D
21. D	21. A	21. C	21. A	21. 27

Right Triangles
1. 3/5
2. 4/5
3. 4/3
4. 32
5. C
6. D
7. A
8. B
9. D
10. B
11. A
12. B
13. B
14. C
15. D
16. A
17. A
18. D
19. B
20. B
21. C

Explanations can be found online at http://www.tpgenius.com/

THIS PAGE IS LEFT INTENTIONALLY BLANK

Section 6
Full-Length Practice Tests

Reading Test

60 MINUTES, 47 QUESTIONS

Mark your responses on this test. Use the "How to Calculate Your Scores in the back of this book to determine your scores.

DIRECTIONS

Each passage or pair of passages below is followed by a number of questions. After reading each passage or pair, choose the best answer to each question based on what is stated or implied in the passage or passages and in any accompanying graphics (such as a table or graph).

Questions 1-9 are based on the following passage.

The following passage is adapted from an article originally published in Scientific American *in 2012. The article explores water-saving measures that were tested in the state of Georgia.*

Fifteen gasoline-powered augers will soon
drill 100 holes in the corn, cotton, and peanut
fields of the Lower Flint River Basin in
Line southwest Georgia. Scientists from the
(5) University of Georgia (UGA) will then slip
half-meter-long PVC pipes into these holes.
The pipes are filled with sensors for soil
moisture and temperature; they are topped by a
flexible antenna that can handle being run over
(10) by a tractor while still being able to relay
information to a computer. Over a two-year
time span, these sensors will provide readings
on soil conditions from 20, 40, and 60
centimeters deep. Combined with more
(15) accurate weather forecasts, the data will help
farmers decide when and where to best use their
irrigations systems.
   "The biggest problem we've got with
irrigation is we [have to] use old wives' tales to
(20) decide when to irrigate," says farmer Marty
Tabb, who will host the probes in a field at his
1,050-he-ctare Bushwater Farm near Colquitt,
Ga., to help him irrigate corn, cotton, and
peanut crops. This technology can help to save
(25) water by producing more crop per drop. "Using
the simplest soil monitor and a computer
program, my peanut yields jumped 20 percent,"
Tabb reports. "I know, just from that, that if we
learn how to water corn, cotton, wheat, we can

(30) save water because we tend to overwater."
   Overwatering is a major problem,
particularly in the Lower Flint River Basin,
which lies in a region gripped by drought. The
area produces the most peanuts and pecans in
(35) the nation, in addition to huge amounts of
cotton and corn. Perhaps more importantly, the
Lower Flint River Basin is the major recharge
zone for the Floridian Aquifer, which provides
water to Florida, Mississippi, Alabama, South
(40) Carolina, and Georgia.
   Farmers in the region have a direct impact
on this vital groundwater. Waters on the surface
and below ground are directly linked: a
downpour can replenish the aquifer, but
(45) excessive pumping of underground water to
irrigate fields can deplete nearby rivers and
streams. When there is plenty of surface water,
the groundwater is also plentiful, but when one
begins to dry up, so does the other. "Because of
(50) the drought and because of us irrigating, we
have pulled water down, and the springs don't
pump anymore," Tabb says.
   In an attempt to cut down on water use
while still maintaining the $2 billion in corn,
(55) cotton, peanuts, and other crops grown in the
region, the Nature Conservancy and the U.S.
Department of Agriculture, along with UGA
and the University of Florida, have teamed up
with more than 1,000 local farmers. They began
(60) by switching some irrigation systems from high
pressure mists to a low pressure system, thus
saving both water and energy. This relatively
simple switch can reduce water use by more
than 22 percent.
(65)   Next, they helped some local farmers
install so-called variable-rate irrigation, which

varies water application rather than simply dumping water equally across an entire field. "Last year that system at my farm, we saved
(70) two to three million gallons of water by having that system cut off over wasteland," Tabb notes. In fact, variable-rate irrigation systems save 15 percent of water use on average. As a result, the technology has begun to spread across the
(75) region and is now being offered as an option for new irrigation systems worldwide.

Despite the success of variable-rate irrigation, it has its drawbacks. It relies on a static map of a given field and does not take
(80) soil type or field conditions into consideration. The new UGA sensor probes, which allow farmers to monitor soil moisture in real time, will help to address this shortcoming. With specific data in hand, farmers will be able to
(85) better target water where it is most needed.

The new technology won't just help farmers in the Lower Flint River Basin; it may also help all those who rely on the water from the Floridian Aquifer. Not only do tens of
(90) thousands of residents of Savannah, Orlando, and other nearby cities rely on the Floridian Aquifer for much of their water, but the Lower Flint River Basin is also home to the largest concentration of amphibian and reptile species
(95) in the entire U.S., many of which are threatened or endangered. When farmers like Tabb conserve water, more of it flows in the region's waterways, providing water for humans and animals alike.

1

As it is used in line 10, "relay" most nearly means

A) hand over.
B) race.
C) communicate.
D) spread.

2

The author most likely included the quotes from Marty Tabb in the second paragraph (lines 18-30) in order to

A) provide expert testimony to establish the benefits of the new sensors.
B) offer a statistical study to establish the necessity of the new sensors.
C) engage the reader by including colloquial language in the passage.
D) suggest that the sensors may not work since the only available evidence is a mere personal anecdote.

3

Based on information in the third paragraph (lines 31-40), it can be reasonably inferred that

A) without the Lower Flint River Basin, the nation would not have access to peanuts and pecans.
B) the Lower Flint River Basin has never experienced a worse period of drought.
C) the biggest problem faced by residents of the Lower Flint River Basin is overwatering.
D) the Lower Flint River Basin is vital to many residents in several states.

4

The relationship between surface water and groundwater (lines 42-43) is most similar to

A) a predatory relationship in which one species hunts another species.
B) a parasitic relationship in which one species lives off of the other without giving anything in return.
C) a symbiotic relationship in which two species are dependent on one another to thrive.
D) a cooperative relationship in which two species choose to work together for a short time.

CONTINUE

5

According to the passage, the Lower Flint River Basin is important because it

A) provides all of the peanuts and pecans grown in the U.S.
B) is the site of a major scientific experiment.
C) is the only source of water for the entire southeast.
D) adds $2 billion to Georgia's agriculture each year.

6

Which of the following provides the best evidence to support the previous question?

A) Lines 1-4 ("Fifteen...Georgia")
B) Lines 33-35 ("The area...nation")
C) Lines 36-40 ("the Lower...Georgia")
D) Lines 53-56 ("In an...region")

7

As it is used in line 67, "application" most nearly means

A) industry.
B) coverage.
C) demand.
D) operation.

8

Which of the following is a widespread impact of the partnership among the Nature Conservancy, the U.S. Department of Agriculture, UGA, and the University of Florida?

A) UGA will install sensors in every field in the region.
B) New, water-saving options are being offered for new irrigation systems worldwide.
C) Residents of cities that rely on the Floridian Aquifer will never have to worry about water supplies.
D) Drought is no longer a concern for farmers in the Lower Flint River Basin.

9

Which of the following provides the best evidence to support the answer to the previous question?

A) Lines 1-4 ("Fifteen...Georgia")
B) Lines 31-33 ("Overwatering...drought")
C) Lines 73-76 ("the technology...worldwide")
D) Lines 87-89 ("it may...Aquifer")

CONTINUE

Questions 10-19 are based on the following passage.

This is an excerpt from Three Men in a Boat *a humorous account of a boating holiday written by Jerome K. Jerome and published in 1889.*

I remember going to the British Museum
one day to read up the treatment for some slight
ailment of which I had a touch—hay fever, I
Line fancy it was. I got down the book, and read all
(5) I came to read; and then, in an unthinking
moment, I idly turned the leaves, and began to
indolently study diseases, generally. I forget
which was the first distemper I plunged into—
some fearful, devastating scourge, I know--and,
(10) before I had glanced half down the list of
"premonitory symptoms," it was borne in upon
me that I had fairly got it.

I sat for awhile, frozen with horror; and
then, in the listlessness of despair, I again
(15) turned over the pages. I came to typhoid
fever—read the symptoms--discovered that I
had typhoid fever, must have had it for months
without knowing it—wondered what else I had
got; turned up St. Vitus's Dance—found, as I
(20) expected, that I had that too—began to get
interested in my case, and determined to sift it
to the bottom, and so started alphabetically—
read up ague, and learnt that I was sickening for
it, and that the acute stage would commence in
(25) about another fortnight. Bright's disease, I was
relieved to find, I had only in a modified form,
and, so far as that was concerned, I might live
for years. Cholera I had, with severe
complications; and diphtheria I seemed to have
(30) been born with. I plodded conscientiously
through the twenty-six letters, and the only
malady I could conclude I had not got was
housemaid's knee.

I felt rather hurt about this at first; it
(35) seemed somehow to be a sort of slight. Why
hadn't I got housemaid's knee? Why this
invidious reservation? After a while, however,
less grasping feelings prevailed. I reflected that
I had every other known malady in the
(40) pharmacology, and I grew less selfish, and
determined to do without housemaid's knee.
Gout, in its most malignant stage, it would
appear, had seized me without my being aware
of it; and zymosis I had evidently been
(45) suffering with from boyhood. There were no
more diseases after zymosis, so I concluded
there was nothing else the matter with me.

I sat and pondered. I thought what an
interesting case I must be from a medical point
(50) of view, what an acquisition I should be to a
class! Students would have no need to "walk

the hospitals," if they had me. I was a hospital
in myself. All they need do would be to walk
round me, and, after that, take their diploma.
(55) Then I wondered how long I had to live. I
tried to examine myself. I felt my pulse. I
could not at first feel any pulse at all. Then, all
of a sudden, it seemed to start off. I pulled out
my watch and timed it. I made it a hundred and
(60) forty-seven to the minute. I tried to feel my
heart. I could not feel my heart. It had stopped
beating. I have since been induced to come to
the opinion that it must have been there all the
time, and must have been beating, but I cannot
(65) account for it. I patted myself all over my
front, from what I call my waist up to my head,
and I went a bit round each side, and a little
way up the back. But I could not feel or hear
anything. I tried to look at my tongue. I stuck
(70) it out as far as ever it would go, and I shut one
eye, and tried to examine it with the other. I
could only see the tip, and the only thing that I
could gain from that was to feel more certain
than before that I had scarlet fever.
(75) I had walked into that reading-room a
happy, healthy man. I crawled out a decrepit
wreck.

I went to my medical man. Rather than
bore him with my list of complaints, I felt it
(80) easier to tell him what was *not* the matter. "I
have not got housemaid's knee. Everything else,
however, I *have* got."

And I told him how I came to discover it
all.
(85) Then he opened me and looked down me,
and hit me over the chest when I wasn't
expecting it—a cowardly thing to do, I call it —
and immediately afterwards, he sat down and
wrote out a prescription.
(90) It read: "Don't stuff up your head with
things you don't understand."

I followed the directions, which the happy
result that my life is still going on.

10

The author can best be described as

A) A layperson learning more about human
anatomy and health.
B) A doctor familiarizing himself with new
developments in medicine.
C) Someone who is easily convinced of things he
reads.
D) A skeptic who is attempting to disprove medical
science.

1

The author went to the library in order to research

A) hay fever.
B) cholera.
C) housemaid's knee.
D) scarlet fever.

2

What is the central theme of the passage?

A) Everyone is in poorer health than they expect.
B) It can be easy to convince yourself that you are sick.
C) Medical science is often untrustworthy.
D) The great amount of medical knowledge available can be overwhelming for patients.

3

The word "acute" in line 24 most nearly means

A) sharp.
B) severe.
C) important.
D) perceptive.

4

As it is used in line 42, "malignant" most nearly means

A) spiteful.
B) cancerous.
C) dangerous.
D) unkind.

15

The narrator's response to his self-diagnosis can best be described as

A) proud.
B) horrified.
C) jocular.
D) indifferent.

16

Which of the following gives the best evidence for the answer to the previous question?

A) Lines 13-15 ("I... pages.")
B) Lines 25-28 ("Bright's... years.")
C) Lines 34-35 ("I... slight.")
D) Lines 48-51 ("I... class!")

17

What role does the fourth paragraph play in the passage?

A) It communicates the narrator's disdain for hospitals.
B) It suggests a new method for medical students to learn about disease.
C) It humorously overstates the narrator's medical problems.
D) It communicates the author's despair at his medical condition.

18

When he shares them with others, the author begins to see his ailments as

A) the results of an overactive imagination.
B) the signs of his impending demise.
C) an overdramatic response to some real but solvable problems.
D) a complicated medical dilemma.

19

Which of the following gives the best evidence for the answer to the previous question?

A) Lines 7-12 ("I forget...got it.")
B) Lines 48-51 ("I sat...class!")
C) Lines 78-80 ("Rather...matter.")
D) Lines 85-91 ("Then...understand.")

CONTINUE

Questions 20-28 are based on the following passage.

The following passages are excerpted from a pair of National Science Foundation articles. The first is from an article titled "Snails in the Waters, Disease in the Villages." The second is from an article titled "'Defective' Virus Leads to Epidemic of Dengue Fever."

Passage 1

Watch where you jump in for a swim or where your bath water comes from, especially if you live in Africa, Asia, or South America.
Line Snails that live in tropical fresh water in these
(5) locations are intermediaries between disease-causing parasitic worms and humans. The worms' infectious larvae emerge from the snails, cruise in shallow water, easily penetrate human skin, and mature in internal organs. The
(10) result is schistosomiasis, the second most socioeconomically devastating disease after malaria.

People in developing countries who don't have access to clean water and good sanitation
(15) facilities are often exposed to the infected snails, and thus the parasitic worms. Over 70 developing nations have identified significant rates of schistosomiasis in human populations.

There has been much debate about how
(20) long treatment should last once someone has schistosomiasis. Current guidelines focus on suppressing the disease's effects by limiting the infection during childhood, but that may not be enough to cure it or to prevent re-infection,
(25) leaving children still at risk for stunted growth and anemia.

Schistosomiasis is usually treated with a single dose of the oral drug praziquantel. World Health Organization (WHO) guidelines
(30) recommend that when more than 10 percent of the children in a village have parasite eggs in their urine or stool—a clear sign of schistosomiasis—everyone in the village should receive treatment. In addition, school-age
(35) children should receive additional treatments every two years.

However, because of the long-term health effects of schistosomiasis, many scientists are critical of this plan. They now argue instead for
(40) regular yearly treatment, saying that current WHO recommendations cannot achieve full suppression of schistosomiasis. In higher-risk villages, repeated annual treatment is necessary for an indefinite period—until the eco-social
(45) factors that foster the disease, such as poor wastewater treatment, are removed. Fixing the water treatment problem can reduce human

diseases much more effectively and at a lower cost than simply focusing on disease treatment.
(50)　　To achieve the goal of the complete elimination of schistosomiasis, scientists need to determine what makes a "wormy village," how often therapy is needed to prevent disease in such locations, and what can be done to
(55) change the environment so that a high-risk village becomes a low-risk one. There is a long way to go before this goal is reached.

Passage 2

It's 2001 in Myanmar (formerly known as Burma), a country in Southeast Asia. Almost
(60) 200 people have died, and more than 15,000 are ill—all having contracted dengue fever. Dengue is a disease transmitted by mosquitoes and caused by four types of the dengue virus. Infection may not result in symptoms; it may
(65) cause mild, flu-like illness; or it may result in potentially deadly hemorrhagic fever.

Dengue virus infects some 50-100 million people annually in Southeast Asia, South America, and parts of the United States. In
(70) Myanmar, dengue is endemic. The disease has occurred there in three- to five-year cycles since the first recorded outbreak in 1970. Each one has been more deadly than the last.

What caused the widespread infection in
(75) Myanmar in 2001, a disease that resulted from one type of dengue virus, DENV-1? For more than a decade, researchers have been working to solve the puzzle.

One potential explanation involves so-
(80) called "defective" viruses. A defective virus results from genetic mutations or deletions that eliminate essential functions. They're generated in viruses with high mutation rates. These defective viruses were once considered
(85) unimportant.

However, in a recent study, scientists reported a significant link between one such defective virus and the high rate of transmission of DENV-1 in Myanmar in 2001. They found
(90) that the normal, functional virus is actually helping the defective virus. While defective viruses can't complete their life cycle on their own, if they're able to get into the same cell with a non-defective virus, they can "hitchhike"
(95) with the non-defective one and propagate.

Pathogens can depend on the presence of other species to spread, or, as in this case, other varieties of the same species. Understanding these interactions is critical for predicting when
(100) the next epidemic might occur—and how to prevent it.

CONTINUE

Why would a defective virus increase transmission of a disease? One hypothesis is that the defective virus may be interfering with (105) the disease-causing virus, making the disease less intense. People then have a milder infection, and because they don't feel as sick, they're more likely to go out of their homes and spread the disease.

(110) The biologists believe that their work will help turn the tide of the next deadly outbreak of dengue in Myanmar—and in other tropical countries around the globe.

20

The primary goal of the scientists in Passage 1 is to

A) eliminate schistosomiasis.
B) kill off the snails in tropical waters.
C) change the WHO guidelines.
D) identify at-risk populations.

21

Which of the following best supports the answer to the previous question?

A) Lines 13-16 ("People...worms")
B) Lines 16-18 ("Over...populations")
C) Lines 21-26 ("Current...anemia")
D) Lines 50-56 ("To achieve...one")

22

According to the passage, why does schistosomiasis typically only impact people in developing nations?

A) Because people in developing nations lack access to adequate healthcare facilities for early treatment of the illness.
B) Because people in developing nations often lack access to the clean water and sanitation facilities that can eliminate the parasite.
C) Because the WHO guidelines in place in developing nations are inadequate.
D) Because villages in developing nations have a large percentage of vulnerable populations like children.

23

As it is used in line 39, "critical" most nearly means

A) serious.
B) crucial.
C) demanding.
D) disparaging.

24

According to the first passage, which of the following is the best way to reduce diseases?

A) Improving water treatment, particularly in developing countries
B) Focusing research on developing cost-effective treatment options
C) Treating patients regularly for an unspecified period of time
D) Identifying the means by which diseases are spread

25

The purpose of the information in lines 58-61 ("It's...fever") is to

A) explain how quickly dengue virus spreads.
B) convince the reader to take action to solve the dengue virus endemic in Myanmar.
C) establish the severity of the dengue virus endemic in Myanmar.
D) show that the dengue virus endemic in Myanmar is not as bad as it is in other areas.

26

Which of the following best establishes the primary idea of the second passage?

A) Lines 58-66 ("It's...fever")
B) Lines 67-70 ("Dengue...endemic")
C) Lines 70-73 ("The disease...last")
D) Lines 74-78 ("What...puzzle")

CONTINUE →

27

As it is used in line 82, "essential" most nearly means

A) requisite.
B) underlying.
C) crucial.
D) cardinal.

28

Which of the following describes the effect of the author's use of the term "hitchhike" in line 94?

A) To use a common term to illustrate a complex process
B) To create imagery through descriptive words
C) To suggest that defective viruses engage in risky behavior similar to hitchhiking
D) To personify the virus in order to better explain its motives

CONTINUE

Questions 29-37 are based on the following passage.

The following is an excerpt from a speech delivered by U.S. Supreme Court Justice Stephen G. Breyer to lawyers and judges at a meeting of the American Bar Association.

Three weeks ago, when Justice O'Connor
and I were at the Ninth Circuit Judicial
Conference, a judge asked us whether we
Line thought judges should participate in community
(5) affairs. Justice O'Connor and I agree about
many things—not everything—and we
certainly agreed about the answer to that one.
Of course they should. Yet more important—so
should lawyers. After all, Roscoe Pound once
(10) defined our profession as a group of men and
women "pursuing a learned art as a common
calling in the spirit of public service." And
many of us remember at least hearing about a
professional golden age when the respected
(15) general practitioner or local judge would serve
on a school board, sponsor a Scout Troop, or
give a Fourth of July speech.
Yet as we spoke, we were both aware of
modern pressures that make it difficult for any
(20) of us, whether judge or lawyer, to live up to that
past ideal. For the judge those pressures may
take the form of workload, keeping us at our
desks, or internally generated concerns about
conflicts of interest that may lead us to believe
(25) the safest way to avoid public criticism is
through total isolation. But ethics rules, which
must be followed, do not mandate total
isolation. Indeed, just after the judicial
conference, Justice O'Connor and I went on to
(30) visit several Indian reservations, where we saw
tribal courts in action. On the Spokane
Reservation we saw a drug court draw upon a
host of community resources in order to prevent
a teenager's recidivism. In the Navajo Nation
(35) we witnessed highly successful mediation
techniques. We also began to understand the
great benefits that a few additional resources
might bring. During these visits, we shared
views and experiences—which, we hope, will
(40) prove beneficial in the continuing effort to
improve the quality of justice (and therefore the
quality of life) on Indian reservations.
Lawyers face different, more immediate,
more serious pressures. Many of my
(45) practitioner friends talk about the "treadmill."
How can a lawyer undertake pro bono work,
engage in law reform efforts, even attend bar
association meetings, if that lawyer must
produce 2,100 or more billable hours each year,
(50) say sixty-five or seventy hours in the office

each week? That kind of number reflects a
pace, which, according to one lawyer, is like
"drinking water from a fire hose." The
treadmill's pressure is partly financial,
(55) aggravated for younger lawyers by law school
loans that may amount to $100,000 or more,
which must be paid back from their earnings in
practice. The pressure also reflects the
increased complexity and specialization of law
(60) itself. . . .
All of us want to resist these isolating
pressures. Perhaps it will help if in the next few
minutes I try to explain why, from my own
perspective, it is so important that we do so. I
(65) shall describe three different "public service"
roles that the lawyer traditionally has played
and which still, taken together, make up that
"spirit of public service" that must continue to
characterize the American Bar.
(70) I shall touch upon the first—pro bono legal
work—only briefly, simply because it is so well
known to you. The Supreme Court is itself a
direct beneficiary of that work, for public
interest organizations and law firms
(75) representing pro bono clients often file briefs.
And they represent clients ranging from death
row prisoners in habeas corpus cases to
property owners in "Takings Clause" cases. The
briefs are almost always helpful, whatever
(80) political or ideological view they represent.
But more broadly, pro bono work means
that those who cannot afford legal
representation to protect their legal rights will
have it. The need is there. A 1994 ABA Report
(85) says that between 70% and 80% of those with
low incomes who needed a lawyer in a civil
case failed to find one. . . .
And the critical importance of satisfying
the resulting need was explained to me in a
(90) sentence two summers ago by a foreign judge.
He told me that most villagers in his country
had never seen a lawyer or a judge. He had
persuaded a local bar group to lend him a small
private plane; and he spent weekends flying to
(95) distant villages, mediating disputes, most of
which he resolved rather quickly. Why?
Because, he explained, by helping make the
legal system work for everyone, he would help
to build public confidence necessary to sustain
(100) the legal system itself.

29

The author's primary purpose in speaking is to

A) explain why judges often isolate themselves from the community.
B) convince his listeners of the importance of public service on the part of lawyers.
C) explain why lawyers often find it difficult to engage in public service.
D) hold himself up as an example of how judges can engage in public service.

30

The author most likely included the quote from Roscoe Pound in lines 11-12 in order to

A) provide expert testimony to prove that public service is mandatory for lawyers.
B) explain why he believes that public service is vital to the legal profession.
C) better illustrate the ideals of the golden age of the legal profession.
D) define the legal profession.

31

As it is used in line 33, "host" most nearly means

A) moderator.
B) crowd.
C) presenter.
D) array.

32

It can be inferred from the passage that

A) the tribal courts operate differently from other courts.
B) Justices Breyer and O'Connor visited the tribal courts to tell tribal judges what they were doing wrong.
C) tribal courts lack access to helpful community resources.
D) tribal courts do not follow judicial rules of ethics.

33

Which of the following provides the best evidence for the answer of the previous question?

A) Lines 26-28 ("But ethics...isolation")
B) Lines 29-31 ("Justice...action")
C) Lines 31-34 ("On the...recidivism")
D) Lines 38-43 ("During...reservations")

34

Based on information in the passage, what does the author mean by the term "treadmill" (line 45)?

A) Lawyers are under constant pressure to perform pro bono work.
B) Lawyers enjoy working constantly in the same way that many other people enjoy exercise.
C) Lawyers must work constantly in order to pay student loans and get ahead, leaving little time for other pursuits.
D) The increased complexity of the legal profession requires that lawyers work constantly to stay ahead of changes.

35

The author likely included the question in lines 46-52 in order to

A) show that the speaker doesn't fully understand the issue himself.
B) present a problem that the speaker intends to solve.
C) pose a question that will be answered later in the speech.
D) illustrate the pressures that prevent many lawyers from doing pro bono work.

36

As it is used in line 55, "aggravated" most nearly means

A) worsened.
B) irritated.
C) enhanced.
D) teased.

37

Based on the passage, which of the following best describes the "isolating pressures" that prevent judges and lawyers from engaging in public service?

A) Judges are forbidden from public service by ethics rules while lawyers lack the "spirit of public service."
B) Judges are too busy sitting on school boards while lawyers are overwhelmed by the complexity of the profession.
C) Judges fear ethics violations while lawyers simply lack the time.
D) Judges are overworked while lawyers fear ethics violations.

CONTINUE

Questions 38-47 are based on the following passage.

The following is adapted from an article titled "Why North Europeans Are the Happiest People on Earth."

According to the 2015 World Happiness Report, a report published by a group of influential economists, the world's happiest
Line countries are Switzerland, Iceland, Denmark,
(5) and Norway. What exactly are these nations doing right that the rest of the world is doing wrong?

Jeffrey Sachs of Columbia University, Richard Layard of the London School of
(10) Economics, and John Helliwell of the University of British Columbia have been publishing the World Happiness Report since 2012. Their goal is to remind governments that success is about more than economic growth
(15) and other such statistics. Certainly people tend to be happier when they're wealthier and healthier, as they tend to be in more developed countries, but there are many other factors that influence well-being. That's what the report
(20) measures: People in various countries are asked how they perceive various aspects of their lives.

After years of conducting these surveys, the authors have identified six variables that account for three-quarters of the differences in
(25) happiness levels among countries: Gross domestic product per capita, social support, healthy life expectancy, freedom to make life choices, generosity, and freedom from corruption. Two of these—social support and
(30) generosity—are relatively independent of economic development or politics, which explains why some fairly poor, institutionally weak countries have happier populations than the strongest Western democracies. For
(35) example, Mexicans are happier than Americans, and Brazilians report being happier than the residents of Luxembourg.

The happiest countries are rich, healthy, free, and populated with generous people who
(40) support one another when there's trouble. One has to wonder if Northern Europe's so-called Law of Jante might not be responsible for the fact that Iceland, Denmark, Norway, Finland, and Sweden are among the world's ten happiest
(45) nations. Though Scandinavians may scoff at the cultural creed that considers individual success to be unworthy, it does make for unusually strong social support networks. It is this cultural phenomenon that the study's authors point to as
(50) an explanation for Iceland's surprising resilience during an economic collapse, as well

as the country's second place in the rankings. Iceland has the highest percentage in the world of people who say they have someone to count
(55) on in times of crisis.

The report includes a chapter that emphasizes the role of "relational goods," such as reciprocity and simultaneity (which describes people taking part in meaningful activities
(60) together), in building happy nations. People are happier when they're socially fulfilled, particularly as members of a group. The happiest countries are participatory. That is true for Switzerland, with its direct democracy and
(65) close-knit local communities, as well as for the Scandinavian countries, which have perhaps the highest social capital in the world. Participation and democracy help to build mutual trust, an important part of social capital, a term that
(70) describes the networks of relationships among people in a society. People are more willing to pay taxes, less likely to become corrupt, and more likely to embrace expansive social safety nets.

(75) Though it might seem that such a social fabric ought to be strong, it is, in fact, quite delicate. The happiest countries in the world have small populations (the biggest country in the top ten is Canada, at 35 million residents).
(80) Bringing smaller countries together into a bigger bloc, such as the European Union, doesn't help to increase social capital. In fact, when some countries in such a union are outperformed by others, their social fabric rips,
(85) trust erodes, and the decline in happiness is greater than economic losses can explain. The ideal example of this is Greece, the biggest happiness loser compared with data for 2005-2007.

(90) One of the policy implications of the findings of Sachs, Layard, and Helliwell is that countries need to nurture their natural social fabric rather than seek to impose contrived rules that might have worked elsewhere. If laws are
(95) passed that run counter to the social and moral rules prevailing in a society, then those laws will fail to produce the desired results because they will not be followed because not all infringers of such rules can be punished. Worse,
(100) such laws are likely to threaten the stability of the social order by trying to impose unnatural change on a culture.

In other words, a country like the U.S. cannot improve happiness simply by passing
(105) laws or establishing government programs that imitate those of countries like Sweden. No matter how much we may like big, ambitious programs, aiming for happiness may mean

CONTINUE

thinking small and being careful with the fragile
(110) web of relationships that make human society
function.

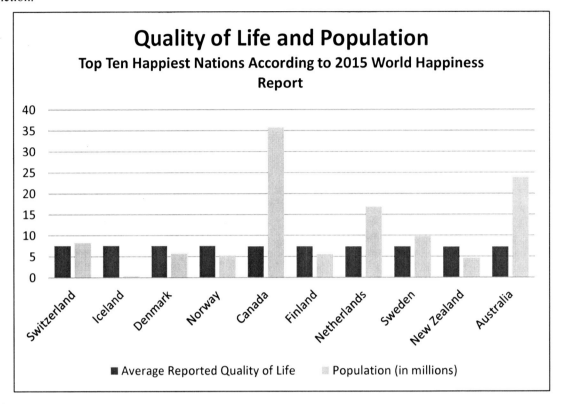

Quality of Life and Population
Top Ten Happiest Nations According to 2015 World Happiness Report

Legend: ■ Average Reported Quality of Life   ▨ Population (in millions)

Nations (left to right): Switzerland, Iceland, Denmark, Norway, Canada, Finland, Netherlands, Sweden, New Zealand, Australia

38

Which of the following best establishes the main idea of the passage?

A) Lines 5-7 ("What...wrong")
B) Lines 8-13 ("Jeffrey...2012")
C) Lines 20-21 ("People...lives")
D) Lines 32-34 ("institutionally...democracies")

39

Which of the following can be inferred from the second paragraph (lines 8-21)?

A) The only factor that should be considered in evaluating a government's success is the happiness of its people.
B) A government's success can best be measured by a country's economic health.
C) Governments use the World Happiness Report when measuring their success or failure.
D) Governments often forget to consider things like happiness when considering their success or failure.

40

As it is used in line 22, "conducting" most nearly means

A) accompanying.
B) administering.
C) transporting.
D) acquitting.

41

How would the author most likely explain why Mexicans are happier than Americans?

A) The Mexican economy is stronger than the American economy.
B) The Mexican government is less corrupt than the American government.
C) The Mexican government is stronger than the American government.
D) Mexicans report enjoying greater social support and generosity than Americans.

CONTINUE ▶

42

Which of the following provides the best evidence in support of the answer to the previous question?

A) Lines 19-21 ("That's...lives")
B) Lines 22-29 ("After...corruption")
C) Lines 29-34 ("Two of these...democracies.")
D) Lines 38-40 ("The...trouble")

43

It can be inferred that the author believes which of the following about the Law of Jante (line 42)?

A) By minimizing the importance of individual success, it encourages group cooperation.
B) It causes a decline in happiness by degrading individual achievement.
C) It is a written law that is strongly enforced in Northern European countries.
D) It was enacted during one of Iceland's economic collapses.

44

Which of the following is most strongly implied by the passage?

A) Smaller countries are more likely to be happier countries.
B) Greece is a part of the European Union.
C) Mexico and Brazil tend to favor reciprocity and simultaneity above all else.
D) Because the United States is a union of many parts, it has a weak social fabric.

45

Which of the following provides the best evidence in support of the answer to the previous question?

A) Lines 34-37 ("For... Luxembourg.")
B) Lines 45-48 ("Though... networks.")
C) Lines 75-79 ("Though... residents.)")
D) Lines 82-89 ("In fact... 2007.")

46

As it is used in line 95, "counter" most nearly means

A) opposite.
B) retaliate.
C) backwards.
D) offset.

47

Based on the graphic, which of the following countries could be considered an outlier based on the information found in the sixth paragraph (lines 75-89)?

A) Switzerland
B) Iceland
C) Sweden
D) Australia

STOP

If you finish before time is called, you may check your work on this section only.

Do not turn to any other section.

Writing and Language Test

35 MINUTES, 44 QUESTIONS

Mark your responses on this test. Use the "How to Calculate Your Scores in the back of this book to determine your scores.

DIRECTIONS

Each passage below is accompanied by a number of questions. For some questions, you will consider how the passage might be revised to improve the expression of ideas. For other questions, you will consider how the passage might be edited to correct errors in sentence structure, usage, or punctuation. A passage or a question may be accompanied by one or more graphics (such as a table or graph) that you will consider as you make revising and editing decisions.

Some questions will direct you to an underlined portion of a passage. Other questions will direct you to a location in a passage or ask you to think about the passage as a whole.

After reading each passage, choose the answer to each question that most effectively improves the quality of writing in the passage or that makes the passage conform to the conventions of standard written English. Many questions include a "NO CHANGE" option. Choose that option if you think the best choice is to leave the relevant portion of the passage as it is.

Questions 1-11 are based on the following passage.

Though American parents spend more time with their children than any other parents in the world, many feel guilty because they don't believe it's enough. There's a widespread cultural assumption that the time parents, particularly mothers, spend with children is key to ensuring a bright future. **1** A new study confirms the importance of parent time in child development.

1

Which of the following provides the best thesis for the passage as a whole?

A) NO CHANGE
B) New research suggests that even the large amounts of time that Americans spend with their children isn't enough.
C) It turns out that parent time is completely unimportant to child development.
D) Groundbreaking new research upends that conventional wisdom.

In fact, it appears that the amount of time parents spend with their children between the ages of 3 and 11 has virtually no impact on how children turn out. This is the primary finding of the first large-scale longitudinal study of parent time, published in April 2015 in the Journal of Marriage and Family, which examined parental time and **2** it's impact on such factors as children's academic achievement, behavior, and emotional well-being.

3 That's not to say that parent time isn't important. Plenty of studies have shown links between quality parent time—such as reading to a **4** child; sharing meals; talking with them, or otherwise engaging with them one-on-one—and positive outcomes for kids. The same is true for parents' warmth and sensitivity toward their children. It's just that the quantity of time doesn't appear to matter.

2

A) NO CHANGE
B) its
C) it
D) its'

3

Which of the following creates the best transition between the second and third paragraphs?

A) NO CHANGE
B) These findings are confusing since other studies show the exact opposite.
C) Other researchers question these findings.
D) Clearly, these findings show that parent time is unimportant.

4

A) NO CHANGE
B) child; sharing meals; talking with them; or otherwise
C) child, sharing meals, talking with them, or otherwise
D) child, sharing meals (talking with them), or otherwise

CONTINUE

The one instance the study identified in which the quantity of time parents spend does indeed matter is during adolescence: the more time a teen spends engaged with **5** their mother, the fewer instances of delinquent behavior. And the more time a teen spends with both parents together in family time, **6** the less likely he or she is to engage in drug and alcohol use and to engage in other risky, dangerous, or illegal behavior. Students who spend plenty of time with family also achieve higher math scores. Interestingly, the study found positive **7** conclusions for teens who spent an average of just six hours a week engaged in family time with **8** parents, so the time required to see beneficial results is minimal.

5

A) NO CHANGE
B) him or her
C) his or her
D) they're

6

A) NO CHANGE
B) the lower the likelihood of the teen engaging in drug and alcohol abuse or engaging in illegal and risky behavior.
C) the less likely they are to do drugs, drink, or do illegal things.
D) the less likely he or she is to abuse drugs and alcohol or engage in other risky behavior.

7

A) NO CHANGE
B) outcomes
C) events
D) consequences

8

A) NO CHANGE
B) parents;
C) parents, for
D) parents, but

CONTINUE

These findings could have significant impacts on modern parenting. The study's findings shook some parents, many of whom had built their lives around the idea that the more time with children, the better. **9** Working mothers today spend as much time with their children as at-home mothers did in the early 1970s. This is despite the fact that modern mothers often work full time outside of the home. **10** They quit or cut back on work, have downsized their houses, or will have struggled to cram it all in. **11** Turns out, all those sacrifices were totally pointless.

Hours of Parent-Child Time per Week

■ Mothers ■ Fathers

Year	Mothers	Fathers
1965	10.5	2.6
1975	7.3	2.4
1985	8.5	3
1995	11.2	4.5
1999	12	6.9
2004	13.9	6.4
2010	13.7	7.2

9

Which of the following best suits the paragraph based on the information in the graph?

A) NO CHANGE
B) Mothers today spend significantly more time with their children than mothers in past decades.
C) Modern fathers still fail to spend more time with their children than they did several decades ago.
D) Mothers spent little time with their children in the 1970s and 1980s.

10

A) NO CHANGE
B) They quit or cut back on work, have downsized their houses, or struggled to cram it all in.
C) They quit or cut back on work, downsized their houses, or struggled to cram it all in.
D) They quit or cut back on work or downsized their houses or struggled to cram it all in.

11

Which of the following provides the best conclusion to the passage as a whole?

A) NO CHANGE
B) Instead, it is building relationships in order to seize quality moments of connection that is most important for both parent and child well-being.
C) And when mothers failed to meet the standards they set for themselves by not being able to balance everything, they realized that it just didn't matter.
D) Who knew that spending time with kids was pointless?

CONTINUE

Questions 12-22 are based on the following passage.

Food is energy for the body. The digestive process breaks complex food structures down into simpler structures, such as sugars, that travel to our cells. The energy stored in the chemical bonds of these simpler molecules powers our **12** bodies. We measure this energy in calories.

In the 19th century, chemist Wilbur Olin Atwater developed the calorie system that we still use today. Every calorie count on every food label you have ever seen is based on Atwater's measurements. What if these measurements are wrong? **13** Even modern research shows that Atwater was very careful in his calculations. To truly calculate the total calories that someone gets out of a given food, you would have to take into account a dizzying array of factors.

12

Which of the following best combines the sentences at the underlined portion?

A) bodies, yet we
B) bodies, and we
C) bodies since we
D) bodies; and we

13

Which of the following best establishes the main idea of the passage as a whole?

A) NO CHANGE
B) There have been many advances in nutritional knowledge since the 19th century.
C) In fact, new research suggests that these calculations are significantly inaccurate.
D) The caloric count for a hamburger could turn out to be different if you looked at different aspects of the meal itself.

CONTINUE

One of the first factors that scientists must consider is the **14** <u>variable</u> digestibility of foods. For instance, nuts are far less easily digested than spinach; as a result, nuts require more energy to digest. But even within the same category of food, digestibility can vary. A new study by Janet A. Novotny at the Department of Agriculture suggests that peanuts, pistachios, and almonds are less completely digested than other foods with similar levels of proteins, carbohydrates, and **15** <u>fats meaning</u> that they relinquish fewer calories than one would expect. **16**

14

A) NO CHANGE
B) fickle
C) irregular
D) wavering

15

A) NO CHANGE
B) fats; meaning
C) fats—meaning
D) fats, meaning

16

The author is considering adding the following sentence at this point:

Almonds, for instance, yield just 129 calories per serving, far less than the 170 calories reported on the label.

Should the author make this addition?

A) Yes, because the sentence provides an example to clarify the idea presented in the previous sentence.
B) Yes, because the sentence meaningfully develops the main idea of the passage.
C) No, because the sentence fails to meaningfully develop the ideas of the paragraph.
D) No, because the sentence is unrelated to the main idea of the paragraph.

CONTINUE

17 Cooking affects the calorie counts of foods, too. One Harvard study showed that cooking made calories in foods more readily accessible. In the study, adult mice were fed either sweet potatoes or lean beef. Some mice received cooked foods while others received raw foods. **18** The mice that ate cooked foods retained or gained significantly more weight when compared to the mice that ate raw foods. This is to be expected: heating hastens the unraveling of proteins, **19** makes them more easily digestible.

[1] Yet even if people eat the exact same food cooked in the exact same way, **20** they will not get the same number of calories out of it. [2] For example, studies from the early 1900s found that some populations have longer colons than others, and since the final stages of nutrient absorption occur in the large intestine, a larger colon means that more calories can be absorbed from the same food. [3] People differ in nearly all traits, and many of those traits impact digestion. [4] People also differ immensely in the community of bacteria that populates the intestines. [5] These bacteria have been shown to not only impact our digestive abilities, but can even cause us to crave specific foods. **21**

17

Which sentence provides the best transition between this paragraph and the previous paragraph?

A) NO CHANGE
B) Yet another complicating factor is the change that the food undergoes when cooked.
C) Beyond the variability of foods themselves, we must also consider the impact that cooking has on our foods.
D) However, the foods we eat have to be cooked.

18

A) NO CHANGE
B) Mice that are fed raw foods often gain less weight than the weight that is gained by mice that eat cooked foods.
C) When food is cooked for the mice, the mice often gain more weight from cooked foods than their weight gain from raw foods.
D) The mice that ate cooked foods retained or gained significantly more weight than those that ate raw foods.

19

A) NO CHANGE
B) making
C) made
D) having made

20

A) NO CHANGE
B) one
C) he
D) he or she

21

To improve the logical flow of the previous paragraph, sentence 3 should be placed

A) where it is now.
B) after sentence 1.
C) after sentence 4.
D) after sentence 5.

CONTINUE

Because of the myriad of minute factors that can alter the number of calories we absorb from any given food item, it would be nearly impossible to develop totally accurate food labels. But one thing is **22** <u>certain, a</u> calorie isn't necessarily a calorie.

22

A) NO CHANGE
B) certain, that a
C) certain because a
D) certain: a

CONTINUE

Questions 23-33 are based on the following passage.

[1] We often think of African politics and governments as being dominated by a single ethnic group. [2] The exclusion of certain groups then **23** translated into ethnic tensions as groups attempt to wrestle power from one another. [3] It makes a certain amount of sense. [4] We rely on this narrative to explain the root cause of the civil wars, revolutions, and coups we've seen in the last half-century. **24**

But a new paper published by economists Patrick Francois, Franceso Trebbi, and Illia Rainer **25** argue that we may have the story backwards. **26** It is not ethnic dominance that causes coups, but coups that cause ethnic dominance. Moreover, they are inclusive because leaders hope to reduce the probability of revolutions and coups against them. The authors **27** administered their analysis based on data that they carefully compiled on the ethnic composition of cabinet ministers in 15 African countries from 1960 to 2004.

23

A) NO CHANGE
B) translates
C) will have translated
D) has translated

24

Which sentence should be eliminated in order to improve the cohesion of the paragraph?

A) Sentence 1
B) Sentence 2
C) Sentence 3
D) Sentence 4

25

A) NO CHANGE
B) argues
C) will argue
D) have argued

26

Which of the following best establishes the main idea of the passage as a whole?

A) NO CHANGE
B) Coups are hostile takeovers of official governments, which happen often in Africa.
C) Ruling coalitions in Africa are, in fact, ethnically inclusive.
D) Ethnic tensions in Africa have been a considerably reliable trend throughout Africa's modern history.

27

A) NO CHANGE
B) conducted
C) regulated
D) transported

CONTINUE

On average, ruling coalitions in Africa are broad, representing roughly 80% of a country's population. Moreover, the study's authors found that an ethnic group's share in the total population matched **28** its share in the cabinet. In other words, an ethnic group making up 20% of the total population held roughly 20% of the cabinet seats. This pattern of ethnic representation also held for the top cabinet posts of Finance, Defense, Justice, Home Affairs, Foreign Affairs, and so on.

These findings also undermine the popular belief that African heads of state disproportionately favor **29** their own ethnic groups in the allocation of cabinet posts. The study's authors found that this ethnic advantage is actual very small. They estimate that heads of state only allocate an additional 2 cabinet posts out of an average 25-member cabinet to their own ethnic group over and above their group's share in the population.

28

A) NO CHANGE
B) it's
C) its'
D) their

29

A) NO CHANGE
B) one's
C) his or her
D) his

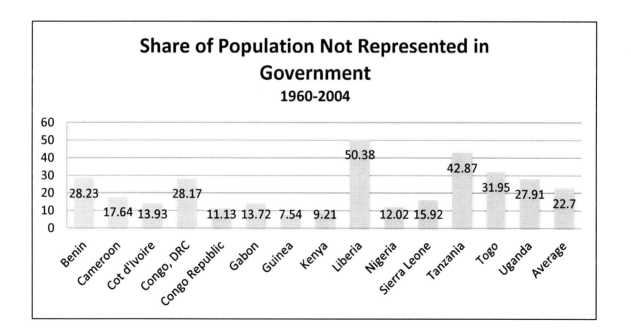

Share of Population Not Represented in Government
1960-2004

CONTINUE

[1] Liberia seems to be the biggest **30** eccentricity in the study. **31** [2] Currently, only about 50% of the country's population is represented in government. [3] Once American help waned, the rule of the Americo-Liberians collapsed. [4] Interestingly, the authors found that most of this ethnic exclusiveness was limited to the period before 1980 when Liberia was ruled by Americo-Liberians, a very small minority of freed American slaves. [5] Americo-Liberians made up just 4% of the **32** population, they were able to set aside about 50% of cabinet posts for themselves. [6] Their minority rule was largely reinforced by outside help from the U.S. **33**

Western views of African politics are, at best, inaccurate and, at worst, prejudicial. We tend to generate over-simplified narratives in an attempt to explain a complex political situation. If western nations are to play a role in the development of African nations, then westerners must take the time to better understand African politics.

30

A) NO CHANGE
B) outlier
C) quirk
D) aberration

31

Which of the following provides accurate information based on the graph?

A) NO CHANGE
B) The population of Liberia is better represented in its government than other countries such as Nigeria or Sierra Leone.
C) In comparison to other African countries, Liberia has a much higher rate of citizens getting involved in their governments.
D) Only about 50% of the population found representation in government during the time period studied.

32

A) NO CHANGE
B) population, yet they
C) population; they
D) population, so they

33

In order to improve the logical flow of the previous paragraph, sentence 3 should be placed

A) where it is now.
B) before sentence 1.
C) after sentence 4.
D) after sentence 5.

CONTINUE

Questions 34-44 are based on the following passage.

34 Although a molecule of DNA holds the complex blueprints for life, it measures just 2.5 billionths of a meter in diameter. DNA isn't simply responsible for a person's eye color or stature; many scientists believe that DNA may also hold the key to understanding and treating many diseases. To accomplish that goal, researchers have turned to nanotechnology. **35**

34

The author is considering eliminating this sentence. Should this change be made?

A) Yes, because the sentence provides no meaningful information to the reader.
B) Yes, because the sentence misleads the reader into believing that DNA is the focus of the passage.
C) No, because the sentence provides context regarding the scale of work in the field of nanotechnology.
D) No, because the sentence provides vital information regarding the role of DNA.

35

The author is considering adding the following clause to the end of this sentence:

, the science of manipulating matter on a miniscule scale.

Should the author make this addition?

A) Yes, because it defines a term that is vital to the reader's understanding of the passage.
B) Yes, because it meaningfully develops the concept of DNA research.
C) No, because it unnecessarily defines a term that is in common use.
D) No, because it introduces a redundancy to the passage.

CONTINUE

Through painstaking work over the last decade, scientists have learned to **36** manipulate and building molecules similar in size to a molecule of DNA. **37** This knowledge has revealed all of the medical applications of nanotechnology.

Regarding cancer alone, nanotechnology may provide multiple means of treatment. One potential treatment involves nanobots **38** molecule-sized robots that target cancer cells. Researchers at Harvard have developed a nanorobot that is designed to transport a collection of molecules. These molecules contain instructions that make cells behave in a particular way. In their study, the researchers successfully demonstrated the delivery of molecules that trigger cell suicide in leukemia and lymphoma cells.

Researchers at Northwestern University have taken a different approach. Scientists used gold to make "nanostars," simple star-shaped nanoparticles that can deliver drugs straight to the nuclei of cancer cells. These drug-loaded nanostars behave like tiny hitchhikers; after being attracted to an over-expressed protein found on the surface of human cervical and ovarian cancer cells, these little hitchhikers deposit their payload **39** promptly into the nuclei of those cells.

Scientists have long known that these kinds of protein-based drugs hold great promise. Unlike conventional cancer treatments, which kill not only the cancerous cells but also the surrounding healthy cells, protein-based drugs can be programmed to deliver specific signals to certain cells, **40** targeting treatment more effectively. The problem with current methods of delivery of such drugs is that the body breaks most of them down before the drugs are able to reach **41** their destination.

36

A) NO CHANGE
B) manipulate and build
C) manipulating and building
D) manipulate, build

37

Which of the following best establishes the main idea of the passage as a whole?

A) NO CHANGE
B) DNA studies have expanded in leaps and bounds thanks to the introduction of nanotechnology.
C) This knowledge is leading to new medicines and diagnostic methods, revealing some of the many possible medical applications of nanotechnology.
D) Nanotechnology allows scientists to work on a previously unimaginably small scale.

38

A) NO CHANGE
B) —molecule-sized robots—
C) molecule-sized robots,
D) (molecule-sized robots)

39

A) NO CHANGE
B) directly
C) openly
D) unswervingly

40

A) NO CHANGE
B) targets
C) will target
D) targeted

41

Which of the following best clarifies the pronoun reference?

A) the methods'
B) the drugs'
C) the body's
D) the delivery's

42 Therefore, researchers at the Massachusetts Institute of Technology (MIT) have begun exploring the possibility of creating self-assembling "nanofactories" that manufacture the necessary protein compounds on demand at target sites. The MIT team came up with this idea while trying to find a way to attack metastatic tumors, those that grow from cancer cells that have **43** journeyed from the original site to other parts of the body. Over 90% of cancer deaths are due to metastatic **44** cancer, so that successful treatments would be groundbreaking. Work has begun on the development of the nanofactories that may one day synthesize cancer drugs exactly where they are needed most—where the cancer grows.

42

Which of the following provides the best transition from the previous paragraph?

A) NO CHANGE
B) To discover this problem
C) To solve this problem
D) However,

43

A) NO CHANGE
B) emigrated
C) wandered
D) migrated

44

A) NO CHANGE
B) cancer, and successful
C) cancer, so successful
D) cancer, successful

STOP

If you finish before time is called, you may check your work on this section only.
Do not turn to any other section.

Math Test – Calculator

25 MINUTES, 17 QUESTIONS

Mark your responses on this test. Use the "How to Calculate Your Scores in the back of this book to determine your scores.

For questions 1-13, solve each problem, choose the best answer from the choices provided, and fill in the corresponding circle on your answer sheet. **For questions 14-17**, solve the problem and enter your answer in the grid on the answer sheet. Please refer to the directions before question 16 on how to enter your answers in the grid. You may use any available space in your test booklet for scratch work.

1. The use of a calculator **is not permitted**.
2. All variables and expressions used represent real numbers unless otherwise indicated.
3. Figures provided in the test are drawn to scale unless otherwise indicated.
4. All figures lie in a plane unless otherwise indicated.
5. Unless otherwise indicated, the domain of a given function f is the set of all real numbers x for which $f(x)$ is a real number.

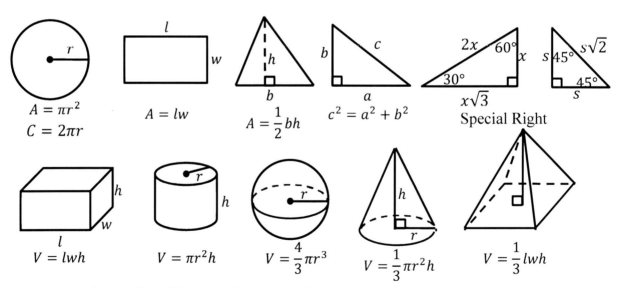

$A = \pi r^2$
$C = 2\pi r$

$A = lw$

$A = \frac{1}{2}bh$

$c^2 = a^2 + b^2$

Special Right

$V = lwh$

$V = \pi r^2 h$

$V = \frac{4}{3}\pi r^3$

$V = \frac{1}{3}\pi r^2 h$

$V = \frac{1}{3}lwh$

The number of degrees of arc in a circle is 360.

The number of radians of arc in a circle is 2π.

The sum of the measures in degrees of the angles of a triangle is 180.

CONTINUE ▶

3

The function $f(x) = x^2 - 2$ is graphed in the xy-plane. If $f(x)$ is translated up 3 units and then flipped over the x-axis, its new vertex is what?

A) $(0, -5)$
B) $(0, -1)$
C) $(0, 1)$
D) $(0, 5)$

If $|x - 3| < \frac{1}{2}$, what is a possible value of $3x$?

A) -9
B) $\frac{21}{2}$
C) $\frac{17}{2}$
D) $\frac{15}{2}$

4

The amount of money, in dollars, Kenji makes each month from his online blog series, y, can be estimated using the equation
$y = 2.25(x - 100) + 193.69$, where x represents the number of subscribers to his blog and $x \geq 100$. Which of the following statements is the best interpretation of the number 2.25 in the context of this problem?

A) The estimated amount of money Kenji makes per subscriber
B) The estimated amount of money Kenji makes for each subscriber after the 100th
C) The estimated amount of money Kenji makes when he has no subscribers
D) The estimated amount of money Kenji makes when he has 100 subscribers

If $xy - 3 = 2z$, $x \neq 0$, $y \neq 0$, and $z \neq 0$, what is y in terms of x and z?

A) $y = \frac{2z - 3}{x}$
B) $y = \frac{2z + 3}{x}$
C) $y = \frac{x}{2z + 3}$
D) $y = \frac{x}{2z - 3}$

5

If $A = x^2 + 6x + 9$, $B = x + 3$, and $x \neq -3$, what is $\frac{A}{2B}$ in terms of x?

A) $\frac{x^2 + 5x + 6}{2}$
B) $\frac{x^2 + 9}{2}$
C) $\frac{x^2 + 6x + 3}{2}$
D) $\frac{x + 3}{2}$

CONTINUE

6

The graph of $y = (x + 3)(3x + 15)$ is a parabola in the xy-plane. In which of the following equivalent equations do the x- and y-coordinates of the vertex of the parabola appear as constants or coefficients?

A) $3x^2 + 24x + 45$
B) $3x(x + 8) + 45$
C) $3(x + 4)^2 - 3$
D) $(3x + 9)(x + 5)$

7

$$5x + 7y = 13$$
$$5y - 2x = -17$$

Based on the system of equations above, what is the value of $7x + 2y$?

A) -4
B) $-\dfrac{15}{13}$
C) 30
D) $\dfrac{1406}{39}$

8

Which of the following is equal to $\cos\left(-\dfrac{\pi}{6}\right)$?

A) $\sin\left(-\dfrac{\pi}{3}\right)$
B) $\sin\left(-\dfrac{\pi}{6}\right)$
C) $\sin\left(\dfrac{\pi}{6}\right)$
D) $\sin\left(\dfrac{\pi}{3}\right)$

9

$$\frac{1}{t} + \frac{3}{t} = \frac{1}{7}$$

Corey and Trevor need to build a new greenhouse for their father. Corey works three times as quickly as Trevor does, and together they can build the greenhouse in seven hours. The equation above represents the situation described. Which of the following describes what the expression $\dfrac{3}{t}$ represents in this equation?

A) The portion of the greenhouse that Corey would complete in one hour
B) The portion of the greenhouse that Trevor would complete in one hour
C) The time, in hours, that it takes for Corey to finish the greenhouse alone
D) The time, in hours, that it takes for Trevor to finish the greenhouse alone

CONTINUE

10

$$\frac{1 - 2(x - 3)}{4} = \frac{3(2 - x) - 5}{7}$$

In the equation above, what is the value of x?

A) $\frac{-39}{2}$

B) $-\frac{21}{13}$

C) 4

D) $\frac{45}{2}$

11

In the xy-plane, if the parabola with equation $y = x^2 - x$ passes through the point (a, a), where a is a constant, what are all of the possible values of a?

A) -1

B) -1 and 0

C) 2

D) 0 and 2

12

Jason needs to buy at least 20 pounds of meat for the cookout he's holding. Hamburger costs $7.50 per pound and chicken costs $5.75 per pound, and Jason can only spend a maximum of $150 on meat. If Jason buys x pounds of hamburger and y pounds of chicken, which of the following lists a solution, (x, y) that meet both of Jason's constraints?

A) $(10, 10), (13, 6)$

B) $(2, 19), (19, 3)$

C) $(12, 8), (15, 7)$

D) $(8, 15), (12, 10)$

13

Which of the following is equivalent to $s^2(\frac{1}{s} - \frac{1}{s^2})$?

A) $s - 1$

B) $1 - s$

C) $s - \frac{1}{s^2}$

D) $\frac{1}{s} - 1$

CONTINUE

DIRECTIONS

For questions 14-17, solve the problem and enter your answer in the grid, as described below, on the answer sheet.

1. Although not required, it is suggested that you write your answer in the boxes at the top of the columns to help you fill in the circles accurately. You will receive credit only if the circles are filled in correctly.

2. Mark no more than one circle in any column.

3. No question has a negative answer.

4. Some problems may have more than one correct answer. In such cases, grid only one answer.

5. **Mixed numbers** such as $3\frac{1}{2}$ must be gridded as 3.5 or 7/2.

   (If [3 1 / 2] is entered into the grid, it will be interpreted as $\frac{31}{2}$, not $3\frac{1}{2}$.)

6. **Decimal answers:** If you obtain a decimal answer with more digits than the grid can accommodate, it may be either rounded or truncated, but it must fill the entire grid.

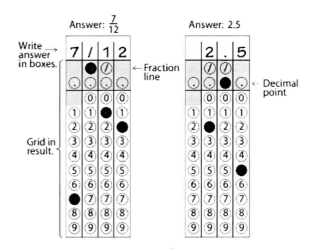

Acceptable ways to grid $\frac{2}{3}$ are:

Answer: 201 – either position is correct

NOTE: You may start your answers in any column, space permitting. Columns you don't need to use should be left blank.

CONTINUE

14

If $\frac{3}{5}a + \frac{2}{3}b = 7$, what is the value of $9a + 10b$?

16

If $(x + 3) + 3(x - 4) = x$ and $x > 0$, what is the value of x?

15

What is the perimeter of the triangle with vertex coordinates in the xy-plane at $(-3, 2)$, $(-3, 5)$, and $(-7, 2)$?

17

What is a possible solution to the equation $\frac{30}{x+4} = \frac{45}{4(x+1)}$?

STOP

If you finish before time is called, you may check your work on this section only.
Do not turn to any other section.

Math Test –Calculator

45 MINUTES, 31 QUESTIONS

Mark your responses on this test. Use the "How to Calculate Your Scores in the back of this book to determine your scores.

DIRECTIONS

For questions **1-27**, solve each problem, choose the best answer from the choices provided, and fill in the corresponding circle on your answer sheet. **For questions 28-31**, solve the problem and enter your answer in the grid on the answer sheet. Please refer to the directions before question 31 on how to enter your answers in the grid. You may use any available space in your test booklet for scratch work.

NOTES

1. The use of a calculator is permitted.
2. All variables and expressions used represent real numbers unless otherwise indicated.
3. Figures provided in the test are drawn to scale unless otherwise indicated.
4. All figures lie in a plane unless otherwise indicated.
5. Unless otherwise indicated, the domain of a given function f is the set of all real numbers x for which $f(x)$ is a real number.

REFERENCE

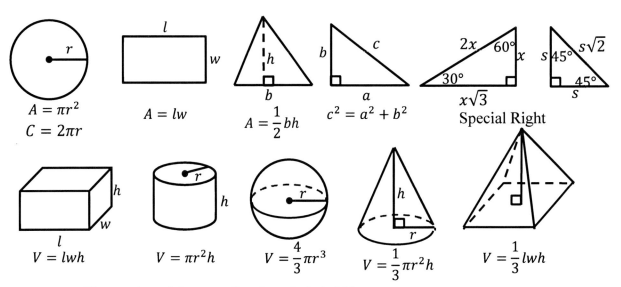

$A = \pi r^2$
$C = 2\pi r$

$A = lw$

$A = \frac{1}{2}bh$

$c^2 = a^2 + b^2$

Special Right

$V = lwh$

$V = \pi r^2 h$

$V = \frac{4}{3}\pi r^3$

$V = \frac{1}{3}\pi r^2 h$

$V = \frac{1}{3}lwh$

The number of degrees of arc in a circle is 360.

The number of radians of arc in a circle is 2π.

The sum of the measures in degrees of the angles of a triangle is 180.

CONTINUE

1

A charity video game livestream needs to earn $10,000. Silver viewers pay $3.50 to watch the stream, while gold viewers pay $5.25 to watch the stream. Which of the following inequalities represents the number of silver viewers s and gold viewers g the charity needs to meet or exceed its goal?

A) $\frac{3.50}{s} + \frac{5.25}{g} > 10,000$

B) $\frac{3.50}{s} + \frac{5.25}{g} \geq 10,000$

C) $3.50s + 5.25g > 10,000$

D) $3.50s + 5.25g \geq 10,000$

2

Sierra is shopping at an organic grocery store. She didn't bring her own grocery bags with her, so the grocery store charges her an untaxed fee of $2.50 for grocery bags. A tax of x percent is applied to the cost of her groceries, $78.53. Which of the following represents Sierra's total charge, in dollars?

A) $\frac{x}{100}(78.53) + 2.50$

B) $\frac{x}{100}(78.53 + 2.50)$

C) $\frac{x+100}{100}(78.53) + 2.50$

D) $\frac{x+100}{100}(78.53 + 2.50)$

3

Group	Mean (min)	Margin of Error (min)
A	125	9.21
B	121	4.32
C	131	2.59
D	152	5.36

A university official randomly selected four different groups of sophomore chemical engineering students and asked each student "How many minutes per day do you typically spend studying?" The results are shown in the table above. Which group most likely had the largest number of students surveyed?

A) Group A
B) Group B
C) Group C
D) Group D

CONTINUE

Questions 4-6 refer to the following information.

The scatterplot below shows the relationship between the mass, in pounds, of a lobster and age, in years, of 12 lobsters.

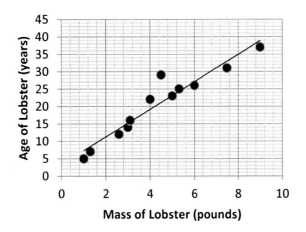

5

Which of the following is the best interpretation of the slope of the line of best fit in the context of this problem?

A) The predicted mass of a one-year-old lobster.
B) The predicted age of a one pound lobster.
C) The predicted mass increase in pounds for every year increase in age.
D) The predicted age increase in years for one pound increase in mass.

4

Based on the line of best fit, a 10-pound lobster would be expected to be approximately how many years old?

A) 1.6
B) 39.0
C) 43.0
D) 47.0

6

Based on the line of best fit, a 6-year-old lobster would have what mass, in pounds?

A) 0.6
B) 1.2
C) 1.8
D) 2.7

CONTINUE

7

$$x^2 + y^2 = 16$$
$$x = -\frac{1}{2}y - 1$$

A system of equations is shown above. How many solutions does the system have?

A) Zero
B) One
C) Two
D) Four

8

Elise is starting a lemonade stand to make money for her trip to Nicaragua. She estimates that her startup costs will be $35, and that it will cost approximately 75 cents to produce a cup of lemonade. If she plans to sell each cup of lemonade for $1.50, what is the minimum number of cups that she must sell to raise at least $200?

A) 134
B) 157
C) 314
D) 470

9

Employee	Salary
Johnson	$60,000
Parvathi	$100,000
Lee	$30,000
Angelo	$60,000
Takas	$45,000
Tsumura	$35,000

What is the positive difference in the mean and median salaries, in dollars, of the employees listed above?

A) $2,500
B) $5,000
C) $7,500
D) $10,000

10

A biologist researched the population of a local group of elephants and recorded the data below:

Year	Population
1995	7
2000	14
2005	28

The population adheres to the same model over time. If P represents the population n years after 1995, then which of the following equations represents the biologist's model of the population over time?

A) $P = 7 + 2n$
B) $P = 7 + 7n$
C) $P = 7(2)^{5n}$
D) $P = 7(2)^{\frac{n}{5}}$

CONTINUE

11

$$m = 2 - n$$
$$3m - 2n = 21$$

Based on the system of equations above, what is the value of n^2?

A) −9
B) −3
C) 3
D) 9

12

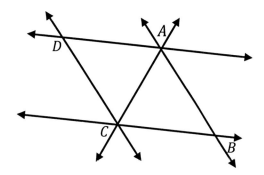

Note: Figure not drawn to scale.

In the figure above, $\triangle ABC \sim \triangle CDA$. Which of the following is NOT necessarily true?

A) $\angle DAB \cong \angle DCB$
B) $\angle ADC \cong \angle ACB$
C) $DA \parallel CB$
D) $DC \parallel AB$

13

A shipping truck at a local distributor has a gas mileage of 15 miles per gallon when the truck travels at an average speed of 60 miles per hour. The truck's gas tank starts with 24 gallons of gas at the beginning of the trip. If the truck travels at an average speed of 60 miles per hour, which of the following functions f models the number of gallons of gas remaining in the tank m minutes after the trip begins?

A) $24 - 4m$
B) $24 - \dfrac{m}{15}$
C) $\dfrac{24 - m}{15}$
D) $\dfrac{24 - 4m}{15}$

14

Jenny needs to buy at least 1,500 hot dog buns for her school's end of the year picnic. Hot dog buns come in two sizes: packs of wheat buns and packs of white buns. Each 12-pack of wheat hot dog buns costs $1.69, while each 18-pack of white hot dog buns costs $1.89. If Jenny has a maximum of $200.00 to spend on the hot dog buns, and the number of wheat and white buns she buys is inconsequential, solving which of the following systems of inequalities yields the number of packs of wheat buns, a, and white buns, b, she could buy?

A) $a + b \geq 1,500$
   $1.69a + 1.89b \leq 200$
B) $12a + 18b \geq 1,500$
   $1.69a + 1.89b \leq 200$
C) $12a + 18b \leq 1,500$
   $1.69a + 1.89b \geq 200$
D) $a + b \leq 1,500$
   $12(1.69a) + 18(1.89b) \geq 200$

CONTINUE

15

When mining a particular region of the United States, the average mass of gold found per cubic meter of dirt unearthed increases linearly with the depth at which the dirt is mined. At a depth of 300 meters, an average of 3.7 g of gold is found per cubic meter of dirt unearthed. At a depth of 500 meters, an average of 4.8 g of gold is found per cubic meter of dirt unearthed. How much gold would be expected to be unearthed, on average, in 10 cubic meters of dirt at a depth of 100 meters?

A) 2.6 g
B) 5.9 g
C) 26.0 g
D) 59.0 g

16

Reaction Time versus Age

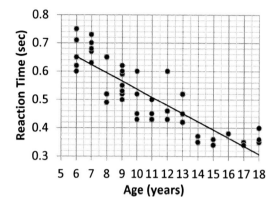

The scatterplot above shows the reaction time, in seconds, of several people based on their age, in years. Based on the line of best fit to the data shown, which of the following values is closest to the average yearly decrease in reaction time, in seconds?

A) 0.01
B) 0.03
C) 0.05
D) 0.07

17

Which of the following equations can be used to find the area of a circle, A, in terms of its circumference, C?

A) $A = \dfrac{C^2}{4\pi}$

B) $A = \dfrac{\pi C^2}{4}$

C) $A = \dfrac{4}{\pi C^2}$

D) $A = \dfrac{4\pi}{C^2}$

CONTINUE

18

If $\dfrac{-2(x-2)+5}{3} = \dfrac{3-(2x-5)}{2}$, then $x =$

A) -6
B) -4
C) 3
D) $\dfrac{9}{2}$

19

A research assistant wants to know if there is an association between time spent watching television and physical fitness for the population of middle school students in the United States. She obtained responses from a random sample of 5,000 middle school students and found convincing evidence of an indirect correlation between time spent watching television and physical fitness. Which of the following conclusions is well supported by the data?

A) Using time spent watching television and physical fitness as defined by the study, an increase in time spent watching television is caused by a decrease in physical fitness for middle school students in the United States.
B) Using time spent watching television and physical fitness as defined by the study, a decrease in time spent watching television is caused by an increase in physical fitness for middle school students in the United States.
C) There is a negative association between time spent watching television and physical fitness for students in the United States.
D) There is a negative association between time spent watching television and physical fitness for middle school students in the United States.

20

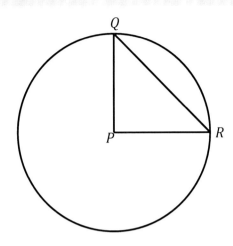

Circle P above contains right triangle QPR. If QR has a length of $12\sqrt{2}$, what is the area of circle P?

A) 24π
B) 72π
C) 144π
D) 288π

21

$$x + y = 3x$$
$$4x - \frac{1}{2}y = 12$$

Which of the following is a solution to the system of equations above?

A) $(8, 4)$
B) $(7, 14)$
C) $(6, 6)$
D) $(4, 8)$

CONTINUE

22

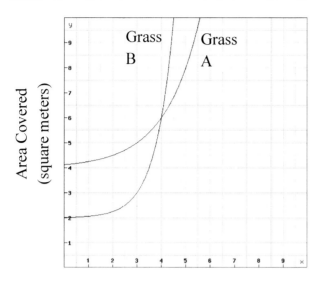

Time (days)

A botanist plants two different varieties of grass on two different lawns in order to measure their rates of growth. After the initial planting of the grass ($t = 0$ days), the botanist measures and records the area covered by the grass every 12 hours. The data for each grass were fit by a smooth curve, as shown above, where each curve represents the area of a lawn covered by grass as a function of time, in days. Which of the following is a correct statement about the data above?

A) Grass B initially covers more of the lawn than Grass A does.

B) After 4 days, both grass varieties covered the same amount of the lawn.

C) After 6 days, both grass varieties covered the same amount of the lawn.

D) For the first 2 days, Grass A spreads more slowly than does Grass B.

Questions 23-25 refer to the following information.

A survey was conducted among a randomly chosen sample of registered voters from four different states about participation in the November 2008 presidential election. The table below displays a summary of the survey results.

Reported Voting by State				
	Voted	Did Not Vote	Did Not Respond	Total
Alabama	951	1,237	36	2,224
Georgia	1,639	2,364	73	4,076
Florida	3,134	4,752	108	7,994
Tennessee	1,030	1,781	43	2,854
Total	6,754	10,134	260	17,148

23

Which of the following is closest to the percent of those surveyed who reported voting?

A) 1.5%

B) 19.7%

C) 39.4%

D) 59.1%

24

Which state had the highest proportion of registered voters who did NOT vote?

A) Alabama

B) Georgia

C) Florida

D) Tennessee

CONTINUE

25

Based on the data, how many times more likely is it for a registered voter in Alabama to not vote than to vote? (Round the answer to the nearest hundredth)

A) 0.67 times as likely
B) 0.77 times as likely
C) 1.30 times as likely
D) 1.50 times as likely

27

$$(x - 3)^{-0.5} = 2$$

Which value of x satisfies the equation above?

A) $3 - \sqrt{2}$
B) $\frac{11}{4}$
C) $\frac{13}{4}$
D) $3 + \sqrt{2}$

26

$$3(2 - x) + 2x = 6(5 + x) - 7x$$

Which of the following is a solution to the equation above?

A) -4
B) 4
C) 12
D) No solution exists.

CONTINUE

For questions 28-31, solve the problem and enter your answer in the grid, as described below, on the answer sheet.

1. Although not required, it is suggested that you write your answer in the boxes at the top of the columns to help you fill in the circles accurately. You will receive credit only if the circles are filled in correctly.

2. Mark no more than one circle in any column.

3. No question has a negative answer.

4. Some problems may have more than one correct answer. In such cases, grid only one answer.

5. **Mixed numbers** such as $3\frac{1}{2}$ must be gridded as 3.5 or 7/2.

   (If 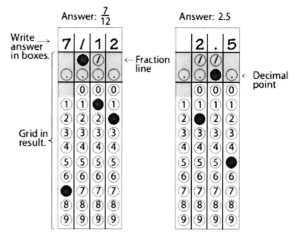 is entered into the grid, it will be interpreted as $\frac{31}{2}$, not $3\frac{1}{2}$.)

6. **Decimal answers:** If you obtain a decimal answer with more digits than the grid can accommodate, it may be either rounded or truncated, but it must fill the entire grid.

Answer: $\frac{7}{12}$ Answer: 2.5

Write answer in boxes.   ← Fraction line
Grid in result.   ← Decimal point

Acceptable ways to grid $\frac{2}{3}$ are:

Answer: 201 – either position is correct

NOTE: You may start your answers in any column, space permitting. Columns you don't need to use should be left blank.

CONTINUE

28

The table below classifies 66 people based on two different physical characteristics.

	Widow's Peak	No Widow's Peak	Total
Attached Earlobes	10	32	42
Detached Earlobes	6	18	24
Total	16	50	66

What fraction of all people in the table with detached earlobes have a widow's peak as well?

29

In the xy-coordinate plane, line FG is perpendicular to line segment DE and intersects DE at its midpoint. DE has endpoints at $(1, 5)$ and $(-3, -1)$. If FG intersects the y-axis at $(0, b)$, what is the value of b?

CONTINUE

Questions 30 and 31 refer to the following information.

A popular cellphone provider offers the following plans for data usage:

Low Usage: $15.00 per month for 200 MB of data. For each 1 MB of data used over 200 MB, a charge of 7.5 cents is added to the user's bill.

High Usage: $25.00 per month for 1 GB of data. For each 1 MB of data used over 1 GB, a charge of 1.5 cents is added to the user's bill.

(Note: 1 GB = 1024 MB)

30

Gregory uses exactly 500 MB of data each month. How much money, to the nearest dollar, would he save per year by switching from the Low Usage plan to the High Usage plan?

31

Hannah currently uses 6 GB of data per month under the High Usage plan. She is considering switching to a competitor's plan. This plan charges $120.00 per month. However, since she is switching from a competitor, the new company is offering her a 20% discount on her data bill. How much money, to the nearest hundredth of a dollar, will Hannah save the first month when she makes her switch?

STOP

If you finish before time is called, you may check your work on this section only.
Do not turn to any other section.

ANSWER KEY

Explanations can be found online at http://www.tpgenius.com/

Section 1: Reading Test		Section 2: Writing and Language Test		Section 3: Math Test – No Calculator	Section 4: Math Test – Calculator Allowed
1. C	26. D	1. C	23. B	1. B	1. D
2. A	27. C	2. B	24. C	2. B	2. C
3. D	28. A	3. A	25. B	3. C	3. C
4. C	29. B	4. C	26. A	4. B	4. C
5. D	30. B	5. C	27. B	5. D	5. D
6. D	31. D	6. D	28. A	6. C	6. A
7. B	32. A	7. D	29. A	7. C	7. C
8. B	33. C	8. A	30. B	8. D	8. C
9. C	34. C	9. B	31. D	9. A	9. A
10. C	35. D	10. C	32. B	10. D	10. D
11. A	36. A	11. B	33. D	11. D	11. D
12. B	37. C	12. B	34. C	12. D	12. B
13. B	38. A	13. C	35. A	13. A	13. B
14. C	39. D	14. A	36. B	14. 105	14. B
15. B	40. B	15. D	37. C	15. 12	15. C
16. A	41. D	16. A	38. B	16. 3	16. B
17. C	42. C	17. B	39. B	17. 0.8 or $\frac{4}{5}$	17. A
18. A	43. A	18. D	40. A		18. C
19. D	44. A	19. B	41. B		19. D
20. A	45. C	20. A	42. C		20. C
21. D	46. A	21. B	43. D		21. D
22. B	47. D	22. D	44. C		22. B
23. D					23. C
24. A					24. D
25. C					25. C
					26. D
					27. C
					28. $\frac{1}{4}$ or 0.25
					29. $\frac{4}{3}$ or 1.33
					30. 150
					31. 5.8

Explanations can be found online at http://www.tpgenius.com/

How to Calculate Your Scores

Once you have completed an assessment, use the following steps to calculate your scores. The score(s) you calculate will be *general estimates* of your official scores for a number of reasons:

- Because standardized test score calculations are based on normative scaling and statistical analysis, your scores will differ depending your official test date – the final score calculations are impacted by the number of students, per-question performance by all students on each test date, and other numerical factors.
- College Board determines the final curve for official tests. Therefore, the scores you calculate for yourself on Test Prep Genius tests are within a general range of scores.

Calculate Your Raw Scores

Evidence-based Reading and Writing Section Raw Score

1) Count the number of correct answers you got on Section 1 (Reading Test). There is no penalty for wrong answers. The number of correct answers is your raw score.
2) Go to the Raw Score Conversion Table on the next page. Look in the "Raw Score" column for your raw score and match it to the number in the "Reading Test Score" column.
3) Do the same with Section 2 (Writing Test) to determine your Writing and Language Test Score. Make sure to use the "Writing Test Score" column.
4) Add your Reading Test Score and your Writing and Language Test Score.
5) Multiply that number by 10. This is your final Evidence-based Reading and Writing Section Score.

Math Section Score

1) Count the number of correct answers you got on Section 3 (Math Test – No Calculator) and Section 4 (Math Test – Calculator). There is no penalty for wrong answers.
2) Add the two numbers together.
3) Use the Raw Score Conversion Table on the next page to your final Math Section Score.

Use the following Raw Score Conversion Table to determine your test scores

Raw Score (# of correct answers)	Math Section Score	Reading Test Score	Writing Test Score	Raw Score (# of correct answers)	Math Section Score	Reading Test Score	Writing Test Score
0	160	8	8	25	560	26	25
1	190	9	9	26	570	26	26
2	210	10	10	27	580	27	27
3	240	11	11	28	580	27	27
4	270	12	12	29	590	28	28
5	290	14	13	30	600	28	28
6	320	15	14	31	610	29	29
7	340	16	14	32	620	29	29
8	360	16	15	33	630	30	30
9	370	17	15	34	640	30	30
10	390	18	16	35	650	31	31
11	400	18	16	36	670	31	32
12	420	19	17	37	680	32	32
13	430	19	18	38	690	32	33
14	440	20	18	39	710	33	34
15	460	20	19	40	720	34	35
16	470	21	20	41	730	34	36
17	480	21	20	42	730	35	37
18	490	22	21	43	740	36	37
19	500	22	21	44	740	37	38
20	510	23	22	45	750	37	
21	520	23	23	46	750	38	
22	530	24	24	47	760	38	
23	540	24	24	48	760		
24	550	25	25				

For Evidenced-based Reading and Writing and Language Test Scores, add them together and multiply by 10 for your final Section Score for Reading and Writing and Language.

Add your two Section Scores together to get your final Score on a 320-1520 scale

Calculating Subscores

The Redesigned, New SAT will offer more detailed information in specific areas within math, reading, and writing. These subscores are reported on a scale of 1-15.

Math: Heart of Algebra

The Heart of Algebra subscore is calculated based on questions from the two Math Tests that focus on linear equations and inequalities.

1) Each practice test's Heart of Algebra questions are specified below. Add up your total correct answers from the specified set of questions for each test to get your raw scores for each test.
    Practice Test 1:

    Math Test – No Calculator: Questions 2-4; 7; 9; 10; 12; 14; 16-17

    Math Test – Calculator: Questions 11; 18; 21; 26-27; 29

2) Use the Subscore Conversion Table on Page 327 to calculate your Heart of Algebra Subscore.

Math: Problem Solving and Data Analysis

The Problem Solving and Data Analysis subscore is calculated based on questions from the two Math Tests that focus on quantitative reasoning, interpretation and synthesis of data, and solving problems with rich and varied contexts.

1) Each practice test's Problem Solving and Data Analysis questions are specified below. Add up your total correct answers from the specified set of questions for each test to get your raw scores for each test.
    Practice Test 1:

    Math Test – No Calculator: No Questions

    Math Test – Calculator: Questions 1-7; 9-10; 13-15; 19; 28; 30-31

2) Use the Subscore Conversion Table on Page 327 to calculate your Problem Solving and Data Analysis Subscore.

Math: Passport to Advanced Math

The Passport to Advanced Math subscore is calculated based on questions from the two Math Tests that focus on topics critical to the ability of students to handle more advanced math topics, such as expressions, complex equations, and analysis of functions.

1) Each practice test's Passport to Advanced Math questions are specified below. Add up your total correct answers from the specified set of questions for each test to get your raw scores for each test.
    Practice Test 1:

    Math Test – No Calculator: Questions 1; 5-6; 8; 11; 13; 15

    Math Test – Calculator: Questions 7; 16-17; 22-25

2) Use the Subscore Conversion Table on Page 327 to calculate your Passport to Advanced Math Subscore.

Writing and Language: Expression of Ideas

The Expression of Ideas subscore is calculated based on questions from the Writing and Language Test that focus on topic development, organization, and rhetorical, effective use of language.

1) Each practice test's Expression of Ideas questions are specified below. Your total number of correct answers in the specified set below is your raw score.

> Practice Test 1: Questions 1; 3; 6-7; 9; 11; 13-14; 16-18; 21; 24; 26-27; 30-31; 33-35; 37; 39; 42-43

2) Use the Subscore Conversion Table on Page 327 to calculate your Expression of Ideas Subscore

Writing and Language: Standard English Conventions

The Standard English Conventions subscore is calculated based on questions from the Writing and Language Test that focus on sentence structure, usage, and punctuation (basic grammar).

1) Each practice test's Standard English Conventions questions are specified below. Your total number of correct answers in the specified set below is your raw score.

> Practice Test 1: Questions 2; 4; 5; 8; 10; 12; 15; 19-20; 22-23; 25; 28-29; 32; 36; 38; 40-41; 44

2) Use the Subscore Conversion Table on Page 327 to calculate your Standard English Conventions Subscore

Writing and Language + Reading: Words in Context

The Words in Context subscore is based on questions from both Reading and Writing Tests that focus on the meaning of words in context and rhetorical word choice.

1) Each practice test's Words in Context questions are specified below. Your total number of correct answers in the specified set below is your raw score.

> Practice Test 1:
>
> Reading Test: Questions 1; 7; 13-14; 23; 27; 31; 36; 40; 46
>
> Writing Test: Questions 7; 14; 27; 30; 34-35; 39; 43

2) Use the Subscore Conversion Table on Page 327 to calculate your Words in Context Subscore

Writing and Language + Reading: Command of Evidence

The Command of Evidence subscore is based on questions from both the Reading and Writing Tests that focus on the student's ability to interpret and use evidence found in passages and informational graphics such as tables, graphs, and charts.

1) Each practice test's Command of Evidence questions are specified below. Your total number of correct answers in the specified set below is your raw score.

> Practice Test 1:
>
> Reading Test: Questions 6; 9; 16; 19; 21; 26; 33; 42; 45
>
> Writing Test: Questions 1; 9; 11; 13; 16; 26; 31; 37

2) Use the Subscore Conversion Table on Page 327 to calculate your Command of Evidence Subscore

Use the following Subscore Conversion Table to calculate your Subscores

Raw Score (# of correct answers)	Expression of Ideas	Standard English Conventions	Heart of Algebra	Problem Solving and Data Analysis	Passport to Advanced Math	Words in Context	Command of Evidence
0	1	1	1	1	1	1	1
1	2	2	3	3	5	2	2
2	3	3	4	4	7	3	3
3	4	3	5	5	8	3	4
4	4	4	6	6	9	4	5
5	5	4	7	7	10	5	6
6	6	5	8	8	11	6	7
7	6	6	8	8	12	6	8
8	7	6	9	9	13	7	8
9	7	7	10	10	14	8	9
10	8	7	10	11	15	9	9
11	8	8	11	11	15	10	10
12	9	8	12	12	15	10	11
13	9	9	13	13	15	11	11
14	10	9	14	14	15	12	12
15	10	10	15	15		13	13
16	11	10	15	15		14	14
17	12	11				15	15
18	12	12				15	
19	13	13					
20	13	15					
21	14						
22	15						
23	15						
24	15						

Calculating Cross-Test Scores

The Redesigned, New SAT also offers detailed information in the form of two Cross-Test scores. These scores are based on questions in the Reading, Writing and Language, and Math Tests that focus on analytical thinking about texts and questions in specific subject areas. Cross-Test Scores are reported on a scale from 1-40.

Analysis in History/Social Studies

1) Each practice test's History/Social Studies questions are specified below. Your total number of correct answers in the specified set below is your raw score.
   Practice Test 1:
   > Reading Test: Questions 29-37; 38-47
   > Writing Test: Questions 1; 9; 11; 26; 31; 33
   > Math Test – No Calculator: No Questions
   > Math Test – Calculator: Questions 9; 16; 19; 23-25; 28

2) Use the Cross-Test Conversion Table on the next page to calculate your Cross-Test Score for Analysis in History/Social Studies.

Analysis in Science

1) Each practice test's Science questions are specified below. Your total number of correct answers in the specified set below is your raw score.
   Practice Test 1:
   > Reading Test: Questions 1-9; 20-28
   > Writing Test: Questions 13; 16; 17; 34-35; 37
   > Math Test – No Calculator: No Questions
   > Math Test – Calculator: Questions 4-6; 10; 23; 27; 37-38

2) Use the Cross-Test Conversion Table on the next page to calculate your Cross-Test Score for Analysis in Science.

Use the following Cross-Test Conversion Table to calculate your Cross-Test Scores

Cross-Test Score Conversion Table					
Raw Score (# of correct answers)	Analysis in History/Social Studies Cross-Test Score	Analysis in Science Cross-Test Score	**Raw Score (# of correct answers)**	Analysis in History/Social Studies Cross-Test Score	Analysis in Science Cross-Test Score
0	8	8	**17**	26	28
1	9	12	**18**	27	28
2	11	15	**19**	28	29
3	12	16	**20**	29	30
4	14	17	**21**	30	31
5	15	18	**22**	30	31
6	16	18	**23**	31	32
7	17	19	**24**	32	33
8	18	20	**25**	32	34
9	19	21	**26**	33	35
10	20	22	**27**	34	36
11	21	23	**28**	35	37
12	22	24	**29**	36	37
13	23	25	**30**	37	38
14	24	26	**31**	37	38
15	25	26	**32**	38	38
16	26	27			

If you enjoyed using this New PSAT Guide, then check out Test Prep Genius's full guide for the New SAT, which includes:

- Over 1000 practice questions
- 3 full-length practice tests

Test Prep Genius 2016 Redesigned SAT Strategy & Practice Guide
This workbook is designed to help you with the New SAT coming in March 2016. With over 1000+ practice problems, 3 full-length tests, and the simplest and most effective lessons you can find, this guide will help you study independently and quickly for the new test.

Find us on Amazon at: http://www.amazon.com/Genius-Redesigned-Strategy-Practice-Guide/dp/1514193973/

Check out our website at: http://www.tpgenius.com/

CPSIA information can be obtained at www.ICGtesting.com
Printed in the USA
BVOW04s0214181215

430586BV00023B/245/P